Focus on GRAMMAR 4B

FOURTH EDITION

Focus on GRAMMAR 4B

FOURTH EDITION

Marjorie Fuchs
Margaret Bonner

ALWAYS LEARNING

PEARSON

To the memory of my parents, Edith and Joseph Fuchs—MF
To my parents, Marie and Joseph Maus, and to my son, Luke Frances—MB

FOCUS ON GRAMMAR 4B: An Integrated Skills Approach, Fourth Edition

Copyright © 2012, 2006, 2000, 1995 by Pearson Education, Inc.
All rights reserved.

Pearson Education, 10 Bank Street, White Plains, NY 10606

Staff credits: The people who made up the *Focus on Grammar 4B, Fourth Edition*
team, representing editorial, production, design, and manufacturing, are Elizabeth Carlson,
Tracey Cataldo, Aerin Csigay, Dave Dickey, Christine Edmonds, Nancy Flaggman, Ann France,
Françoise Leffler, Lise Minovitz, Barbara Perez, Robert Ruvo, and Debbie Sistino.

Cover image: Shutterstock.com
Text composition: ElectraGraphics, Inc.
Text font: New Aster

PEARSON LONGMAN ON THE **WEB**

Pearsonlongman.com offers online
resources for teachers and students. Access
our Companion Websites, our online catalog,
and our local offices around the world.

Visit us at **pearsonlongman.com**.

Printed in the United States of America

ISBN 10: 0-13-216940-1
ISBN 13: 978-0-13-216940-0

1 2 3 4 5 6 7 8 9 10—V082—16 15 14 13 12 11

ISBN 10: 0-13-216966-5 (with MyLab)
ISBN 13: 978-0-13-216966-0 (with MyLab)

1 2 3 4 5 6 7 8 9 10—V082—16 15 14 13 12 11

CONTENTS

WELCOME TO *FOCUS ON GRAMMAR*

Now in a new edition, the popular five-level *Focus on Grammar* course continues to provide an integrated-skills approach to help students understand and practice English grammar. Centered on thematic instruction, *Focus on Grammar* combines controlled and communicative practice with critical thinking skills and ongoing assessment. Students gain the confidence they need to speak and write English accurately and fluently.

NEW for the FOURTH EDITION

VOCABULARY

Key vocabulary is highlighted, practiced, and recycled throughout the unit.

PRONUNCIATION

Now, in every unit, pronunciation points and activities help students improve spoken accuracy and fluency.

LISTENING

Expanded listening tasks allow students to develop a range of listening skills.

UPDATED CHARTS and NOTES

Target structures are presented in a clear, easy-to-read format.

NEW READINGS

High-interest readings, updated or completely new, in a variety of genres integrate grammar and vocabulary in natural contexts.

NEW UNIT REVIEWS

Students can check their understanding and monitor their progress after completing each unit.

MyFocusOnGrammarLab

An easy-to-use online learning and assessment program offers online homework and individualized instruction anywhere, anytime.

Teacher's Resource Pack   One compact resource includes:

THE TEACHER'S MANUAL: General Teaching Notes, Unit Teaching Notes, the Student Book Audioscript, and the Student Book Answer Key.

TEACHER'S RESOURCE DISC: Bound into the Resource Pack, this CD-ROM contains reproducible Placement, Part, and Unit Tests, as well as customizable Test-Generating Software. It also includes reproducible Internet Activities and PowerPoint® Grammar Presentations.

THE *FOCUS ON GRAMMAR* APPROACH

The new edition follows the same successful four-step approach of previous editions. The books provide an abundance of both controlled and communicative exercises so that students can bridge the gap between identifying grammatical structures and using them. The many communicative activities in each Student Book provide opportunities for critical thinking while enabling students to personalize what they have learned.

- **STEP 1: GRAMMAR IN CONTEXT** highlights the target structures in realistic contexts, such as conversations, magazine articles, and blog posts.
- **STEP 2: GRAMMAR PRESENTATION** presents the structures in clear and accessible grammar charts and notes with multiple examples of form and usage.
- **STEP 3: FOCUSED PRACTICE** provides numerous and varied controlled exercises for both the form and meaning of the new structures.
- **STEP 4: COMMUNICATION PRACTICE** includes listening and pronunciation and allows students to use the new structures freely and creatively in motivating, open-ended speaking and writing activities.

Recycling

Underpinning the scope and sequence of the *Focus on Grammar* series is the belief that students need to use target structures and vocabulary many times, in different contexts. New grammar and vocabulary are recycled throughout the book. Students have maximum exposure and become confident using the language in speech and in writing.

Assessment

Extensive testing informs instruction and allows teachers and students to measure progress.

- **Unit Reviews** at the end of every Student Book unit assess students' understanding of the grammar and allow students to monitor their own progress.
- Easy to administer and score, **Part and Unit Tests** provide teachers with a valid and reliable means to determine how well students know the material they are about to study and to assess students' mastery after they complete the material. These tests can be found on MyFocusOnGrammarLab, where they include immediate feedback and remediation, and as reproducible tests on the Teacher's Resource Disc.
- **Test-Generating Software** on the Teacher's Resource Disc includes a bank of *additional* test items teachers can use to create customized tests.
- A reproducible **Placement Test** on the Teacher's Resource Disc is designed to help teachers place students into one of the five levels of the *Focus on Grammar* course.

COMPONENTS

In addition to the Student Books, Teacher's Resource Packs, and MyLabs, the complete *Focus on Grammar* course includes:

Workbooks Contain additional contextualized exercises appropriate for self-study.

Audio Program Includes all of the listening and pronunciation exercises and opening passages from the Student Book. Some Student Books are packaged with the complete audio program (mp3 files). Alternatively, the audio program is available on a classroom set of CDs and on the MyLab.

THE *FOCUS ON GRAMMAR* UNIT

Focus on Grammar introduces grammar structures in the context of unified themes. All units follow a **four-step approach**, taking learners from grammar in context to communicative practice.

STEP 1 GRAMMAR IN CONTEXT

This section presents the target structure(s) in a natural context. As students read the **high-interest texts**, they encounter the form, meaning, and use of the grammar. **Before You Read** activities create interest and elicit students' knowledge about the topic. **After You Read** activities build students' reading vocabulary and comprehension.

Vocabulary exercises improve students' command of English. Vocabulary is **recycled** throughout the unit.

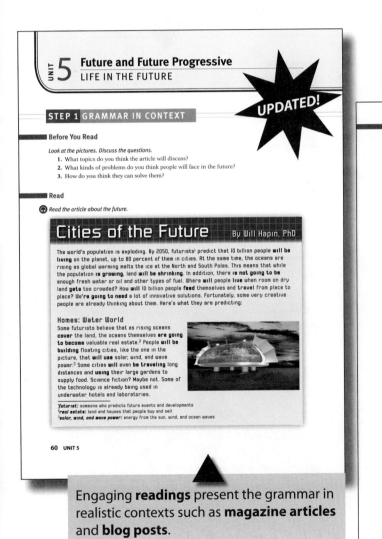

Engaging **readings** present the grammar in realistic contexts such as **magazine articles** and **blog posts**.

Reading comprehension tasks focus on the meaning of the text and draw students' attention to the target structure.

STEP 2 GRAMMAR PRESENTATION

This section gives students a comprehensive and explicit overview of the grammar with detailed **Grammar Charts** and **Grammar Notes** that present the form, meaning, and use of the structure(s).

Grammar Charts present the structure in a clear, easy-to-read format.

Grammar Notes give concise, simple **explanations** and **examples** to ensure students' understanding.

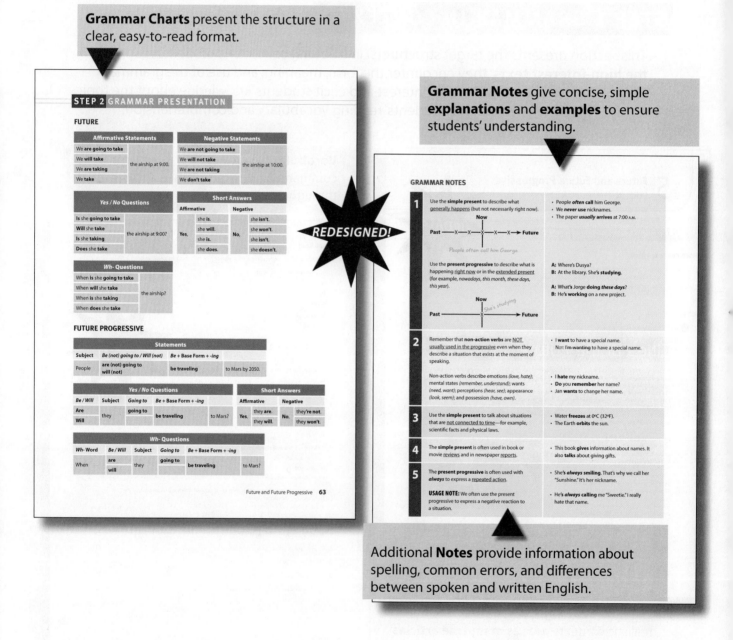

Additional **Notes** provide information about spelling, common errors, and differences between spoken and written English.

Controlled practice activities in this section lead students to master form, meaning, and use of the target grammar.

EXERCISE 1: Discover the Grammar

Match the facts with the speculations and conclusions.

Facts

___e___ **1.** The original title of *Chariots of the Gods?* was *Erinnerungen an die Zukunft*.

_____ **2.** Erich von Däniken visited every place he described in his book.

_____ **3.** In 1973, he wrote *In Search of Ancient Gods*.

_____ **4.** He doesn't have a degree in archeology.

_____ **5.** *Chariots of the Gods?* was published the same year as the Apollo moon landing.

_____ **6.** In the 1900s, writer Annie Besant said beings from Venus helped develop culture on Earth.

_____ **7.** Von Däniken's books sold millions of copies.

_____ **8.** As soon as von Däniken published his book, scientists attacked his theories.

Speculations and Conclusions

a. He must have made a lot of money.

b. He may have known about her unusual ideas.

c. He could have learned about the subject on his own.

d. He must have traveled a lot.

e. He must have written his book in German.

f. This great event had to have increased sales of the book.

g. He must not have had scientific evidence for his beliefs.

h. He might have written some other books too.

Discover the Grammar activities develop students' recognition and understanding of the target structure before they are asked to produce it.

EXERCISE 2: Questions and Statements

(Grammar Notes 1–4)

Circle the correct words to complete the review of Erich von Däniken's book, Chariots of the Gods?

Who could have make / made the Nazca lines? Who
   1.
could have carve / carved the Easter Island statues?
   2.
According to Erich von Däniken, ancient achievements
like these are mysteries because our ancestors could not
have / had created these things on their own. His
   3.
conclusion: They must / couldn't have gotten help from
   4.
space visitors.

"Here comes another one."

Von Däniken's readers may not realize that experiments
have contributed to our understanding of some of these
"mysteries." Von Däniken asks: How may / could the Nazcans have planned the lines from
   5.
the ground? Archeologists now speculate that this civilization might have / has developed flight.
   6.
They think ancient Nazcans may draw / have drawn pictures of hot-air balloons on pottery. To test
   7.

(continued on next page)

An **Editing** exercise ends every Focused Practice section and teaches students to find and correct typical mistakes.

EXERCISE 6: Editing

Read this article about cars of the future. There are ten mistakes in the use of the future and future progressive. The first mistake is already corrected. Find and correct nine more.

The SkyCar

Flying Cars

Your class starts in 10 minutes, but you're stuck in
traffic. Don't panic. With just a press of a button, your
                                              lift
car will ~~lifts~~ off the ground, and you'll be on your way
to school. No bad roads, no stop signs, no worries!

Welcome to the future! It seems like science fiction, but it isn't. Engineers have been working on
flying cars for decades, and they have already solved many of the big challenges. They predict that
we'll all be use these amazing vehicles one day.

According to *Car Trends Magazine*, one model, part car and part plane, is going be on the
market in the not-so-distant future. It will look like a regular car when it's on the road, but its
wings will unfold when the driver will decide to take to the skies. It will runs on the same fuel for
both land and air travel, and you'll be able to keep it in your garage. (But you're still going need an
airport to take off and land.)

A better model will be a vertical takeoff and landing vehicle (VTOL). You won't need to go to
the airport anymore, and all controls will being automatic. Imagine this: You'll be doing your
homework while your car will be getting you to school safely and on time.

And what does this future dream car cost? Well, fasten your seatbelts—the price will going to be
sky-high. At first it will be about a million dollars, but after a few years, you'll be able to buy one
for "only" $60,000. Don't throw away your old driver's license just yet!

A **variety of exercise types** engage students and guide them from recognition and understanding to accurate production of the grammar structures.

STEP 4 COMMUNICATION PRACTICE

This section provides practice with the structure in **listening** and **pronunciation** exercises as well as in communicative, open-ended **speaking** and **writing** activities that move students toward fluency.

Listening activities allow students to hear the grammar in natural contexts and to practice a range of listening skills.

STEP 4 COMMUNICATION PRACTICE

EXERCISE 7: Listening

A | *Some friends are at a high school reunion. They haven't seen one another for 25 years. Read the statements. Then listen to the conversation. Listen again and circle the correct words to complete the statements.*

1. People at the reunion have / haven't changed a lot.

2. Ann is wearing a lot of jewelry / a scarf.

3. It's the man / woman who first recognizes Kado.

4. Bob and Pat are the students who worked on the school paper / ran for class president.

5. Asha is looking at a photo / Bob.

6. Asha is the woman who married Pete Rizzo / Raza Gupta.

7. The man and woman know / don't know who is sitting between Asha and Pat.

B | *Look at the picture. Then listen again to the conversation and write the correct name next to each person.*

| Ann | Asha | Bob | Kado | Pat | Pete |

EXPANDED!

Pronunciation Notes and **exercises** improve students' spoken fluency and accuracy.

EXERCISE 8: Pronunciation

A | *Read and listen to the Pronunciation Note.*

> **Pronunciation Note**
>
> In **writing**, we use **commas** around **nonidentifying adjective clauses.**
> In **speaking**, we **pause** briefly **before and after** nonidentifying adjective clauses.
> **EXAMPLE:** Marta, who lives across from me, has become a good friend. →
> "Marta [PAUSE] who lives across from me [PAUSE] has become a good friend."

NEW!

B | *Listen to the sentences. Add commas if you hear pauses around the adjective clauses.*

1. My neighbor who is an introvert called me today.

2. My neighbor who is an introvert called me today.

3. My brother who is one year older than me is an extrovert.

4. My sister who lives in Toronto visits us every summer.

5. My friend who is in the same class as me lent me a book.

6. The book which is about personality types is really interesting.

7. The article that won a prize is in today's newspaper.

8. My boyfriend who hates parties actually agreed to go to one with me.

C | *Listen again and repeat the sentences.*

EXERCISE 9: Discussion

A | *Take the quiz in Exercise 2.*

B | *Work with a partner. Discuss your answers to the quiz. What do you think your answers show about your personality?*

> **EXAMPLE:** **A:** Question 1. People who talk a lot tire me. That's true.
> **B:** I think that means you're probably an introvert. It wasn't true for me. I myself talk a lot, and I enjoy people who talk a lot too.

evil a bad thing

EXERCISE 12: Writing

A | *Write a two-paragraph essay about a friend. You may want to begin your essay with one of the quotations from Exercise 11. Use adjective clauses with subject relative pronouns. You can use the essay in Exercise 6 as a model.*

> **EXAMPLE:** Do friends have to be people who have the same interests or personality? I don't think so. My friend Richie and I are best friends who are complete opposites. He's an extrovert who can walk into a room that is full of strangers with no problem. In an hour, they'll all be new friends. I'm an introvert who . . .

B | *Check your work. Use the Editing Checklist.*

> **Editing Checklist**
>
> Did you use . . . ?
> ☐ *who* or *that* for people
> ☐ *which* or *that* for places and things
> ☐ *whose* to show possession or relationship
> ☐ the correct verb form in adjective clauses
> ☐ identifying adjective clauses to identify a noun
> ☐ nonidentifying adjective clauses to give more information about a noun
> ☐ commas to separate nonidentifying adjective clauses

NEW!

Speaking activities help students synthesize the grammar through discussions, debates, games, and problem-solving tasks, developing their fluency.

Writing activities encourage students to produce meaningful writing that integrates the grammar structure.

An **Editing Checklist** teaches students to correct their mistakes and revise their work.

219

UNIT 5 Review

Check your answers on page UR-2.
Do you need to review anything?

NEW!

A | *Circle the correct words to complete the sentences.*

1. Our daughter will turns / turn 15 next week.

2. Are / Do you going to go to work today?

3. What will you be doing / do at 3:00 this afternoon?

4. The sun will / is going to rise at 6:22 tomorrow morning.

5. Be careful! Your coffee will / is going to spill!

6. While you're / 'll be driving to work tomorrow, we'll be flying to Beijing.

7. Roboid will let us know when he finished / finishes cooking dinner.

B | *Complete the conversation with the future or future progressive form of the verbs in parentheses or with a short answer. Use the future progressive when possible.*

A: What _____ you _____ at 10:00 tomorrow morning?
                          1. (do)

B: 10:00? Well, let's see. My plane _____ at 9:45, so at 10:00,
                                2. (leave)

    I _____ on the plane.
         3. (sit)

A: So I guess you _____ to the office at all tomorrow.
                   4. (not come)

B: Doesn't look like it. Why? _____ that _____ a problem?
                                      5. (cause)

A: _____, it _____. It _____ fine. Have a good trip.
                      6.   7. (be)

B: Thanks. I _____ you in a couple of weeks.
           8. (see)

C | *Find and correct five mistakes.*

A: How long are you going to staying in Beijing?

B: I'm not sure. I'll let you know you as soon as I'll find out, OK?

A: OK. It's going to be a long flight. What will you did to pass the time?

B: I'll be work a lot of the time. And I'm going to try t[...]

A: Good idea. Have fun, and I'm emailing you all the [...]

PART III

From Grammar to Writing
AVOIDING REPETITION WITH SENTENCE ADDITIONS

When you write, one way to **avoid repetition** is to use **sentence additions**.

EXAMPLES: Brasília is a capital city. Washington, D.C. is a capital city. →
Brasília is a capital city, *and so* is Washington, D.C.

Brasília's shape is modern. Washington's shape isn't modern. →
Brasília's shape is modern, *but* **Washington's isn't**.

1 | *Read this student's essay comparing and contrasting Brasília and Washington, D.C. Underline once additions that express similarity. Underline twice additions that express contrast.*

BRASÍLIA AND WASHINGTON, D.C.

Citizens of Brasília and citizens of Washington, D.C. live on different continents, but their cities still have a lot in common. Brasília is its nation's capital, and so is Washington. Brasília did not exist before it was planned and built as the national capital. Neither did Washington. Both cities were designed by a single person, and both have a definite shape. However, 20th-century Brasília's shape is modern—that of an airplane—but the shape of 18th-century Washington isn't. Its streets form a wheel.

The cities reflect their differences in location and age. Brasília is located in a dry area in the highlands, while Washington was built on wet, swampy land. As a result, Brasília has moderate temperatures all year, but Washington doesn't. Washington is famous for its cold winters and hot, humid summers. Brasília was built 600 miles from the Atlantic coast in order to attract people to an unpopulated area. Washington, near the Atlantic coast, includes old towns that had already existed. Brasília is home to many famous theaters and museums, and so is the city of Washington. However, as a new city, Brasília has not yet become its nation's real cultural center. Washington hasn't either. Washington is its country's capital, but it is not its country's most popular city. Neither is Brasília. Many people still prefer the excitement of Rio and New York.

The *Focus on Grammar* Unit **xiii**

SCOPE AND SEQUENCE

UNIT	READING	WRITING	LISTENING
1 page 2 **Grammar:** Simple Present and Present Progressive **Theme:** Names	A school newsletter article: *What's in a Name?*	A profile to introduce yourself to your class	Two friends discussing photos
2 page 13 **Grammar:** Simple Past and Past Progressive **Theme:** First Meetings	An article: *Super Couples*	Two paragraphs about a relationship that is important to you	A woman explaining how she met her husband
3 page 26 **Grammar:** Simple Past, Present Perfect, and Present Perfect Progressive **Theme:** Hobbies and Interests	A personal website: *Jumping for Joy*	A few paragraphs about yourself for a personal website	A couple planning their honeymoon trip
4 page 38 **Grammar:** Past Perfect and Past Perfect Progressive **Theme:** Musicians	An article: *The People's Conductor*	Two paragraphs about a musician or singer	A radio host interviewing several young musicians
PART I From Grammar to Writing, page 55 **Editing for Verb Forms:** Write a paragraph about a phase you went through.			
5 page 60 **Grammar:** Future and Future Progressive **Theme:** Life in the Future	An article: *Cities of the Future*	A paragraph about your life 10 years from now	A discussion about organizing a conference
6 page 79 **Grammar:** Future Perfect and Future Perfect Progressive **Theme:** Money and Goals	A transcript of a TV finance show: *Money Talks*	Activities and goals of some of your classmates for a class website	A couple discussing how to save money for a family vacation
PART II From Grammar to Writing, page 96 **Avoiding Sentence Fragments:** Write a letter to a friend about some plans you are making.			

SPEAKING	PRONUNCIATION	VOCABULARY	
Find Someone Who . . .	Stressing contrasting or new information	actually convince* institute*	style* (n) title
What About You? The first time you met someone who became influential in your life *Ask and Answer:* Important events in your life	Intonation and pauses in sentences with time clauses	couple* cover (v) influential	opponent recover* research* (n)
What About You? Talk about your hobbies and interests *Ask and Answer:* What did you plan to accomplish last week?	Reduction of *has he* ("hazee") and *did he* ("didee") *have you* ("havya") and *did you* ("didja")	celebrate engaged extreme	fantastic historic introduce
What About You? Compare your day yesterday with a classmate's *Conversation:* Talk about things you had never done before . . . *Game:* Find the Differences	Pronunciation of the contraction of *had* ('d) after pronouns and nouns	conduct* (v) contract* (n) enthusiastic	ethnic* participate* transform*
Reaching Agreement: Finding a time to get together *Discussion:* Which activities will robots be doing and not doing? *Information Gap:* Dr. Eon's Calendar	Stress for contrasting information	challenge* (n) creative* innovative*	technology* vehicle* vertical
Conversation: What will some of the people in your life have achieved by the end of this year, month, or week? *What About You?* Three goals you would like to achieve in the next five years	Reduction of *have* ("of") in the future perfect and future perfect progressive	budget (n) credit* (n) debt	minimum* purchase* (n) statistics*

* = AWL (Academic Word List) items

SPEAKING	PRONUNCIATION	VOCABULARY	
Information Gap: London and Vancouver *Conversation:* How well do you know your classmates?	Rising or falling intonation in tag questions	adjustment* attract bother	originally provide structure* (n)
Discussion: Are the man and woman a good match? *Picture Discussion:* Imagine the conversations of reunited twins *Find Someone Who . . .* *Compare and Contrast:* Look at pictures of a pair of twins and find their similarities and differences *What Do You Think?* Which is more important, nature or nurture?	Stress in additions and short responses of similarity and difference	coincidence* despite* factor*	identical* image* outgoing
Information Gap: The Right Job? *Questionnaire:* Compare your answers on a fast-food questionnaire with your partner's *Cross-Cultural Comparison:* Describe a food from your culture. Then choose foods to include in an international food festival. *Problem Solving:* Solutions to social problems	Intonation to express sincerity or sarcasm	appealing consequence* globe*	objection region* reliability*
Discussion: Who helped you learn something? *For or Against:* Keeping animals captive	Reductions and linking of pronouns: *let her* ("let'er"), *made him* ("made'im"), *got them* ("got'em")	complicated former humane	physical* punishment reward (n)

* = AWL (Academic Word List) items

UNIT	READING	WRITING	LISTENING
11 page 172 **Grammar:** Phrasal Verbs: Review **Theme:** Feng Shui	An article: *Wind and Water*	Two paragraphs about how you feel in your home, office, dorm, or classroom	A couple talking about their home
12 page 186 **Grammar:** Phrasal Verbs: Separable and Inseparable **Theme:** Telemarketing	An article: *Welcome Home!*	A paragraph about an experience you have had on the phone	A telemarketing call
PART V **From Grammar to Writing,** page 200 **Using the Appropriate Level of Formality:** Write a letter to a landlord about problems in a building lobby.			
13 page 206 **Grammar:** Adjective Clauses with Subject Relative Pronouns **Theme:** Friends and Personality Types	An article: *Extroverts and Introverts*	A two-paragraph essay about a friend	A conversation between classmates at a high school reunion
14 page 221 **Grammar:** Adjective Clauses with Object Relative Pronouns or *When* and *Where* **Theme:** The Immigrant Experience	Two book reviews: *Torn Between Two Worlds*	One or two paragraphs about a place you remember from your childhood	An author describing her childhood room
PART VI **From Grammar to Writing,** page 237 **Adding Details with Adjective Clauses:** Write an essay about a famous person.			
15 page 240 **Grammar:** Modals and Similar Expressions: Review **Theme:** Social Networking	An article: *Facebook or Face Time? The Pros and Cons of Social Networking*	A blog post about your plans for the week	Two friends discussing Facebook

SPEAKING	PRONUNCIATION	VOCABULARY	
Problem Solving: How would you like to change your classroom or your school? *Compare and Contrast:* Describe the differences in Before and After pictures of a room	Linking final consonant sounds to beginning vowel sounds in phrasal verbs	complex* consultant* environment*	harmful theory*
For or Against: Telemarketing calls *Discussion:* What do you think about an ad, a piece of junk mail, spam, or an Internet offer?	Stress in separable phrasal verbs	authorities* constantly* eliminate*	equivalent* identify* tactic
Discussion: What do your answers on a personality quiz mean? *Questionnaire:* A friend is someone who . . . *Quotable Quotes:* Friends and personality types	Pausing before and after nonidentifying adjective clauses	contradict* define* personality	require* sensitive unique*
What About You? Share photos of people and places with your classmates. *Quotable Quotes:* Home	Breaking long sentences into thought groups	connection generation* immigrant*	issue* poverty translation
Discussion: What do you think of a student's profile on a social networking site? *Reaching Agreement:* Designing a class website *Problem Solving:* What would you do to survive on a desert island? *For or Against:* The advantages and disadvantages of online social networking	Reductions of: *have to* ("hafta"), *have got to* ("have gotta"), *ought to* ("oughta"), *be able to* ("be able ta")	comment* (n) content (n) involved*	network* (v) privacy resource*

* = AWL (Academic Word List) items

UNIT	READING	WRITING	LISTENING
16 page 257 **Grammar:** Advisability in the Past **Theme:** Regrets	An article: *Useless Regrets*	Three paragraphs about a dilemma that you have faced	A woman recording her regrets at the end of the day
17 page 270 **Grammar:** Speculations and Conclusions About the Past **Theme:** Unsolved Mysteries	An article: *Close Encounters*	A paragraph speculating about an event	Archeology students speculating about objects they have found

PART VII From Grammar to Writing, page 285
Organizing Ideas from Freewriting: Write a letter to a person you had a problem with.

UNIT	READING	WRITING	LISTENING
18 page 290 **Grammar:** The Passive: Overview **Theme:** Geography	An article: *Geography: The Best Subject on Earth*	An essay about a country you know well	Short conversations between two travel writers
19 page 308 **Grammar:** The Passive with Modals and Similar Expressions **Theme:** The International Space Station	An article: *Close Quarters*	Two paragraphs about your neighborhood, your school, or your workplace	Conversations from a science fiction movie
20 page 323 **Grammar:** The Passive Causative **Theme:** Personal Services	An article: *Body Art*	An email describing what you have recently done or have had done	A college student talking to her father about her new apartment

PART VIII   From Grammar to Writing, page 337
Changing the Focus with the Passive: Write a research report about a famous building.

SPEAKING	PRONUNCIATION	VOCABULARY	
Game: Find the Problems *Survey:* Sense of Obligation *Problem Solving:* What should the people have done in these situations?	Reductions of *have* in past modals: *should have* ("shoulda"), *could have* ("coulda"), *might have* ("mighta"), *ought to have* ("oughta of")	process* (n) psychology* ruined	strategy* technique* unrealistic
Picture Discussion: Speculate on what ancient objects are and how people might have used them *For or Against:* Do you agree or disagree with Erich von Däniken's theories?	Reductions of *have* in past modals: *could have* ("could of"), *may have* ("may of"), *couldn't have* ("couldn't of")	conclusion* contribute* encounter* (n)	estimate* (v) evidence* speculate*
Quotable Quotes: International proverbs *Information Gap:* The Philippines *Game:* Trivia Quiz	Stressing corrected information	decade* edition* explorer	inhabitant mission publication*
Reaching Agreement: What rules should be made for living in close quarters? *Problem Solving:* What things must be done to get a student lounge in order? *For or Against:* Spending money on space projects	Dropping the final "t" in *must be, mustn't be, couldn't be,* and *shouldn't be*	assemble* benefit* (v) cooperate*	period* perspective* undertaking*
Making Plans: A car trip to another country *Compare and Contrast:* Describe what a model had done to change her appearance *Cross-Cultural Comparison:* The types of things people do or get done to change their appearance	Contrast: Contractions of *have* in the present perfect (*She's cut her hair.*) and Uncontracted use of *have* in the passive causative (*She has her hair cut.*)	appearance event option*	permanent remove* risk (n)

* = AWL (Academic Word List) items

SPEAKING	PRONUNCIATION	VOCABULARY	
Reaching Agreement: Ordering T-shirts from a store's website *Cross-Cultural Comparison:* Shopping *Discussion:* What do you do when you want to make an important purchase? *For or Against:* Shopping in a "store with doors" and shopping online	Intonation and pauses in conditional statements	consumer* dispute (v) policy*	precaution secure* (adj) site*
Problem Solving: What are possible solutions to everyday problems? *Cross-Cultural Comparison:* Superstitions about luck	Intonation in conditional *yes / no* and *wh-* questions	anticipate* attitude* confident	insight* percent* widespread*
What About You? What would you do if . . . ? *Problem Solving:* Giving Advice *Discussion:* What three wishes would you make?	Contractions of *would* ("d") Dropping the final "t" after *wouldn't*	consent* (v) embarrassed enchanted	furious grant* (v) respond*
What About You? How a single decision or event changed your life or the life of someone you know *Problem Solving:* What would you have done in certain situations? *Discussion:* What is a situation in your life that you regret?	Reduction of *have* ("of") Contractions for: *had* ("d"), *had not* ("hadn't"), *would not* ("wouldn't"), *could not* ("couldn't")	alternate* (adj) intelligent* occur*	outcome* parallel* (adj) version*
Discussion: Is it OK to lie in certain circumstances? *Questionnaire:* Honesty *Game:* To Tell the Truth *Quotable Quotes:* Lying and telling the truth	Stress and intonation to express belief and disbelief about what someone said	average (adj) aware* justify*	majority* reveal*

* = AWL (Academic Word List) items

UNIT	READING	WRITING	LISTENING
26 page 417 **Grammar:** Indirect Speech: Tense Changes **Theme:** Extreme Weather	A news article: *The Flood of the Century*	A paragraph reporting someone else's experience with extreme weather	A winter storm warning
27 page 432 **Grammar:** Indirect Instructions, Commands, Requests, and Invitations **Theme:** Health Problems and Remedies	A radio interview: *Here's to Your Health: The Snooze News*	A paragraph about a dream	A conversation about treatment at a headache clinic
28 page 445 **Grammar:** Indirect Questions **Theme:** Job Interviews	An article: *The Stress Interview*	A report of an interview with someone working in a job that might interest you	A job interview
29 page 461 **Grammar:** Embedded Questions **Theme:** Travel Tips	An interview: *The Tip: Who? When? and How Much?*	A paragraph about a situation that confused or surprised you	A call-in radio program about tipping

PART X   **From Grammar to Writing,** page 478
Using Direct and Indirect Speech: Write a letter of complaint.

SPEAKING	PRONUNCIATION	VOCABULARY	
Game: Telephone *Interview:* Experiences with severe weather conditions	Stress on content words	bear (v) collapse* (v) damage (n)	evacuate optimistic restore*
Problem Solving: What advice would you give for some minor health problems? *Picture Discussion:* Which instructions did Jeff follow?	Stress in affirmative and negative indirect instructions, commands, requests, and invitations	astonishing fatigue (n) interfere	monitor* (v) persist* remedy (n)
Role Play: A Job Interview *Questionnaire:* Work Values *What About You?* A personal experience with a school or job interview	Intonation in direct and indirect *yes / no* questions	appropriate* (adj) candidate evaluation*	handle (v) potential* (adj) pressure (n)
Information Gap: Eating Out *Discussion:* What is your opinion about tipping? *What About You?* The problems you had when you did something for the first time *Role Play:* Information Please!	Intonation in direct and embedded *wh-* questions	clarify* custom depend on	logical* ordinary ultimate*

* = AWL (Academic Word List) items

ABOUT THE AUTHORS

Marjorie Fuchs has taught ESL at New York City Technical College and LaGuardia Community College of the City University of New York and EFL at the Sprach Studio Lingua Nova in Munich, Germany. She has a master's degree in Applied English Linguistics and a certificate in TESOL from the University of Wisconsin-Madison. She has authored and co-authored many widely used books and multimedia materials, notably *Crossroads, Top Twenty ESL Word Games: Beginning Vocabulary Development, Families: Ten Card Games for Language Learners, Focus on Grammar 3: An Integrated Skills Approach, Focus on Grammar 3 CD-ROM, Focus on Grammar 4 CD-ROM, Longman English Interactive 3* and *4, Grammar Express Basic, Grammar Express Basic CD-ROM, Grammar Express Intermediate, Future 1: English for Results,* and workbooks for *The Oxford Picture Dictionary High Beginning* and *Low Intermediate, Focus on Grammar 3* and *4,* and *Grammar Express Basic.*

Margaret Bonner has taught ESL at Hunter College and the Borough of Manhattan Community College of the City University of New York, at Taiwan National University in Taipei, and at Virginia Commonwealth University in Richmond. She holds a master's degree in library science from Columbia University, and she has done work toward a PhD in English literature at the Graduate Center of the City University of New York. She has authored and co-authored numerous ESL and EFL print and multimedia materials, including textbooks for the national school system of Oman, *Step into Writing: A Basic Writing Text, Focus on Grammar 3: An Integrated Skills Approach, Focus on Grammar 4 Workbook, Grammar Express Basic, Grammar Express Basic CD-ROM, Grammar Express Basic Workbook, Grammar Express Intermediate, Focus on Grammar 3 CD-ROM, Focus on Grammar 4 CD-ROM, Longman English Interactive 4,* and *The Oxford Picture Dictionary Low-Intermediate Workbook.*

ACKNOWLEDGMENTS

Before acknowledging the many people who have contributed to the fourth edition of *Focus on Grammar*, we wish to express our gratitude to those who worked on the first, second, and third editions, and whose influence is still present in the new work. Our continuing thanks to:

- **Joanne Dresner**, who initiated the project and helped conceptualize the general approach of *Focus on Grammar*
- Our editors for the first three editions: **Nancy Perry**, **Penny Laporte**, **Louisa Hellegers**, **Joan Saslow**, **Laura Le Dréan**, and **Françoise Leffler**, for helping to bring the books to fruition
- **Sharon Hilles**, our grammar consultant, for her insight and advice on the first edition

In the fourth edition, *Focus on Grammar* has continued to evolve as we update materials and respond to the valuable feedback from teachers and students who have been using the series. We are grateful to the following editors and colleagues:

- The Pearson *FOG* team, in particular **Debbie Sistino** for overseeing the project and for her down-to-earth approach based on years of experience and knowledge of the field; **Lise Minovitz** for her enthusiasm and alacrity in answering our queries; and **Rosa Chapinal** for her courteous and competent administrative support.
- **Françoise Leffler**, our multi-talented editor, for her continued dedication to the series and for helping improve *Focus on Grammar* with each new edition. With her ear for natural language, eye for detail, analytical mind, and sense of style, she is truly an editor *extraordinaire*.
- **Robert Ruvo** for piloting the book through its many stages of production
- **Irene Schoenberg** and **Jay Maurer** for their suggestions and support, and Irene for generously sharing her experience in teaching with the first three editions of this book
- **Irene Frankel** for reviewing Unit 29 and offering us some good tips of her own
- **Sharon Goldstein** for her intelligent, thoughtful, and practical suggestions

Finally, we are grateful, as always, to **Rick Smith** and **Luke Frances** for their helpful input and for standing by and supporting us as we navigated our way through our fourth *FOG*.

REVIEWERS

We are grateful to the following reviewers for their many helpful comments:

Aida Aganagic, Seneca College, Toronto, Canada; **Aftab Ahmed**, American University of Sharjah, Sharjah, United Arab Emirates; **Todd Allen**, English Language Institute, Gainesville, FL; **Anthony Anderson**, University of Texas, Austin, TX; **Anna K. Andrade**, ASA Institute, New York, NY; **Bayda Asbridge**, Worcester State College, Worcester, MA; **Raquel Ashkenasi**, American Language Institute, La Jolla, CA; **James Bakker**, Mt. San Antonio College, Walnut, CA; **Kate Baldrige-Hale**, Harper College, Palatine, IL; **Leticia S. Banks**, ALCI-SDUSM, San Marcos, CA; **Aegina Barnes**, York College CUNY, Forest Hills, NY; **Sarah Barnhardt**, Community College of Baltimore County, Reisterstown, MD; **Kimberly Becker**, Nashville State Community College, Nashville, TN; **Holly Bell**, California State University, San Marcos, CA; **Anne Bliss**, University of Colorado, Boulder, CO; **Diana Booth**, Elgin Community College, Elgin, IL; **Barbara Boyer**, South Plainfield High School, South Plainfield, NJ; **Janna Brink**, Mt. San Antonio College, Walnut, CA; **AJ Brown**, Portland State University, Portland, OR; **Amanda Burgoyne**, Worcester State College, Worcester, MA; **Brenda Burlingame**, Independence High School, Charlotte, NC; **Sandra Byrd**, Shelby County High School and Kentucky State University, Shelbyville, KY; **Edward Carlstedt**, American University of Sharjah, Sharjah, United Arab Emirates; **Sean Cochran**, American Language Institute, Fullerton, CA; **Yanely Cordero**, Miami Dade College, Miami, FL; **Lin Cui**, William Rainey Harper College, Palatine, IL; **Sheila Detweiler**, College Lake County, Libertyville, IL; **Ann Duncan**, University of Texas, Austin, TX; **Debra Edell**, Merrill Middle School, Denver, CO; **Virginia Edwards**, Chandler-Gilbert Community College, Chandler, AZ; **Kenneth Fackler**, University of Tennessee, Martin, TN; **Jennifer Farnell**, American Language Program, Stamford, CT; **Allen P. Feiste**, Suwon University, Hwaseong, South Korea; **Mina Fowler**, Mt. San Antonio Community College, Rancho Cucamonga, CA; **Rosemary Franklin**, University of Cincinnati, Cincinnati, OH; **Christiane Galvani**, Texas Southern University, Sugar Land, TX; **Chester Gates**, Community College of Baltimore County, Baltimore, MD; **Luka Gavrilovic**, Quest Language Studies, Toronto, Canada; **Sally Gearhart**, Santa Rosa Community College, Santa Rosa, CA; **Shannon Gerrity**, James Lick Middle School, San Francisco, CA; **Jeanette Gerrity Gomez**, Prince George's Community College, Largo, MD; **Carlos Gonzalez**, Miami Dade College, Miami, FL; **Therese Gormley Hirmer**, University of Guelph, Guelph, Canada; **Sudeepa Gulati**, Long Beach City College, Long Beach, CA; **Anthony Halderman**, Cuesta College, San Luis Obispo, CA; **Ann A. Hall**, University of Texas, Austin, TX; **Cora Higgins**, Boston Academy of English, Boston, MA; **Michelle Hilton**, South Lane School District, Cottage Grove, OR; **Nicole Hines**, Troy University, Atlanta, GA; **Rosemary Hiruma**, American Language Institute, Long Beach, CA; **Harriet Hoffman**, University of Texas, Austin, TX; **Leah Holck**, Michigan State University, East Lansing, MI; **Christy Hunt**, English for Internationals, Roswell, GA; **Osmany Hurtado**, Miami Dade College, Miami, FL; **Isabel Innocenti**, Miami Dade College, Miami, FL; **Donna Janian**, Oxford Intensive School of English, Medford, MA; **Scott Jenison**, Antelope Valley College, Lancaster, CA; **Grace Kim**, Mt. San Antonio College, Diamond Bar, CA; **Brian King**, ELS Language Center, Chicago, IL; **Pam Kopitzke**, Modesto Junior College, Modesto, CA; **Elena Lattarulo**, American Language Institute, San Diego, CA; **Karen Lavaty**, Mt. San Antonio College, Glendora, CA; **JJ Lee-Gilbert**, Menlo-Atherton High School, Foster City, CA; **Ruth Luman**, Modesto Junior College, Modesto, CA; **Yvette Lyons**, Tarrant County College, Fort Worth, TX; **Janet Magnoni**, Diablo Valley College, Pleasant Hill, CA; **Meg Maher**, YWCA Princeton, Princeton, NJ; **Carmen Marquez-Rivera**, Curie Metropolitan High School, Chicago, IL; **Meredith Massey**, Prince George's Community College, Hyattsville, MD; **Linda Maynard**, Coastline Community College, Westminster, CA; **Eve Mazereeuw**, University of Guelph, Guelph, Canada; **Susanne McLaughlin**, Roosevelt University, Chicago, IL; **Madeline Medeiros**, Cuesta College, San Luis Obispo, CA; **Gioconda Melendez**, Miami Dade College, Miami, FL; **Marcia Menaker**, Passaic County Community College, Morris Plains, NJ; **Seabrook Mendoza**, Cal State San Marcos University, Wildomar, CA; **Anadalia Mendoza**, Felix Varela Senior High School, Miami, FL; **Charmaine Mergulhao**, Quest Language Studies, Toronto, Canada; **Dana Miho**, Mt. San Antonio College, San Jacinto, CA; **Sonia Nelson**, Centennial Middle School, Portland, OR; **Manuel Niebla**, Miami Dade College, Miami, FL; **Alice Nitta**, Leeward Community College, Pearl City, HI; **Gabriela Oliva**, Quest Language Studies, Toronto, Canada; **Sara Packer**, Portland State University, Portland, OR; **Lesley Painter**, New School, New York, NY; **Carlos Paz-Perez**, Miami Dade College, Miami, FL; **Ileana Perez**, Miami Dade College, Miami, FL; **Barbara Pogue**, Essex County College, Newark, NJ; **Phillips Potash**, University of Texas, Austin, TX; **Jada Pothina**, University of Texas, Austin, TX; **Ewa Pratt**, Des Moines Area Community College, Des Moines, IA; **Pedro Prentt**, Hudson County Community College, Jersey City, NJ; **Maida Purdy**, Miami Dade College, Miami, FL; **Dolores Quiles**, SUNY Ulster, Stone Ridge, NY; **Mark Rau**, American River College, Sacramento, CA; **Lynne Raxlen**, Seneca College, Toronto, Canada; **Lauren Rein**, English for Internationals, Sandy Springs, GA; **Diana Rivers**, NOCCCD, Cypress, CA; **Silvia Rodriguez**, Santa Ana College, Mission Viejo, CA; **Rolando Romero**, Miami Dade College, Miami, FL; **Pedro Rosabal**, Miami Dade College, Miami, FL; **Natalie Rublik**, University of Quebec, Chicoutimi, Quebec, Canada; **Matilde Sanchez**, Oxnard College, Oxnard, CA; **Therese Sarkis-Kruse**, Wilson Commencement, Rochester, NY; **Mike Sfiropoulos**, Palm Beach Community College, Boynton Beach, FL; **Amy Shearon**, Rice University, Houston, TX; **Sara Shore**, Modesto Junior College, Modesto, CA; **Patricia Silva**, Richard Daley College, Chicago, IL; **Stephanie Solomon**, Seattle Central Community College, Vashon, WA; **Roberta Steinberg**, Mount Ida College, Newton, MA; **Teresa Szymula**, Curie Metropolitan High School, Chicago, IL; **Hui-Lien Tang**, Jasper High School, Plano, TX; **Christine Tierney**, Houston Community College, Sugar Land, TX; **Ileana Torres**, Miami Dade College, Miami, FL; **Michelle Van Slyke**, Western Washington University, Bellingham, WA; **Melissa Villamil**, Houston Community College, Sugar Land, TX; **Elizabeth Wagenheim**, Prince George's Community College, Lago, MD; **Mark Wagner**, Worcester State College, Worcester, MA; **Angela Waigand**, American University of Sharjah, Sharjah, United Arab Emirates; **Merari Weber**, Metropolitan Skills Center, Los Angeles, CA; **Sonia Wei**, Seneca College, Toronto, Canada; and **Vicki Woodward**, Indiana University, Bloomington, IN.

PART VII

MODALS: REVIEW AND EXPANSION

"Why can't you use Facebook, like everyone else?"

I should've used a longer piece of paper...

"Here comes another one."

Modals and Similar Expressions: Review

SOCIAL NETWORKING

Before You Read

Look at the cartoon and the title of the article. Discuss the questions.

1. What is the man doing? What does the woman think he should do?
2. What do you think the title means?
3. Do you use social networking sites? Which ones?
4. Do you use them for connecting with friends or for school or business?

Read

 Read the article about social networking.

facebook or face time¹?

The Pros and Cons of Social Networking

By Netta Seiborg

Blaire Thomas's school friends **can find out** what she is doing almost every minute by checking Facebook. Vince Stevenson stays in touch with his family through MySpace. Vince says, "I **had to join**. My grandkids all use MySpace." Magda Tilia, an English teacher in Romania, uses Ning for her class. Her students **are able to discuss** lessons and **chat** with other students in France, Turkey, and Greece. She says, "Students **don't have to use** the Ning site. Class is just more fun for the ones who do."

The growth of social networking all over the world is exciting, but networking **may not** always **be** a good thing. Both children and adults **have to remember** that real-life

"Why can't you use Facebook, like everyone else?"

relationships are more important than virtual² ones. Also, safety and privacy are big issues for everyone, but especially for teenagers and pre-teens³ who are just learning to use the Internet.

¹*face time:* time spent with someone in the same place, face-to-face
²*virtual:* on the Internet
³*pre-teen:* someone between the ages of 10 and 12

facebook or face time?

Parents **must teach** children about keeping personal information private. However, used with care, social networking **can be** a great tool for staying connected and improving your personal and professional life. Here are some ways to get the most out of social networking while avoiding some of the problems.

Making friends on Facebook or MySpace isn't that different from making friends at work or school. You **have to make** the effort to "meet" people with similar interests. Are you a tennis fan? Is *Survivor* a reality TV show you **could** never **miss**? If so, why don't you join those interest groups and begin conversations with people there? Once you've made some friends, you **should keep** posting new content on your own page: comments, photos, and videos that people **can respond** to.

However, while you're having fun getting to know people, you **should** never **forget** that what you post on the Internet is public information. Employers and schools often look at the social networking sites of applicants. Even if your page is only available to friends, embarrassing stuff **can** still **become** public. So maybe you**'d better think** twice before posting those party photos. Once they're out there, you **can't take** them back!

When you're networking for jobs, you **might need** a separate site. On your job-seeking site, you **must stay** absolutely professional. For example, you **should** never **use** abbreviations—remember, ur talking 2 other professionals! And you probably **shouldn't post** all your activities on this professional page, either—your colleagues **don't have to know** that you're eating chicken nuggets at 2:14 A.M.

Social networking is a great resource for students. When you're applying to school, your profile **should show** activities that will interest college admissions officers. You **can** also **network** by chatting with current students. They **could give** you an inside view of the school you're interested in. Once in school, you **can form** study groups, **organize** your schedule, and much more. But be careful: You **might** also **find** yourself wasting valuable study time.

Recently, Blaire has decided she**'s got to cut back** on her Facebook use. "I'm always chatting, and not doing homework," she said. Is she sorry she got so involved? "Not really. Everyone **ought to learn** how to use social networking. It's a big world out there, and you **can learn** a lot. You just **have to know** when to say 'enough is enough,' sign off, and get back to your *real* life."

After You Read

A | **Vocabulary:** *Match the words with their definitions.*

_____ 1. **comment**

_____ 2. **content**

_____ 3. **involved**

_____ 4. **network**

_____ 5. **privacy**

_____ 6. **resource**

a. something valuable or useful

b. taking part in something

c. a statement of an opinion

d. the protection of personal information

e. the ideas, information, and pictures in a book or on a website

f. to connect with people who also know each other

B | Comprehension: *Check (✓)* **True** *or* **False.** *Correct the false statements.*

	True	False
1. Vince joined MySpace because he wanted to stay in touch with his friends.	☐	☐
2. It's very important for parents to teach children about Internet privacy.	☐	☐
3. It's not a good idea to post certain photos because private posts sometimes become public.	☐	☐
4. On a site you use for job seeking, it's a good idea to post messages with abbreviations.	☐	☐
5. Social networking doesn't have much to offer college students.	☐	☐
6. Blaire thinks it's not important for everyone to learn how to use social networking.	☐	☐

STEP 2 GRAMMAR PRESENTATION

MODALS AND SIMILAR EXPRESSIONS: REVIEW

Ability: *Can* and *Could*

Subject	Modal	Base Form of Verb	
She	can (not)	join	now.
	could (not)		last year.

Ability: *Be able to**

Subject	*Be able to*		Base Form of Verb	
She	is (not)	able to	join	now.
	was (not)			last year.

Advice: *Should, Ought to, Had better*

Subject	Modal	Base Form of Verb	
You	should (not) ought to had better (not)	use	Ning.

Necessity: *Must* and *Can't*

Subject	Modal	Base Form of Verb	
You	must (not) can't	post	photos.

Necessity: *Have (got) to**

Subject	*Have to* *Have (got) to*	Base Form of Verb	
They	(don't) have to have got to	post	photos.
He	has to has got to		

*Unlike modals, which have one form, *be* in *be able to* and *have* in *have (got) to* change for different subjects.

Conclusions: *May, Might, Could, Must, Can't*			
Subject	Modal	Base Form of Verb	
They	**may (not)** **might (not)** **could (not)** **must (not)** **can't**	**know**	him.

Conclusions: *Have (got) to**			
Subject	*Have to* *Have got to*	Base Form of Verb	
They	**have to** **have got to**	**know**	him.
He	**has to** **has got to**		

*Unlike modals, which have one form, *have* in *have (got) to* changes for different subjects.

Future Possibility: *May, Might, Could*			
Subject	Modal	Base Form of Verb	
It	**may (not)** **might (not)** **could**	**happen**	soon.

GRAMMAR NOTES

1 **Modals** are auxiliary ("helping") verbs. Use modals and similar expressions to express:

a. **social functions** such as describing **ability**, giving **advice**, and expressing **necessity**

- We **can learn** to use it. *(ability)*
- She **should join** Facebook. *(advice)*
- You **must respond** to him. *(necessity)*

b. **logical possibilities** such as coming to **conclusions** and talking about **future possibilities**

- It **could be** the best site. *(conclusion)*
- I **might join**. *(future possibility)*

REMEMBER: Modals have **only one form**. They do not have -s in the third person singular. Always use **modal** + **base form** of the verb.

- She **might post** photos.
- NOT: She ~~mights~~ post photos.
- NOT: She might ~~to post photos~~.

2 Use the following **modals** for **ability**:

a. *can* or *be able to* for **present ability** (*can* is much more common)

- She **can speak** French.
- We **aren't able to view** his site.

b. *could* or *was / were able to* for **past ability**

- Before she took lessons, she **could speak** French, but she **wasn't able to speak** English.

c. *can*, *will be able to*, or *be going to be able to* for **future ability**

- She **can register** for class soon.
- She**'ll be able to register** for class soon.
- She**'s going to be able to attend** class soon.

REMEMBER: Use the correct form of *be able to* for all other verb forms.

- Since her lessons, she **has been able to chat** online in English.

(continued on next page)

3 Use the following **modals** for **advice**:

a. *should* and *ought to*
(*should* is much more common)

- You **should watch** *Survivor* tonight.
- Terri **ought to watch** it too.

b. *had better* for **urgent advice**—when you believe that something bad will happen if the person does not follow the advice

- You**'d better stop** watching so much TV or your grades will suffer.

c. *should* to **ask for advice**

- **Should** I **join** Facebook?

d. *shouldn't* and *had better not* for **negative advice**

- You **shouldn't spend** so much time online.
- You**'d better not stay up** too late.

---

4 Use the following **modals** for **necessity**:

a. *have to* and *have got to*
(in conversation and informal writing)

- I **have to get** an email address to join.
  (email message to a friend)

USAGE NOTE: We often use *have got to* to express strong feelings.

- You**'ve got to see** this! It's really funny!
  (friend talking to another friend)

b. *must*
(in writing, such as forms, signs, manuals)

- You **must be** at least 13 years old to join.
  (instructions for joining a networking site)
- Students **must post** their homework assignments by next Friday.
  (teacher to students on an online course site)

USAGE NOTE: When we use *must* in **spoken** English, the speaker is usually:

- in a position of power

- You **must go** to bed right now, Tommy!
  (mother talking to her young son)

- expressing urgent necessity

- You **must see** a doctor about that cough.
  (friend talking to a friend)

c. *must not* or *can't* for **prohibition**

- Students **must not leave** before the test ends.
  (written instructions on a test form)
- You **can't leave** yet, Jeff. The test isn't over.
  (teacher speaking to a student)

USAGE NOTE: We often use *can't* for prohibition in **spoken** English.

BE CAREFUL! The meanings of *must not* and *don't have to* are very different.

- Use *must not* to express **prohibition**.

- They **must not stay up** past 10:00.
  (They are not allowed to stay up past 10:00.)

- Use *don't have to* to say that something is **not necessary**.

- They **don't have to stay up** past 10:00.
  (It isn't necessary for them to stay up past 10:00.)

Use *have to*, *have got to*, and *must* for the present or future. Use the correct form of *have to* for all other verb forms.

- Bob **had to get** an email address to join.
  (simple past)
- He **has had to change** his password twice.
  (present perfect)

5 Use the following **modals and similar expressions** for **conclusions** ("best guesses"). They show how certain we are about our conclusions.

AFFIRMATIVE	VERY CERTAIN	NEGATIVE
must		can't, couldn't
have (got) to		must not
may		may not
might, could	LESS CERTAIN	might not

Use:

a. *must*, *have to*, and *have got to* when you are **very certain** that something is true

- That **must be** Blaire in that photo. It looks just like her.
- It **has to be** her. She used the same photo on her Facebook profile.

b. *may*, *might*, and *could* when you are **less certain**

- She **may want** her picture on Bob's page.
- They **could be** friends.

c. *can't* and *couldn't* when you are almost 100% certain that something is **impossible**

- Vince **can't be** a member of the *Survivor* fan group. He doesn't watch TV.
- It **couldn't be** that hard to do social networking. Millions of people do it.

d. *must not* when you are **slightly less certain**

- He **must not belong** to MySpace. I couldn't find his name.

e. *may not* and *might not* when you are **even less certain**

- He **may not use** his real name. A lot of people don't.

For **questions** about conclusions, use *can*, *could*, or expressions such as *Do you think . . . ?* or *Is it possible that . . . ?*
In **answers**, you can use *must (not)*, *have (got) to*, *may(not)*, *might (not)*, *could(n't)*, and *can't*.

- **A: Could** Magda's students **be** online now?
- **B:** No, they **can't be**. The lab is closed.
- **A:** *Do you think she knows* how to set up an online study group?
- **B:** She **must**. She set up a group for her class.

6 Use the following **modals** for **future possibility**:

a. *may*, *might*, and *could* to express the possibility that something **will happen** (The three modals have very similar meanings.)

- Terry **may get** online later. I'm not sure.
- He **might go** to the library tonight.
- Or he **could decide** to go to sleep early.

b. *may not* and *might not* to express the possibility that something **will not happen**

- I **may not** join Facebook.
- It **might not be** a good site for me.

BE CAREFUL! *Couldn't* means that something is **impossible**.

- Terry **couldn't go** to the library tonight. It's closed on Sunday.

We usually do not begin **questions** about possibility with *may*, *might*, or *could*. Instead we use *will* or *be going to* and phrases such as *Do you think . . . ?* or *Is it possible that . . . ?* However, we often use *may*, *might*, or *could* in **short answers** to these questions.

- **A:** *Will* Josh *join* our Facebook study group?
- **B:** He **might not**. He's very involved with his job right now.
- **A:** *Do you think it'll help* us pass chemistry?
- **B:** It **could**. People say study groups help.

EXERCISE 1: Discover the Grammar

A | *Read the FAQ about joining Facebook. Underline the modals and similar expressions.*
Also underline the verbs that follow.

◯ ◯ ◯   FAQs about facebook

How do I join Facebook?

It's easy. You just <u>have to complete</u> an online form with some basic information—your name, birthday, relationship status, etc. Oh, and you must have an email address.

Are there any age restrictions?

Yes. You must be 13 or older to join.

I'm worried about privacy. Do I really have to provide personal information such as my date of birth?

Yes you do. But you will be able to hide personal information if you'd like.

Do I have to post a photo of myself?

It's not required, but most people do. To get the full benefit of making connections, you ought to give as much information as you feel comfortable with. Remember: Facebook is a great resource, so get involved!

Can someone post a photo of me without my permission?

Yes. As long as it doesn't break any of Facebook's rules, people don't have to ask. However, if the photo is embarrassing, a lot of users feel the poster *really* ought to get permission.

What if I don't like a photo that someone has posted of me?

Unfortunately, Facebook cannot remove a photo if it hasn't broken any rules. If you're unhappy, however, you can choose to remove your name from it.

There must be some dangers in social networking. What should I do to protect myself?

The number 1 rule is this: You must not give your password to anyone. Ever.

Also, you should never give out information that strangers could use to contact you in the real world. And remember: Facebook tries to make the environment as safe as possible, but one day you may encounter objectionable content.[1]

---

[1]*objectionable content:* information and pictures that may upset people

B | *Write the underlined verbs in the correct column.*

MEANING	VERBS		
Ability	1. _____	3. _____	
	2. _____	4. _____	
Advice	1. _____	3. _____	
	2. _____	4. _____	
Necessity	1. *have to complete*	3. _____	5. _____
	2. _____	4. _____	6. _____
Prohibition	1. _____		
Future Possibility	1. _____		
	2. _____		
Conclusions	1. _____		

EXERCISE 2: Affirmative and Negative Modals

(Grammar Notes 1–5)

Circle the correct words to complete these posts on a social networking site.

1. Blaire Thomas wrote at 6:30 am

I <u>can't</u> / <u>shouldn't</u> believe I slept this late again! This <u>might / has got to</u> stop—or I'm going
    a.   **b.**
to flunk my early class.

Aneesh Hussain wrote at 6:35 am

LOL! You<u>'d better</u> / <u>may</u> stop posting and get going, girl! We have tests today.
           c.

Adam Hall wrote at 6:55 am

Hey, maybe you <u>should / must</u> get off Facebook a little earlier every night.
             d.

2. Vince Stevenson wrote at 7:00 am

I just saw the weather forecast. Looks like we <u>couldn't / 'll be able to</u> do that fishing trip
                                           a.
this weekend. Tell the kids to get their stuff ready Friday night—they <u>must / can't</u> sleep late
                                                         b.
on Saturday!

(continued on next page)

Ellie Stevenson wrote at 7:30 am

Good Morning, Dad. Macy says we <u>ought to / must not</u> bring the video camera—she's sure
                                        c.
she'll catch the biggest fish. Ben's bringing some friends, so we<u>'ll have to / won't have to</u>
                                                                              d.
find the big cooler. Do you have it?

Ben Stevenson wrote at 4:00 pm

Grandpa, I think our boat <u>may not / can't</u> be big enough. Dylan wants to come with us too.
                                  e.
What do you think? <u>Should / May</u> we rent a bigger one?
                          f.

---

3. Magda Tilia wrote at 9:00 pm

Hi, Class. Great work today! I <u>can / ought to</u> see your English improving every week. Next
                                        a.
week <u>couldn't / could</u> be the last time you <u>can / should</u> chat with your Eukliedis High School
        b.   c.
friends in Greece—they're going on summer break. So please show up online for them.
See you Friday—and remember, I <u>must / 'd better not</u> get your journals by then. I'll make
                                        d.
comments and send them back right away.

Lucian Banika wrote at 9:30 pm

Ms. Tilia, I won't <u>have to / be able to</u> come to class on Friday because of a family problem.
                          e.
I <u>could / must</u> leave my journal in your mailbox on Thursday. Is that OK?
      f.

---

4. Blaire Thomas wrote at 8:01 pm

It's 8:00—time for *Survivor*! I guess all you fans <u>must / must not</u> be in front of your TVs
                                                            a.
right now. Who's your favorite contestant so far? Who <u>should / may</u> they kick off the island
                                                                b.
tonight? Any comments?

Ben Sutter wrote at 8:15 pm

My favorite is Christine. She <u>may not / must</u> be the best contestant, but she's pretty good,
                                      c.
and she works hard. Mel <u>has to / could</u> be the one they kick off. I'm sure of it—there's no
                                d.
excuse for keeping him.

Sara Fry wrote at 9:00 pm

Hi Everybody. I'm posting from my Smart Phone. I'm on a camping trip so I <u>can / couldn't</u>
                                                                                    e.
watch *Survivor* tonight. Let me know what happened, please. And Blaire—you
<u>must / shouldn't</u> go to sleep now!
      f.

EXERCISE 3: Affirmative and Negative

Complete these posts to a reality TV message board. Rewrite the phrases in parentheses.
Use modals and similar expressions.

REALITY TV MESSAGE BOARD

[Follow-Ups] [Post a Reply] [Message Board Index]

bigfan: Any comments about *Pop Idols* last night? I _____*couldn't believe*_____ Jennifer

1. (didn't have the ability to believe)

Tasco didn't win!

aisha: I watched it, and you _____ more wrong. Jason deserved the prize.

2. (it's impossible for you to be)

He's a star. Jennifer isn't.

Kitsdad: Tonight on *Get a Job*, Ronald Trunk interviewed Lateesha and Sam. Too bad Trunk

_____ only one of them. I think he _____

3. (has the ability to keep)   4. (will possibly get rid of)

Lateesha, but I really think Sam _____ the one.

5. (it's a good idea for Sam to be)

winz1: Everybody knows that Sam was really sick last week. He _____

6. (it was necessary for him to go)

to the doctor! If you don't know that, then you _____ very much

7. (it's very certain that you don't know)

about the show.

Elly: *Survivor* is starting again soon! I love that show, and now that I'm not in school anymore, I

_____ missing classes to watch. They _____

8. (it won't be necessary to worry about)   9. (will possibly go)

to Palau this year, but it's not certain yet. I wish *I* were going to Palau!

bigfan: Elly, you _____ the show. You _____

10. (it would be a good idea to get on)   11. (it's possible for you to win)

a million dollars!

EXERCISE 4: Editing

Read the article about Wikipedia. There are ten mistakes in the use of modals. The first mistake is already corrected. Find and correct nine more.

Wikipedia (pronounced WIK-i-PEE-dee-a) It's fast (*wiki* means *quick* in Hawaiian), it's convenient (you ~~must not~~ *don't have to* go to the library), and, best of all, it's free. It's the world's most popular online encyclopedia, and you don't even have to register to use it. It's called "the free encyclopedia that anyone can edits." Volunteers around the world contribute to the millions of articles on its website, which are usually more up-to-date than what you may find in a book. You can't also click on hyperlinks to get more information. But, critics say, users ought be aware that the content may not always be 100 percent accurate. A "paper" encyclopedia has professional editors who fact check every article. Not so with Wikipedia. As a result, many teachers say their students should rely on it when they write reports. It's wrong to think that just because an article is on a famous website, it must be reliable. It mights be a good starting point when researching a topic, but writers should then check the facts with other sources. Then there is always the issue of plagiarism.[1] Remember: Wikipedia information is free to use and edit, but you don't have to copy other people's writing without giving them credit. It's against the law!

Along with the freedom of Wikipedia come some dangers. People can "vandalize" articles. This means that they maliciously[2] insert wrong information into a text or remove important facts. Wikipedia says it deals quickly with these attacks, but, again, users has to be aware that information could be wrong.

Online encyclopedias have changed the way we get information. May they one day replace paper encyclopedias? It's possible. But for now, it might be a good idea to hold on to that library card. In the meantime, it's safe to say that despite some disadvantages, an online encyclopedia can't be a very useful resource if you are careful and use common sense.

---

[1] **plagiarism:** using someone else's words in your own work without giving that person credit
[2] **maliciously:** doing something to deliberately hurt someone

EXERCISE 5: Listening

A | *Read the statements. Then listen to the conversation. Listen again and check (✓)* **True** *or* **False***. Correct the false statements.*

	True	False
1. The woman ~~uses~~ *doesn't use* Facebook.	☐	☑
2. The woman is very busy.	☐	☐
3. The man thinks Facebook is dangerous.	☐	☐
4. The woman would like to make new friends online.	☐	☐
5. The man thinks the woman should join Facebook.	☐	☐
6. The man and woman can chat online on Facebook.	☐	☐
7. The woman promises to consider joining.	☐	☐

B | *Complete the conversation with modals that you think are possible. Then listen again and check your work. If the conversation uses a different modal, write the modal that you hear.*

A: Lea, you really _____*must*_____ join Facebook. You're my only friend who isn't on it.
                        1.

B: I just don't have time for it. There are too many other things that I _____ do.
                                                                                          2.

A: You _____ have *some* free time.
              3.

B: Sure I do. But I _____ afford to spend it online. Besides, isn't it a little dangerous?
                       4.

A: Not really. Of course, you _____ be careful and use common sense. Just like
                                  5.

   with other things.

B: Well, I guess you _____ be right.
                         6.

A: Trust me. It's a lot of fun. And you _____ meet a lot of interesting people that
                                           7.

   way. Like me, for example!

B: I _____ join Facebook to meet interesting people. But on second thought,
        8.

   I suppose it _____ be fun to reconnect with old friends.
                9.

A: Exactly. You really _____ give it some thought. Will you think about it?
                          10.

B: _____ we _____ chat online if I join?
                         11.

A: Sure.

B: In that case, I _____ !
                      12.

EXERCISE 6: Pronunciation

A | *Read and listen to the Pronunciation Note.*

B | *Listen to the short conversations and write the words you hear. Use full forms.*

1. **A:** You _____ join Facebook. It's a lot of fun.

   B: I know. But first I _____ get a new email address.

2. **A:** Do you _____ post a photo of yourself?

   B: No. But you _____ give information about yourself.

3. **A:** You _____ see Jason's new photos. They're great.

   B: I've heard about them, but I _____ sign on last night.

4. **A:** Will you _____ email me the photos?

   B: No problem. I just _____ find them on my computer.

5. **A:** I _____ write a report about social networking.

   B: You _____ look it up on Wikipedia first.

C | *Listen again to the conversations and repeat each question and statement. Then practice the conversations with a partner.*

EXERCISE 7: Discussion

Look at Blaire Thomas's profile on a social networking site. Work with a partner and discuss the site. Use modals. Answer these questions:

- What information shouldn't Blaire have on her profile? What should she keep?
- Does she have too many social networking friends? Why or why not?
- What skills and talents do you think Blaire has?
- What can you guess about her interests?

Blaire shares other profile information with her friends. Click here to make friends.

Blaire Thomas
Female, Age 17
Orlando, Florida, USA

Networks: Waterfront High School
Disney Resorts
Interests: My guitar class, part-time job at Disney Resorts, working out with friends
Danny and Mica
Music: Anything on the guitar, High School Musical, Taylor Swift, Jonas Brothers
Movies: *The Social Network, Avatar, Date Night, La Gloire de Mon Père, Amelie*
TV: *Survivor!* I must be this show's biggest fan!
Books: Books? What are they?

Blaire's bumper stickers

  My friends are pretty awesome.

Hang up and drive! It's never too late to have a happy childhood.

Blaire has 840 Friends (top 3)

Blaire's quizzes and games:
Desert Island
Know-it-All

Ben   Sara   Jesse

EXAMPLE: **A:** She should protect her privacy better. For example, she shouldn't give so much personal information.
B: That's true. It could be dangerous to give your full name and . . .
A: I think Blaire might . . .

EXERCISE 8: Reaching Agreement

Work in small groups. Imagine you are designing a class website. What will you include?
What issues will you have to consider? For example:

- information that you should and shouldn't include about students and your class

- people who can and can't post on the site (for example, classmates, teacher, friends, and family)

- content and features that students might or might not want (for example, photos, videos, chat, discussion forums, fun quizzes and games)

- links to other Internet sites that could be helpful resources (for example, online dictionaries and information about other countries)

- ways that you can get your classmates involved in the website

EXAMPLE: **A:** We should post photos of class members.
              B: But we'd better not give too much personal information.
              C: Students might like to post recipes from their countries.

EXERCISE 9: Problem Solving

A | *Many social networking sites have fun quizzes that people link to their pages. Take this quiz about surviving on a desert island.*

IMAGINE YOU ARE IN A GROUP ON A REALITY TV SHOW CALLED <u>DESERT ISLAND</u>. WHAT SHOULD YOU DO? TAKE THE QUIZ.

1. You only have time to grab one thing. What *must* you have to survive?
- ○ We've got to bring a knife.
- ○ We'll need a fishing rod.
- ○ We should take a mirror.
- ○ Other

2. You've just arrived on the island. What should you do first?
- ○ We'd better take a nap.
- ○ We ought to find fresh water.
- ○ We should build a campfire.
- ○ Other

3. There are no fast-food places on the island. What's for dinner?
- ○ Maybe we can catch some fish.
- ○ Yuck. There must be a village nearby.
- ○ We could eat insects.
- ○ Other

4. The island is getting boring. How can you pass the time?
- ○ We could explore the island.
- ○ We should practice swimming.
- ○ We've got to build a shelter.
- ○ Other

5. There are other people on the island! You hear their voices. What should you do?
- ○ We should say hello.
- ○ Watch first. They may be friendly.
- ○ Avoid them. They may not be friendly.
- ○ Other

6. Planes and ships sometimes pass by. How can you attract their attention?
- ○ We've got to build a big fire on the beach.
- ○ We should scream loudly.
- ○ We could use a mirror to signal them.
- ○ Other

B | *Work in small groups. Compare your choices and decide what your group should do.*

EXAMPLE: **A:** We have to bring a mirror. With a mirror, we can start a fire . . .
B: We'd better not take a nap. We've got to . . .
C: For dinner, we ought to . .

EXERCISE 10: For or Against

A | *In a group, discuss the advantages and the disadvantages of online social networking. You can use these ideas and your own knowledge and experience.*

- How can social networking help people?
- What should you do to get the most benefit from networking?
- What are some of the problems?
- What are some of the things you must do to be safe and protect your privacy?
- Do the advantages outweigh the disadvantages?

B | *Share your ideas in a discussion with the whole class.*

EXAMPLE: **A:** You can find out other students' opinions about schools.
B: You could also learn about jobs.
C: You might even . . .

EXERCISE 11: Writing

A | *Write a post for a personal blog about your plans for the week. Write about things that you are* **going to do, might do, should do,** *and* **have to do.**

EXAMPLE: Next week is going to be a busy week. I have exams on Monday and Wednesday, so I really should study this weekend. I've got to bring that math grade up. I've finally chosen some colors, so on Saturday I'm going to paint the living room. I can't do it myself in one weekend, so I posted my plan on Facebook. Some friends might help me paint . . .

B | *Check your work. Use the Editing Checklist.*

Editing Checklist
Did you use . . . ? ☐ modals for ability ☐ modals for advice ☐ modals for necessity ☐ modals for possibility ☐ the base form of verbs after modals

Check your answers on page UR-4.

Do you need to review anything?

A | *Circle the correct words to complete the conversations.*

- **A:** Were you able to <u>get / got</u> in touch with Carla?
     1.

  B: No, but I left her a message on Facebook. She <u>couldn't / may</u> see it there.
     2.

- **A:** You <u>'ve got / must</u> to see my photos of our class trip. They're really funny.
     3.

  B: I <u>can't / not able to</u> log on right now. I'll check them out later.
     4.

- **A:** Could my MySpace page <u>helps / help</u> me get into college?
     5.

  B: It <u>might be / might</u>. You ought to <u>post / posted</u> information about your school activities.
     6.   **7.**

- **A:** The rules say that to join this site you <u>must not / don't have to</u> be under 13.
     8.

  B: So you're still too young. But you'll <u>can / be able to</u> join next month.
     9.

B | *Rewrite the phrases in parentheses using modals and similar expressions.*

1. You _____ personal information on the Internet.
   (it's a very bad idea to give)

2. We _____ today or we won't be able to attend classes.
   (it's urgent that we register)

3. Sasha _____ online. I'm sure she's studying for her test.
   (it's almost certain that Sasha isn't)

4. Takumi _____ more sleep. He fell asleep in class again today.
   (it's absolutely necessary that Takumi get)

5. Sorry, you _____ here. See the sign?
   (it's against the rules to eat)

6. Paulo _____ to the party tonight, but he hasn't decided yet.
   (will possibly come)

C | *Find and correct five mistakes.*

1. Could that being Amelie in this photograph?

2. No, that's impossible. It doesn't look anything like Amelie. It doesn't have to be her.

3. I don't know this person. I guess I'd not better accept him as a friend on my Facebook page.

4. With MySpace, I must not call to keep in touch with friends. It's just not necessary.

5. May hi5 be as popular as Facebook someday?

Advisability in the Past
REGRETS

Before You Read

Look at the photo. Discuss the questions.

1. How do you think the woman feels?
2. What is she thinking about?
3. What are some typical things that people have regrets about?

Read

Read the article from a popular psychology magazine.

Useless Regrets

For all sad words of tongue or pen
*The saddest are these: "It **might have been**."*
—John Greenleaf Whittier

"It **might have been**." These are not only the saddest words, but perhaps the most destructive. According to recent ideas in psychology, our feelings are mainly the result of the way we *think* about reality, not reality itself.

According to Nathan S. Kline, M.D., it's not unusual to feel deep regret about things in the past that you think you **should have done** and did not do—or the opposite, about things you did and feel you **should not have done**. In fact, we learn by thinking about past mistakes. For example, a student who fails a test learns that he or she **should have studied** more and can improve on the next test.

However, thinking too much about past mistakes and missed opportunities can create such bad feelings that people become paralyzed[1] and can't move on with their lives. Arthur Freeman, Ph.D., and Rose DeWolf have labeled this process "woulda/coulda/shoulda thinking," and they have written an entire book about this type of disorder.

I **should've been** rich and famous by now.

I **ought to have applied** to college.

I **could've become** a doctor.

My parents **shouldn't have discouraged** me.

(continued on next page)

───────────

[1]*paralyzed:* not able to think clearly and make decisions or act

Useless Regrets

In *Woulda/Coulda/Shoulda: Overcoming Regrets, Mistakes, and Missed Opportunities*, Freeman and DeWolf suggest challenging regrets with specifics. "Instead of saying, 'I **should've done** better,'" they suggest, "Write down an example of a way in which you **might have done** better. Exactly what **should** you **have done** to produce the results you were hoping for? Did you have the skills, money, experience, etc., at the time?" Perhaps the student who **should have studied** more was exhausted from job and family responsibilities and really couldn't spend more time studying.

When people examine their feelings of regret about the past, they often find that many of them are frequently based on simple misunderstandings of a situation. A mother regrets missing a football game in which her son's leg was injured. She blames herself and the officials. "I **should've gone**," she keeps telling herself. "I **could've prevented** the injury.

They **might** at least **have telephoned** me as soon as it happened." Did she *really* have the power to prevent her son's injury? **Should** the officials **have called** her *before* looking at the injury? Probably not.

Once people realize how unrealistic their feelings of regret are, they are more ready to let go of them. Psychologist David Burns, M.D., suggests specific strategies for dealing with useless feelings of regret and getting on with the present. One amusing technique is to spend 10 minutes a day writing down all the things you regret. Then say them all aloud (better yet, record them), and listen to yourself.

After you recognize how foolish most feelings of regret sound, the next step is to let go of them and to start dealing with the problems you face right now.

I **shouldn't have told** that joke in the office. My career is ruined.

I **ought to have cleaned** the house instead of going out this weekend. My mother's right. I'm just lazy.

My boyfriend **could have told** me he was going out of town this weekend. He's an inconsiderate[2] jerk.[3] I **should** never **have started** going out with him.

---

[2]*inconsiderate:* not caring about other people's needs or feelings
[3]*jerk:* (informal) a stupid or very annoying person

After You Read

A | **Vocabulary:** *Circle the letter of the word or phrase closest in meaning to the words in* **blue.**

1. Rosa has a new **strategy** for finding a new job.
   a. plan of action
   b. suit
   c. Internet site

2. Sarah wants to help people, so she has decided to major in **psychology**.
   a. the science of how to eat in a healthy way
   b. the study of exercise and movement
   c. the study of how people think and feel

3. Jeb's career wasn't **ruined** because he told that joke. He's still got the same job.
   a. improved
   b. destroyed
   c. changed

4. Petros's goal to learn English in two months is **unrealistic**.
   a. impossible
   b. not popular
   c. really smart

5. The teacher mentioned several good **techniques** for learning vocabulary.
   a. DVDs
   b. methods
   c. schools

6. When I was applying to school, the **process** seemed long and difficult.
   a. series of steps
   b. application form
   c. school catalog

B | **Comprehension:** *Circle the correct word or phrase to complete each statement.*

1. Some psychologists say that it is our thoughts / real situations that cause our feelings.

2. Thoughts like "I should have studied more" can get a student to give up / improve.

3. "Woulda/Shoulda/Coulda" thinking often paralyzes / helps people.

4. Arthur Freeman and Rose DeWolf suggest ignoring / questioning regrets.

5. The thought "I could have prevented the injury" was realistic / unrealistic.

6. Dr. David Burns suggests a strategy for dealing with regrets that might make you cry / laugh.

7. Saying regrets aloud can make them sound silly / intelligent.

ADVISABILITY IN THE PAST:
Should Have, Ought to Have, Could Have, Might Have

Statements				
Subject	**Modal***	*Have*	**Past Participle**	
He	should (not) ought (not) to could might	**have**	**told**	her.

Contractions		
should have	=	**should've**
could have	=	**could've**
might have	=	**might've**
should not have	=	**shouldn't have**

*Should, *ought to, could,* and *might* are modals. Modals have only one form. They do not have *-s* in the third person singular.

Yes / No Questions				
Should	**Subject**	*Have*	**Past Participle**	
Should	he	**have**	**told**	her?

Short Answers							
Affirmative				**Negative**			
Yes,	he	**should**	**have.**	**No,**	he	**shouldn't**	**have.**

Wh- Questions					
Wh- Word	*Should*	**Subject**	*Have*	**Past Participle**	
When	**should**	he	**have**	**told**	her?

GRAMMAR NOTES

1 Use the modals **should have**, **ought to have**, **could have**, and **might have** to talk about **past advisability**.

   a. These past modals often express **regret** about something that happened, especially when we use them with **I** or **we**.

- **I should've applied** to college.
  (*I didn't apply, and now I'm sorry.*)
- **We could've gone** to a much better school.
  (*We didn't go to a better school. Now we regret our choice.*)

   b. These past modals often **express blame** or **criticism** about something that happened, especially when we use them with **you**, **she**, **he**, or **they**.

- **You shouldn't have sent** that letter. It hurt her.
  (*You sent the letter. That was wrong.*)
- **They could have called** us. We waited for hours.
  (*They didn't call. That was inconsiderate.*)

USAGE NOTE: We use **should have**, **ought to have**, and **could have** for **regret** or **blame**. **Might have** (with *you*, *she*, *he*, or *they*) usually expresses **blame**.

- **I ought to have studied** more.
  (*I didn't study. I regret it.*)
- **He might've told** me. I needed to know.
  (*He didn't tell me. That was wrong.*)

2 In **affirmative statements**, use **should have**, **ought to have**, **could have**, and **might have**. *Should have* is the most common form.

- He **should have taken** the math exam.
- He **could've left** home earlier.

In **negative statements**, use **shouldn't have** and **ought not to have**. *Shouldn't have* is more common.
Do NOT use *couldn't have* or *might not have* for past advisability.

- He **shouldn't have missed** the exam.
- He **ought not to have left** so late.

   Not: He ~~could'nt have~~ left so late. That was a mistake.

In **questions** (both *yes / no* and *wh-* questions), use **should have**. Notice that **short answers** include **modal + have**.

- A: **Should** he **have** called the teacher?
- B: Yes, he **should've**.
  Not: Yes, he ~~should~~.
- A: When **should** he **have** called?
- B: Before the test started.

3 We use the **contractions should've**, **could've**, and **might've** in speech, emails, and informal notes.

- I **should've** answered sooner.
  (*informal note*)

We sometimes use "**shoulda**," "**coulda**," "**mighta**," and "**oughta**" in **very informal** notes, emails, and text messages.

- I **shoulda** answered sooner.
  (*email to friend*)

BE CAREFUL! Do NOT use these forms in **formal** writing.

- I **should have** answered sooner.
  (*business letter*)

REFERENCE NOTE
Could have and **might have** are also used for **speculations about the past** (see Unit 17).

EXERCISE 1: Discover the Grammar

Read each numbered statement. Circle the letter of the sentence that is similar in meaning.

1. I shouldn't have called him.
   - **a.** I called him.
   - **b.** I didn't call him.

2. My parents ought to have moved away from that neighborhood.
   - **a.** They're going to move, but they're not sure when.
   - **b.** Moving was a good idea, but they didn't do it.

3. I should have studied psychology.
   - **a.** I didn't study psychology, and now I regret it.
   - **b.** I studied psychology, and it was a big mistake.

4. He might have warned us about the traffic.
   - **a.** He didn't know, so he couldn't tell us.
   - **b.** He knew, but he didn't tell us.

5. Felicia could have been a vice president by now.
   - **a.** Felicia didn't become a vice president.
   - **b.** Felicia is a vice president.

6. They shouldn't have lent him their car.
   - **a.** They refused to lend him their car.
   - **b.** They lent him their car.

7. I ought not to have bought that sweater.
   - **a.** I bought the sweater.
   - **b.** I didn't buy the sweater.

EXERCISE 2: Statements, Questions, and Short Answers   *(Grammar Note 2)*

A class is discussing an ethical problem. Read the problem. Complete the discussion with the correct form of the verbs in parentheses or with short answers. Choose between affirmative and negative.

PROBLEM: Greg, a college student, worked successfully for a clothing store for a year. He spent most of his salary on books and tuition. One week he wanted some extra money to buy a sweater to wear to a party. He asked for a raise, but his boss, Mr. Thompson, refused. The same week, Greg discovered an extra sweater in a shipment he was unpacking. It was very stylish and just his size. Greg "borrowed" it for the weekend and then brought it back. Mr. Thompson found out and fired him.

TEACHER: _____*Should*_____ Mr. Thompson _____*have given*_____ Greg a raise?
1. (should / give)

STUDENT A: Yes, he _____*should have*_____. After all, Greg had worked there for a whole
2.

year. Mr. Thompson _____*shouldn't have refused*_____ at that point.
3. (should / refuse)

STUDENT B: But maybe Mr. Thompson couldn't afford to give Greg a raise. Anyway, Greg still

_____ the sweater. It wasn't his.
4. (should / take)

TEACHER: What strategy _____ Greg _____ instead?
5. (should / use)

STUDENT C: He _____ Mr. Thompson to sell him the sweater. Then
6. (might / ask)

he _____ for it slowly, out of his salary.
7. (could / pay)

STUDENT A: He _____ his old clothes to the party. His behavior was
8. (ought to / wear)

destructive. He just hurt himself by taking the sweater.

TEACHER: Well, _____ Mr. Thompson _____ Greg?
9. (should / fire)

STUDENT B: No, he _____. Greg had been a good employee for a
10.

year, and he brought the sweater back. Now Greg's reputation might be ruined.

TEACHER: How _____ Mr. Thompson _____ the situation?
11. (should / handle)

STUDENT C: He _____ Greg. He _____ just
12. (ought to / warn)

_____ Greg without any warning.
13. (should / fire)

EXERCISE 3: Affirmative and Negative Statements

(Grammar Note 2)

Complete Greta's regrets or complaints about the past using the modals in parentheses.
Choose between affirmative and negative.

1. I didn't go to college. Now I'm depressed about my job.

(should) _I should have gone to college._____

2. My brother quit his job. He thought he could find another job right away. I knew that was
unrealistic, but I didn't warn him. How inconsiderate of me.

(might) _____

3. I feel sick. I ate all the chocolate.

(should) _____

(continued on next page)

4. Christina didn't come over. She didn't even call. My entire evening was ruined.

(might) _____

5. I tried to tell Christina how I felt, but it was useless. She just didn't listen to me.

(could) _____

6. I jogged 5 miles yesterday, and now I'm exhausted.

(should) _____

7. I didn't apply for a good job because the application process was so long. I gave up.

(should) _____

8. I didn't do the laundry yesterday, so I don't have any clean socks. Everyone else gets their laundry done on time. Why can't I?

(ought to) _____

9. I didn't invite Cynthia to the party. Now she's angry at me.

(should) _____

10. Yesterday was my birthday, and my brother didn't send me a card. I'm hurt.

(might) _____

EXERCISE 4: Editing

(Grammar Notes 1–3)

Read this journal entry. There are six mistakes in the use of modals. The first mistake is already corrected. Find and correct five more.

December 15

About a week ago, Jennifer was late for work again, and Doug, our boss, told me he
                                                                              have
wanted to fire her. I was really upset. Of course, Jennifer shouldn't ~~had~~ been late so

often, but he might has talked to her about the problem before he decided to let her

go. Then he laughed and told me to make her job difficult for her so that she would

quit. He thought it was amusing! I just pretended I didn't hear him. What a mistake!

It was unrealistic to think the problem would just go away. I ought confronted him

right away. Or I could at least have warned Jennifer. Anyway, Jennifer is still here, but

now I'm worried about my own job. Should I have telling Doug's boss? I wonder. Maybe

I should handle things differently last week. The company should never has hired this

guy. I'd better figure out some techniques for handling these situations.

STEP 4 COMMUNICATION PRACTICE

EXERCISE 5: Listening

A | *Jennifer is taking Dr. David Burns's advice by recording all the things she regrets at the end of the day. Look at Jennifer's list. Then listen to her recording. Listen again and check (✓) the things she did.*

TO DO

- ☐ Do homework
- ☑ Walk to work
- ☐ Make $100 bank deposit
- ☐ Buy coat
- ☐ Call Aunt Rose
- ☐ Call Ron
- ☐ Go to supermarket
- ☐ Finish David Burns's book

B | *Read these statements from Jennifer's recording. Then listen and complete the statements.*

1. I _____ could've done _____ my homework.

2. I _____ to work today.

3. I really _____ that $100 deposit today.

4. I _____ that new coat.

5. I _____ at least _____ to wish her a happy birthday.

6. I _____ to the supermarket.

7. I _____ that David Burns book.

EXERCISE 6: Pronunciation

A | *Read and listen to the Pronunciation Note.*

Pronunciation Note

In **past modals**, we sometimes pronounce **have** or its contraction **'ve** like the word "a." We only do this in fast, informal conversation.

Examples:
I **should have** called you.	→ "I **shoulda** called you."
They **could have** helped more.	→ "They **coulda** helped more."
He **might have** told me sooner.	→ "He **mighta** told me sooner."

We sometimes pronounce **ought to have** like "oughta of."

Example: They **ought to have** come on time. → "They **oughta of** come on time."

Advisability in the Past **265**

1. **A:** Doug _____ sent that email.

   B: I know. But you _____ told him that yesterday.

2. **A:** We _____ taken the train.

   B: You're right. We _____ been home by now.

3. **A:** I guess I _____ accepted that job.

   B: Well, maybe you _____ waited a few days before deciding.

4. **A:** You _____ washed that T-shirt in cold water.

   B: I guess I _____ read the label before I washed it.

5. **A:** I _____ asked my sister to lend me some money

   B: She's your *sister*! She _____ *offered* to help.

C | *Practice the conversations with a partner.*

EXERCISE 7: Game: Find the Problems

Work with a partner. Look at the picture of Jennifer's apartment. What should she have done? What shouldn't she have done? Write as many sentences as you can in five minutes. When you are done, compare your answers with those of your classmates.

EXAMPLE: **A:** She should have paid the electric bill.
            B: She shouldn't have left the window open.

EXERCISE 8: Survey

A | *A sense of obligation is a feeling that you (or someone else) should have done or shouldn't have done something. How strong is your sense of obligation? Take this test and find out.*

Sense of Obligation Survey (S.O.S.)

INSTRUCTIONS: Read each situation. Circle the letter of your most likely response.

1. You want to lose 10 pounds, but you just ate a large dish of ice cream.
   a. I shouldn't have eaten the ice cream. I have no willpower.
   b. I deserve to enjoy things once in a while. I'll do better tomorrow.

2. Your friend quit her job. Now she's unemployed.
   a. Maybe she was really depressed at work. It's better that she left.
   b. She shouldn't have quit until she found another job.

3. You had an appointment with your doctor. You arrived on time but had to wait more than an hour.
   a. My doctor should have scheduled better. My time is valuable too.
   b. Maybe there was an emergency. I'm sure it's not my doctor's fault.

4. You bought a coat for $140. A day later you saw it at another store for $100.
   a. That was really bad luck.
   b. I should have looked around before I bought the coat.

5. Your brother didn't send you a birthday card.
   a. He could have at least called. He's so inconsiderate.
   b. Maybe he forgot. He's really been busy lately.

6. You just got back an English test. Your grade was 60 percent.
   a. That was a really difficult test.
   b. I should have studied harder.

7. You just found out that an electrician overcharged you.
   a. I should have known that was too much money.
   b. How could I have known? I'm not an expert.

8. You forgot to do some household chores that you had promised to do. Now the person you live with is angry.
   a. I shouldn't have forgotten. I'm irresponsible.
   b. I'm only human. I make mistakes.

9. You got a ticket for driving 5 miles per hour above the speed limit.
   a. I ought to have obeyed the speed limit.
   b. The police officer could've overlooked it and not given me the ticket. It was only 5 miles over the speed limit.

10. You went to the movies but couldn't get a ticket because it was sold out.
   a. I should've gone earlier.
   b. Wow! This movie is really popular!

SCORING
Give yourself one point for each of these answers:

1. **a**	6. **b**
2. **b**	7. **a**
3. **a**	8. **a**
4. **b**	9. **a**
5. **a**	10. **a**

The higher your score, the stronger your sense of obligation.

B | *Now interview a classmate and compare your survey results.*

EXAMPLE: **A:** What was your answer to Question 1?
B: I said I shouldn't have eaten the ice cream. What about you?

EXERCISE 9: Problem Solving

Work in small groups. Read and discuss each case. Did the people act properly or should they have done things differently?

Case 1: Sheila was in her last year of college when she decided to run for student council president. During her campaign, a school newspaper reporter asked her about something he had discovered about her past. In high school, Sheila had once been caught cheating on a test. She had admitted her mistake and repeated the course. She never cheated again. Sheila felt that the incident was over, and she refused to answer the reporter's questions. The reporter wrote the story without telling Sheila's side, and Sheila lost the election.

> **EXAMPLE:** **A:** Should Sheila have refused to answer questions about her past?
> **B:** I don't think so. It's useless to refuse to answer reporters' questions. They always report about it anyway.
> **C:** I agree. She should've . . .

Case 2: Mustafa is a social worker who cares deeply about his clients. Recently, there was a fire in his office building. After the fire, the fire department declared the building unsafe and wouldn't allow anyone to go back in. Mustafa became worried and depressed because all his clients' records were in the building. He needed their names, telephone numbers, and other information in order to help them. He decided to take the risk, and he entered the building to get the records. His supervisor found out and fired him.

Case 3: Pierre's wife has been sick for a long time. One day, the doctor told Pierre about a new medicine that might save her life. He warned Pierre that the medicine was still experimental, so Pierre's insurance would not pay for it. At the pharmacy, Pierre discovered that the medicine was so expensive that he didn't have enough money to pay for it. The pharmacist refused to let Pierre pay for it later. At first, Pierre was paralyzed by fear and hopelessness. Then he took extra work on nights and weekends to pay for the medicine. Now he's too exhausted to take care of his wife as well as he had before.

EXERCISE 10: Writing

A | *Write three paragraphs about a dilemma that you have faced.*

- **Paragraph 1:** Describe the problem and what you did.
- **Paragraph 2:** Evaluate what you should or should not have done.
- **Paragraph 3:** Write about what you learned.

B | *Check your work. Use the Editing Checklist.*

Editing Checklist

Did you use . . . ?

☐ *should have*, *ought to have*, *could have*, *might have* + **past participle** for affirmative statements

☐ *should not have* and *ought not to have* + **past participle** for negative statements

Check your answers on page UR-4.
Do you need to review anything?

A | Circle the correct words to complete the sentences.

1. I got a C on my test. I should <u>had / have</u> studied more.

2. I <u>ought / should</u> to have asked for help.

3. Dara <u>could / couldn't</u> have offered to help me. She's very good at math.

4. The teacher might have <u>gave / given</u> me a little more time.

5. I was tired. I <u>couldn't / shouldn't</u> have stayed up so late the night before.

6. What <u>should I / I should</u> have done differently?

B | Rewrite the sentences with the correct form of the modals in parentheses. Choose between affirmative and negative.

1. I regret that I didn't study for the math test.

   (should) _____

2. It was wrong of you not to show me your class notes.

   (could) _____

3. I regret that I stayed up so late the night before the test.

   (should) _____

4. It was wrong of John not to call you.

   (ought to) _____

5. I blame you for not inviting me to join the study group.

   (might) _____

C | Find and correct nine mistakes.

   I shouldn't have stay up so late. I overslept and missed my bus. I ought have asked Erik for a ride. I got to the office late, and my boss said, "You might had called." She was right. I shouldn't have called. At lunch my co-workers went out together. They really could of invited me to join them. Should have I said something to them? Then, after lunch, my mother called. She said, "Yesterday was Aunt Em's birthday. You could've sending her a card!" I really think my mother might has reminded me. Not a good day! I shouldn't have just stayed in bed.

UNIT 17

Speculations and Conclusions About the Past

UNSOLVED MYSTERIES

STEP 1 GRAMMAR IN CONTEXT

Before You Read

Look at the photo. Discuss the questions.

1. What do you think the design represents?
2. Who do you think made it? When?

Read

Read about one writer's theories on ancient cultures.

CLOSE ENCOUNTERS

In 1927, Toribio Mexta Xesspe of Peru **must have been** very surprised to see lines in the shapes of huge animals and geometric[1] forms on the ground below his airplane. Created by the ancient Nazca culture, these beautiful forms (over 13,000 of them) are too big to recognize from the ground. However, from about 600 feet in the air, the giant forms take shape. Xesspe **may have been** the first human in almost a thousand years to recognize the designs.

Since their discovery, many people have speculated about the Nazca lines. Without airplanes, how **could** an ancient culture **have made** these amazing pictures? What purpose **could** they **have had**?

Nazca lines

---

[1]**geometric:** using lines or shapes from geometry, such as circles, rectangles, and squares

One writer, Erich von Däniken, has a theory as amazing as the Nazca lines themselves. According to von Däniken, visitors from other planets brought their civilization to the Earth thousands of years ago. When these astronauts[2] visited ancient cultures here on Earth, the people of those cultures **must have believed** that the visitors were gods. Since the Nazcans **could have built** the lines according to instructions from an aircraft, von Däniken concludes that the drawings **might have marked** a landing strip for the spacecraft of the ancient astronauts. Von Däniken writes, "The builders of the geometrical figures **may have had** no idea what they were doing. But perhaps they knew perfectly well what the 'gods' needed in order to land."

In his book *Chariots[3] of the Gods?* von Däniken offers many other "proofs" that ancient cultures had contact with visitors from other planets. Giant statues on Easter Island provide von Däniken with strong evidence of the astronauts' presence. Von Däniken estimates that the island **could** only **have supported** a very small population. After examining the simple tools that the islanders probably used, he concludes that even 2,000 men working day and night **could not have been** enough to carve the figures out of hard stone. In addition, he says that at least part of the population **must have worked** in the fields, **gone** fishing, and **woven** cloth. "Two thousand men alone **could not have made** the gigantic statues." Von Däniken's conclusion: Space visitors **had to have built** them.

Archeologists,[4] among others, are skeptical[5] and prefer to look for answers closer to home. However, von Däniken's theories continue to fascinate people, both believers and nonbelievers. And even nonbelievers must admit that visitors from space **might have contributed** to human culture. After all, no one can prove that they didn't.

Easter Island: Statues of space visitors?

---

[2]***astronaut:*** someone who travels and works in a spacecraft

[3]***chariot:*** a vehicle with two wheels, pulled by a horse, used in ancient times in battles and races

[4]***archeologist:*** someone who studies ancient societies by examining the remains of their buildings, tools, and other objects

[5]***skeptical:*** having doubts whether something is true; not believing something

After You Read

A | Vocabulary: *Complete the sentences with the words from the box.*

conclusion	contribute	encounter	estimate	evidence	speculate

1. Dr. Shane has good _____ to support her theory about the Nazca lines.

2. Please _____ ideas for the class project. We need to hear everyone's thoughts.

3. I _____ that there were about 50 people at the party. I don't know the exact number, but the restaurant was very crowded.

4. It's fun to _____ about space aliens, but there are almost no facts to support their existence.

5. After looking at the facts, we came to the _____ that space visitors didn't build the statues.

6. Rob had an interesting _____ with his old roommate at the concert. He didn't expect to see him, and they had a great time talking.

B | Comprehension: *How certain was Erich von Däniken about his ideas? Check (✓) the correct column for each statement.*

	Certain	Possible	Impossible
1. The Nazca people believed that the visitors were gods.	☐	☐	☐
2. The Nazca lines marked a landing strip for ancient astronauts.	☐	☐	☐
3. There were enough people on Easter Island to carve the huge statues.	☐	☐	☐
4. Space visitors built the statues.	☐	☐	☐

SPECULATIONS AND CONCLUSIONS ABOUT THE PAST:
May have, Might have, Could have, Must have, Had to have

Statements				
Subject	**Modal* / *Had to***	***Have***	**Past Participle**	
They	**may (not)** **might (not)** **could (not)** **must (not)** **had to**	**have**	**seen**	the statues.

* *May, might, could,* and *must* are modals. Modals have only one form. They do not have -s in the third person singular.

Contractions	
may have	= **may've**
might have	= **might've**
could have	= **could've**
must have	= **must've**
could not	= **couldn't**

NOTE: We usually do not contract *may not have, might not have,* or *must not have.*

Questions			
Do / Be	**Subject**	**Verb**	
Did	they	**carve**	these statues?
Were			aliens?

Short Answers			
Subject	**Modal / *Had to***	***Have***	***Been***
They	**may (not)** **might (not)** **could (not)**	**have.**	
	must (not) **had to**	**have**	**been.**

Yes / No Questions: *Could*				
Could	**Subject**	***Have***	**Past Participle**	
Could	he	**have**	**seen**	aliens?
			been	an alien?

Short Answers			
Subject	**Modal / *Had to***	***Have***	***Been***
He	**may (not)** **might (not)** **could (not)**	**have.**	
	must (not) **had to**	**have**	**been.**

Wh- Questions				
***Wh-* Word**	***Could***	***Have***	**Past Participle**	
Who	**could**	**have**	**built**	the statues?
What			**happened**	to these people?

GRAMMAR NOTES

1	Use **may have**, **might have**, and **could have** to talk about **past possibilities**. These **speculations** about past situations are usually based on only a few facts.	**FACT:** Archeologists found many pictures of creatures with wings. **SPECULATIONS:** • Space beings **may have visited** that civilization. • The pictures **might have marked** a landing strip for a spacecraft. • The pictures **could have shown** mythological creatures.
2	Use **must have** and **had to have** when you are almost certain about your **conclusions**. In **negative conclusions**, do NOT use *didn't have to have*. Use **must not have** instead.	**FACT:** The Easter Island statues are made of stone. **CONCLUSIONS:** • The islanders **must have had** very sharp tools. • They **had to have been** skilled stoneworkers. • The stones **must not have been** easy to move. NOT: The stones ~~didn't have to have been~~ . . .
3	**Couldn't have** often expresses a feeling of disbelief or **impossibility**.	• He **couldn't have believed** space visitors helped them! It doesn't make any sense.
4	**Questions** about past possibility usually use **could have**. They do not usually use *may have* or *might have*.	• **Could** the Nazcans **have drawn** those lines? NOT COMMON: ~~Might~~ the Nazcans have drawn . . . ?
5	In **short answers** to questions about past possibility use: a. **been** when the questions include a form of **be** b. **modal** + **have** when the questions do NOT include forms of *be*	 A: **Was** Mexta Xesspe surprised when he saw the Nazca lines? B: He **must have been**. No one knew about them at that time. A: **Did** archeologists **measure** the drawings? B: They **must have**. They studied them.
6	We sometimes use "**coulda**" in **very informal** notes, emails, and text messages. **BE CAREFUL!** Do NOT use "*coulda*" in **formal** writing.	• I think you **coulda** been right about my research topic. *(informal email)* NOT: Dear Professor Johnson, I think you ~~coulda~~ been right . . . *(formal note)*

REFERENCE NOTE
Could have and **might have** are also used for **past advisability** (see Unit 16).

EXERCISE 1: Discover the Grammar

Match the facts with the speculations and conclusions.

Facts

_e_ **1.** The original title of *Chariots of the Gods?* was *Erinnerungen an die Zukunft.*

_____ **2.** Erich von Däniken visited every place he described in his book.

_____ **3.** In 1973, he wrote *In Search of Ancient Gods.*

_____ **4.** He doesn't have a degree in archeology.

_____ **5.** *Chariots of the Gods?* was published the same year as the Apollo moon landing.

_____ **6.** In the 1900s, writer Annie Besant said beings from Venus helped develop culture on Earth.

_____ **7.** Von Däniken's books sold millions of copies.

_____ **8.** As soon as von Däniken published his book, scientists attacked his theories.

Speculations and Conclusions

a. He must have made a lot of money.

b. He may have known about her unusual ideas.

c. He could have learned about the subject on his own.

d. He must have traveled a lot.

e. He must have written his book in German.

f. This great event had to have increased sales of the book.

g. He must not have had scientific evidence for his beliefs.

h. He might have written some other books too.

EXERCISE 2: Questions and Statements

(Grammar Notes 1–4)

Circle the correct words to complete the review of Erich von Däniken's book, Chariots of the Gods?

"Here comes another one."

Who could have <u>make / (made)</u> the Nazca lines? Who

1.
could have <u>carve / carved</u> the Easter Island statues?

2.
According to Erich von Däniken, ancient achievements

like these are mysteries because our ancestors could not

<u>have / had</u> created these things on their own. His

3.
conclusion: They <u>must / couldn't</u> have gotten help from

4.
space visitors.

Von Däniken's readers may not realize that experiments

have contributed to our understanding of some of these

"mysteries." Von Däniken asks: How <u>may / could</u> the Nazcans have planned the lines from

5.
the ground? Archeologists now speculate that this civilization might <u>have / has</u> developed flight.

6.
They think ancient Nazcans may <u>draw / have drawn</u> pictures of hot-air balloons on pottery. To test

7.

(continued on next page)

the theory, archeologists built a similar balloon with Nazca materials. The balloon soared[1] high

enough to view the Nazca lines, showing that Nazcans themselves could / couldn't have designed the
                                                                      8.
pictures from the air.

But what about the Easter Island statues? Did / Could islanders have carved the huge statues
                                                   9.
from hard rock with primitive tools? And how could only 2,000 people had / have moved them?
                                                                               10.

---

[1] *soar:* to fly very fast or very high up in the sky

EXERCISE 3: Affirmative and Negative Statements   (*Grammar Notes 1–4*)

Complete the rest of the review of Chariots of the Gods? *Use the verbs in parentheses.*

Explorers thought that Easter Island's ancient culture _____ *must have been* _____
                                                                    1. (must / be)

simple. They assumed that the island _____ many natural
                                              2. (must not / have)

resources, so it _____ a civilization. They were wrong. Studies
                       3. (couldn't / support)

have shown that a large population and a complex culture _____
                                                                    4. (could / develop)

on the island. Large palm trees once grew there. Islanders _____
                                                                    5. (must / make)

large boats from the trees. They _____ in deep water from the
                                          6. (must / fish)

boats because ancient garbage dumps are full of the bones of deep sea fish. Ancient islanders

_____ very well, and archeologists have estimated that as many
            7. (must / eat)

as 15,000 people _____ on the island. From the trees, they also
                          8. (may / live)

_____ ropes to pull their statues. In 1994, DNA tests proved that
            9. (could / make)

the islanders _____ from Polynesia, where there is a tradition of
                       10. (had to / come)

ancestor worship. Doubts still remained—in the language of Rapa Nui (Easter Island), the giant

statues are called *the living faces of our ancestors.* But how _____ the Rapa Nui

people _____ these lifeless images "living faces"? Then Sergio Rapu, a Rapa Nui
          11. (could / call)

archeologist, realized that the statues _____ coral[1] eyes. Pieces of
                                                 12. (must / have)

coral that he had found fit one of the statues perfectly, and its face seemed to come to life. Scientists

are still experimenting with ways islanders _____ the huge images.
                                                     13. (might / move)

However, now no one says, "The people of Rapa Nui _____ these
                                                            14. (couldn't / create)

amazing statues."

---

[1] *coral:* a hard red, white, or pink substance formed from the shells of very small ocean creatures that live in warm water—often
used to make jewelry

276   UNIT 17

EXERCISE 4: Meaning

(Grammar Notes 1–3)

Read about these puzzling events. Then rewrite the answers to the questions about their causes. Substitute a modal phrase for the underlined words. Use the modals in parentheses.

Dinosaurs existed on the Earth for about 135 million years. Then, about 65 million years ago, these giant reptiles all died in a short period of time. What could have caused the dinosaurs to become extinct?

1. It's likely that the Earth became colder. (must)

   The Earth must have become colder.

2. Probably, dinosaurs didn't survive the cold. (must not)

   _____

3. It's been suggested that a huge meteor hit the Earth. (might)

   _____

In 1924, Albert Ostman went camping alone in Canada. Later, he reported that he had an encounter with a Bigfoot (a large, hairy creature that looks human). He said the Bigfoot had kidnapped him and taken him home, where the Bigfoot family treated him like a pet. Ostman escaped after several days. What do you think happened? Could a Bigfoot really have kidnapped Ostman?

4. A Bigfoot didn't kidnap Albert Ostman—that's impossible. (couldn't)

   _____

5. Ostman probably saw a bear. (must)

   _____

6. It's possible that Ostman dreamed about a Bigfoot. (could)

   _____

7. Some people think that he made up the story. (might)

   _____

8. Most likely the man changed the photo. (have to)

   _____

In 1932, a man was taking a walk around Scotland's beautiful Loch Ness. Suddenly, a couple hundred feet from shore, the water bubbled up and a huge monster appeared. The man took a photo. When it was developed, the picture showed something with a long neck and a small head. Since then, many people have reported similar sightings. What do you think? Did the man really see the Loch Ness monster?

9. Perhaps the man saw a large fish. (might)

   _____

10. It's possible that the man saw a dead tree trunk. (may)

    _____

11. It's very unlikely that a dinosaur was in the lake. (couldn't)

    _____

EXERCISE 5: Short Answers

(Grammar Note 5)

Some archeology students are asking questions in class. Use the modals in parentheses to write short answers.

1. **A:** Were the Nazcans really able to fly?

   B: ___*They might have been*___. There's some evidence that they had hot-air
   (might)
   balloons made of cloth.

2. **A:** Is it possible that the Nazca lines were ancient streets?

   B: _____. Some of them just lead to the tops of mountains
   (could not)
   and then end suddenly.

3. **A:** Do you think the Nazcans used them during

   religious ceremonies?

   B: _____. But we
   (might)
   have no proof.

4. **A:** Do you think the people on Rapa Nui built the

   giant statues themselves?

   B: _____. They
   (could)
   had the knowledge and the tools.

5. **A:** Did the original settlers of Rapa Nui come from Polynesia?

   B: _____. There's a lot of scientific evidence to support this.
   (must)

6. **A:** Erich von Däniken says that many ancient artifacts show pictures of astronauts. Could

   these pictures have illustrated anything closer to Earth?

   B: _____. It's possible that the pictures show people dressed
   (may)
   in local costumes.

7. **A:** Did von Däniken believe his own theories?

   B: _____. Many of his ideas came from science fiction.
   (may not)

8. **A:** Was von Däniken upset by all the criticism he received?

   B: _____. After all, it created more interest in his books.
   (might not)

9. **A:** Do you think von Däniken helped increase general interest in archeology?

   B: _____. Just look at how many of you are taking this class!
   (must)

EXERCISE 6: Editing

Read this student's essay about Easter Island. There are ten mistakes in the use of modals.
The first mistake is already corrected. Find and correct nine more.

Rapa Nui (Easter Island) is a tiny island in the middle of the Pacific. To get there, the first

settlers had to ~~had~~ *have* traveled more than 1,000 miles in open boats. Some scientists

believed only the Polynesians of the Pacific Islands could have make the journey. Others

thought that Polynesians couldn't have carved the huge stone statues on Rapa Nui. They

speculated that Mayans or Egyptians maybe have traveled there. (Some people even

said that space aliens might helped!) Finally, a University of Oslo scientist was able to

study the DNA from ancient skeletons. Professor Erika Halberg announced, "These

people has to have been the descendants[1] of Polynesians."

   We now know that the islanders built the statues, but we have also learned that they

must had solved even more difficult problems. The first settlers came sometime between

the years 400 and 700. At first, Rapa Nui must be a paradise with its fishing, forests, and

good soil. Their society may have grown too fast for the small island, however. Botanical

studies show that by the 1600s they had cut down the last tree. The soil must not have

washed away, so they couldn't farm. And with no wood to build boats, they couldn't

have able to fish. For a period of time, people starved and fought violently, but when the

Dutch discovered Rapa Nui in 1722, they found a peaceful, healthy population growing

fields of vegetables. How the islanders could have learned in this short period of time to

live peacefully with so few resources? For our troubled world today, this might be the

most important "mystery of Easter Island."

---

[1]*descendant:* someone related to people who lived a long time ago

EXERCISE 7: Listening

A | *Some archeology students are speculating about objects they have found at various sites. Read the statements. Then listen to the conversations. Listen again and check (✓)* **True** *or* **False** *for each statement. Correct the false statements.*

	True	False

                                              cutting

1. The woman thinks that people might have used the tool for ~~building~~ things. ☐ ☑

2. The man thinks people could have worn this object around their necks. ☐ ☐

3. The woman thinks this object might have been a hole for shoelaces. ☐ ☐

4. The man thinks this piece came from the bottom of an object. ☐ ☐

5. The woman thinks that the people who made this object were very smart. ☐ ☐

6. The man thinks this object is a rock. ☐ ☐

B | *Look at the pictures. Listen again to the conversations and match the pictures with the correct conversation.*

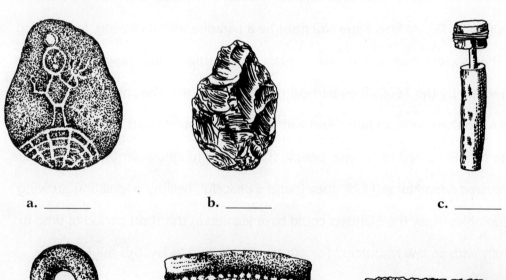

a. _____   b. _____   c. _____

d. _____   e. _____   f. ___1___

EXERCISE 8: Pronunciation

A | *Read and listen to the Pronunciation Note.*

> **Pronunciation Note**
>
> In **past modals**, we usually pronounce ***have*** or its contraction **'ve** like "**of**."
>
> EXAMPLES: This **could have** been a tool.   → "This **could of** been a tool."
> It **may have** happened a long time ago. → "It **may of** happened a long time ago."
> They **couldn't have** lived here long.   → "They **couldn't of** lived here long."
>
> You can also pronounce ***could have*** "coulda" and ***might have*** "mighta."
>
> In **writing**, we use ***could have***, ***couldn't have***, ***may have***, and ***might have***,
> NOT could of, couldn't of, may of, or might of.

B | *Listen to the short conversations. Write the contracted forms of the past modals.*

1. **A:** What was that used for?

   B: I'm not sure. It _____ been a spoon.

2. **A:** I called Rahul yesterday afternoon, but there was no answer.

   B: Oh. He _____ gone to the museum.

3. **A:** Is Sara still on Easter Island?

   B: I'm not sure. She _____ left already.

4. **A:** I think I saw John yesterday.

   B: You _____ seen him. He's in Peru.

5. **A:** Do you agree with the author's conclusion?

   B: I don't know. He _____ been wrong.

6. **A:** Alice got an A on her archeology test.

   B: She _____ been happy.

7. **A:** Could they have sailed that far in small boats?

   B: Sure they _____. They were expert sailors.

C | *Listen again to each conversation and repeat the response. Then practice the conversations with a partner. Use short forms.*

EXERCISE 9: Picture Discussion

Work in small groups. Look at the objects that archeologists have found in different places. Speculate on what they are and how people might have used them. After your discussion, share your ideas with the rest of the class.

1. Archeologists found this object in the sleeping area of an ancient Chinese house. It's about the size of a basketball.

   EXAMPLE: **A:** I think people might have used this as a footstool. It's the right size.
   B: You're right. The floor must have gotten very cold at night.
   C: People could have rested their feet on this.

◄ 2. Archeologists found this in Turkey. People in many places have used objects like this on their clothing for thousands of years. This one is about 3,000 years old. It's the size of a small cell phone.

3. These objects were used by ancient Egyptians. The ► handles are each about the length of a toothbrush.

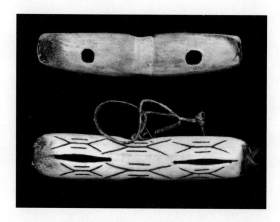

◄ 4. People in the Arctic started using these around 2,000 years ago. They used them when they were hunting or traveling. They are small enough to put in your pocket.

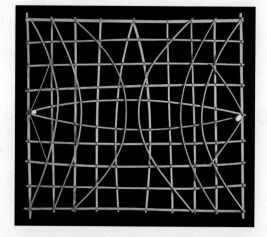

5. Polynesian people used these when they traveled. ► They made them with sticks, coconut fiber, and seashells. This one is about 30 centimeters (1 foot) wide and 30 centimeters long.

Answers: 1. a pillow; **2.** a large pin used to hold clothing together; **3.** a razor and a mirror for shaving; **4.** eye protection against bright light reflected from snow and ice; **5.** a chart showing islands and wave patterns in the ocean

EXERCISE 10: For or Against

A | *Reread the article that begins on page 270. Do you agree or disagree with Erich von Däniken's theory? Discuss your opinion with a partner.*

B | *Have a class discussion. How many students think space creatures might have visited the Earth? How many think space creatures couldn't have affected human culture?*

EXERCISE 11: Writing

A | *Read the paragraph about an unsolved mystery. Then complete the next paragraph. Use modals to speculate about the event. In your conclusion, state which explanation is most likely and why.*

> In 1991, hikers in the Italian Alps discovered a body in some melting ice. The body, which had been in the ice for more than 5,000 years, was in almost perfect condition. The "Ice Man" had several broken ribs. He had been wearing warm winter clothing, and had been carrying a knife, an ax, dried meat, and medicines. He had been making a bow and arrows, but he had not finished them.
>
> What could have happened to the Ice Man? There have been many speculations. The Ice Man might have . . .

EXAMPLE: The Ice Man might have brought his animals into the mountains to feed. . . .

B | *Check your work. Use the Editing Checklist.*

Editing Checklist

Did you use . . . ?
- ☐ *may have*, *might have*, and *could have* for past possibilities
- ☐ *must have* and *had to have* for things in the past you are almost certain about
- ☐ *couldn't have* to show disbelief or impossibility
- ☐ *could have* for questions about past possibility

UNIT 17 Review

Check your answers on page UR-4.

Do you need to review anything?

A | *Circle the correct words to complete the sentences.*

1. Mayans built large cities. They <u>must / must not</u> have had an advanced civilization.

2. Their civilization disappeared. It <u>might not / might not have</u> rained enough to grow crops.

3. Look at this bowl. They could <u>of / have</u> used this to serve food.

4. You must have <u>taken / took</u> a hundred photos today.

5. Trish didn't come on the tour. She <u>may / couldn't</u> have been sick. She wasn't feeling well.

6. I can't find my wallet. I could <u>had / have</u> dropped it in the hotel gift shop.

7. Carla <u>must / couldn't</u> have gotten our postcard. We just mailed it yesterday.

B | *Rewrite the sentences in parentheses using past modals.*

1. Dan didn't call me back yesterday. He _____.
   (Maybe he didn't get my message.)

2. Selina got a C on the test. She _____.
   (It's almost certain that she didn't study.)

3. Why didn't Fahad come to dinner? He _____.
   (It's not possible that he forgot our date.)

4. Myra _____. I saw a woman there who looked like her.
   (It's possible that Myra was at the movies.)

5. The server didn't bring our dessert. She _____.
   (She probably forgot.)

6. Jan didn't say hello to me today. He _____.
   (It's almost certain that he didn't see me.)

C | *Find and correct seven mistakes.*

Why did the Aztecs build their capital city in the middle of a lake? Could they had wanted the protection of the water? They might have been. Or the location may has helped them to control nearby societies. At first it must have being an awful place, full of mosquitoes and fog. But it must no have been a bad idea—the island city became the center of a very powerful empire. To succeed, the Aztecs had to have became fantastic engineers quite quickly. When the Spanish arrived, they couldn't have expect the amazing palaces, floating gardens, and well-built canals. Unfortunately, they destroyed the city anyway.

PART VII

From Grammar to Writing

ORGANIZING IDEAS FROM FREEWRITING

Freewriting is a **way to develop ideas** about a topic. To freewrite, write for a specified length of time without stopping. Don't worry about mistakes. Then organize the ideas in your freewriting.

EXAMPLE: **Can't** stop thinking about **M's** wedding in Quito last year. *(freewriting)* ➔
I can't stop thinking about **Miguel's** wedding in Quito last year. *(formal writing)*

1 | *Read Clara's freewriting about a problem she had with her cousin Miguel. Underline her ideas about Miguel's reasons for what he did. Bracket ([ ]) her ideas about the appropriateness of Miguel's and her own behavior.*

> Can't stop thinking about Miguel's wedding in Quito
> last year. Still feeling hurt and confused. Why
> didn't he invite me? Or even tell me about it? [This
> was a family reunion, and he should have sent
> everyone an invitation.] He knows I'm a student, and
> he must have thought I couldn't afford the airfare
> to Ecuador. He could've sent me an invitation and
> let me decide for myself. On the other hand, I
> should have called him to discuss it. He might have
> even decided that I couldn't afford to send a gift.
> He shouldn't have decided for me. He couldn't have
> been angry with me! I've got to let him know how I
> feel. I should write a letter.

2 | *Clara decided to write a letter to Miguel. Read her outline in Exercise 3. Write the paragraph number where Clara decides to do each of the following:*

_3_ **1.** discuss the appropriateness of Miguel's behavior

_____ **2.** introduce the problem

_____ **3.** suggest resolving the problem

_____ **4.** speculate on reasons for Miguel's behavior

3 | Complete Clara's letter with ideas from Exercise 1.

Dear Miguel,

I'm sorry that I haven't written for some time, but I'm still feeling hurt and confused. Miguel, why didn't you invite me to your wedding last year? You didn't even tell me about it!

Maybe your reasons for not inviting me were actually thoughtful. You know I'm a student, and ____you must have thought I couldn't afford the airfare.____

_____

_____

_____

However, I believe you should have handled the situation in a different way. This was a family reunion, and you should have sent everyone an invitation.

_____

_____

_____

We ought to solve this as soon as possible. I miss you. Please write as soon as you get this letter.

Love,

Clara

4 | Before you write . . .

1. Think of a problem you had with someone (for example, a friend, relative, neighbor). Freewrite about the problem: the reasons it might have happened and what you and other people could have done differently.

2. Choose ideas and organize them.

5 | Write a letter to the person you had the problem with. Include ideas from your freewriting in Exercise 4. Use past modals to speculate about reasons for your problem and to express regrets and obligations.

6 | *Exchange letters with a partner. Write a question mark* **(?)** *over anything in the letter that seems wrong. Then answer the following questions.*

	Yes	No
1. Did the writer correctly use past modals to speculate about reasons?	☐	☐
2. Did the writer correctly use past modals to express appropriateness?	☐	☐
3. Did the writer express his or her feelings and ideas clearly?	☐	☐

7 | *Work with your partner. Discuss each other's editing questions from Exercise 6. Then rewrite your letter and make any necessary corrections.*

PART VIII

THE PASSIVE

 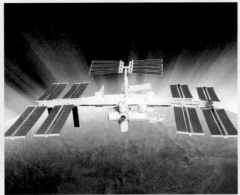 

289

STEP 1 GRAMMAR IN CONTEXT

Before You Read

Look at the title of the article and the photo. Discuss the questions.

1. What is geography?
2. Have you ever studied geography in school? If yes, did you enjoy it?
3. Is geography an important subject? Why or why not?

Read

🔊 *Read the article about* National Geographic, *a famous magazine.*

GEOGRAPHY
The Best Subject on Earth

Geography is the study of the Earth and its people. It sounds exciting, doesn't it? Yet for decades, students yawned just hearing the word. They **were forced** to memorize the names of capital cities, important rivers and mountains, and natural resources.[1] They **were taught** where places were and what **was produced** there. But they **weren't shown** how our world looks and feels.

And then came *National Geographic.* From the Amazon rain forests to the Sahara Desert, and from Baalbek to Great Zimbabwe, the natural and human-made wonders[2] of our world **have** now **been brought** to life **by** its fascinating reporting and beautiful photographs, such as this one, which **was taken by** photojournalist[3] Reza Deghati of a man planting a palm tree in Saudi Arabia.

---
[1]*natural resources:* a country's land, minerals, and energy
[2]*wonder:* something that makes you feel surprise and admiration
[3]*photojournalist:* someone who takes photos and writes reports for newspapers and magazines

GEOGRAPHY
The Best Subject on Earth

The National Geographic Society **was formed** in Washington, D.C., in 1888 **by** a group of professionals including geographers, explorers, teachers, and mapmakers. Nine months later, the first *National Geographic* magazine **was published** so that the Society could fulfill its mission: to spread knowledge of and respect for the world, its resources, and its inhabitants.

In 1995, the first foreign-language edition of *National Geographic* **was published** in Japan. Today, the magazine **is printed** in more than 30 languages and **sold** all over the world. *National Geographic* also puts out a number of special publications. *National Geographic Explorer*, for example, **has been created** for classrooms. Other publications feature travel and adventure. *National Geographic* TV programs **are watched** in over 160 million homes in more than 140 countries.

The study of geography has come a very long way since 1888. The Society's mission **has been fulfilled**. In fact, it **has** even **been extended** to include worlds beyond Earth. From the deep seas to deep space, geography has never been more exciting!

After You Read

A | Vocabulary: *Match the words with their definitions.*

_____ 1. mission

_____ 2. decade

_____ 3. publication

_____ 4. inhabitant

_____ 5. explorer

_____ 6. edition

a. 10 years

b. a book or magazine sold to the public

c. someone who travels for the purpose of discovery

d. an important purpose

e. the total number of copies of a magazine or book printed at the same time

f. one of the people living in a particular place

B | Comprehension: *Answer the questions.*

1. Who memorized names of capital cities?_____

2. What brought the wonders of our world to life?_____

3. Who took the photo of the Saudi man planting a palm tree?_____

4. Who formed the National Geographic Society?_____

5. Who watches *National Geographic* TV? _____

6. How has the Society's mission changed?_____

THE PASSIVE

Active	Passive
Millions of people **buy** it.	It **is bought** by millions of people.
Someone **published** it in 1888.	It **was published** in 1888.
They **have reached** their goal.	Their goal **has been reached**.

Passive Statements

Subject	*Be (not)*	Past Participle	*(By + Object)*	
It	**is (not)**	**bought**	**by** millions of people.	
It	**was (not)**	**published**		in 1888.
Their goal	**has (not) been**	**reached**.		

Yes / No Questions

Be / Have	Subject	*(Been +)* Past Participle	
Is		**sold**	
Was	it		in Japan?
Has		**been sold**	

Short Answers

Affirmative			Negative		
		is.			**isn't.**
Yes,	it	**was.**	**No,**	it	**wasn't.**
		has (been).			**hasn't (been).**

Wh- Questions

Wh- Word	*Be / Have*	Subject	*(Been +)* Past Participle
Where	**is**	it	**sold**?
	was		
	has		**been sold**?

GRAMMAR NOTES

1
Active and **passive** sentences often have similar meanings, but a **different focus**.

a. **Active** sentences focus on the **agent** (the person or thing <u>doing</u> the action).

b. **Passive** sentences focus on the **object** (the person or thing <u>receiving</u> the action).

ACTIVE:
- Millions of **people** read the magazine. (*The focus is on people.*)

PASSIVE:
- The **magazine** is read by millions of people. (*The focus is on the magazine.*)

2 Form the **passive** with a form of:
be + **past participle**.

- It *is printed* in more than 30 languages.
- It *was* first **published** in 1888.
- It *has been* **sold** all over the world.

TRANSITIVE VERB + OBJECT

- Ed Bly **wrote** *that article*.
- That article **was written** by Ed Bly.
  (passive form)

BE CAREFUL! Only **transitive verbs** (verbs that have objects) have passive forms.

INTRANSITIVE VERB

- It **seemed** interesting.
  NoT: It ~~was~~ seemed interesting.
  (no passive form)

Intransitive verbs do NOT have passive forms.

3 Use the **passive** in the following situations:

a. When the **agent** (the person or thing doing the action) is <u>unknown or not important</u>.

- The magazine **was started** in 1888.
  (I don't know who started it.)
- The magazine **is sold** at newsstands.
  (It is not important who sells it.)

b. When you want to <u>avoid mentioning</u> the agent.

- Some mistakes **were made** in that article.
  (I know who made the mistakes, but I don't want to blame the person.)

4 Use the passive with *by* if you mention the **agent**. Only mention the agent when it is <u>important to know who it is</u>.

- The photographs in this article are wonderful. They **were taken** *by a famous photographer*.
- One of the first cameras **was invented** *by Alexander Wolcott*.

BE CAREFUL! In most cases, you do **NOT need to mention an agent** in passive sentences. Do NOT include an agent unnecessarily.

- Ed Bly took a really great photo. It **was taken** last February, but it won't appear until May.
  NoT: It was taken last February ~~by him~~ . . .

STEP 3 FOCUSED PRACTICE

EXERCISE 1: Discover the Grammar

Read the statements. Check (✓) **Active** *or* **Passive.**

	Active	Passive
1. The first *National Geographic* magazine was published in October 1888.	☐	☑
2. Today, millions of people read it.	☐	☐
3. The magazine is translated from English into 32 other languages.	☐	☐
4. My cousin reads the Russian edition.	☐	☐

(continued on next page)

5. Some of the articles are written by famous writers.   ☐   ☐

6. *Young Explorer*, another publication, is written for kids.   ☐   ☐

7. It is known for its wonderful photography.   ☐   ☐

8. A *National Geographic* photographer took the first underwater color photos.   ☐   ☐

9. Photographers are sent all over the world.   ☐   ☐

10. They take pictures of people and nature.   ☐   ☐

11. *National Geographic* is sold at newsstands.   ☐   ☐

EXERCISE 2: Active or Passive

(Grammar Notes 1–3)

The chart shows some of the 33 language editions that National Geographic *publishes. Use the chart to complete the sentences. Some sentences will be active; some will be passive.*

Language	Number of Speakers*
Chinese (all varieties)	1,231
English	460
Indonesian	23.2
Japanese	122
Korean	66.3
Russian	144
Spanish	329
Turkish	50.8

*first language speakers in millions

1. Spanish *is spoken by 329 million people* _____.

2. Around 144 million people _____.

3. Indonesian _____.

4. _____ Chinese.

5. _____ by more than 66 million people.

6. _____ 122 million people.

7. 460 million people _____.

8. _____ more than 50 million people.

EXERCISE 3: *Wh-* Questions and Statements

(Grammar Note 2)

A | *Jill Jones, a magazine journalist, is preparing for a trip to Bolivia. Look at the online travel quiz she is going to take. Complete the questions with the correct form of the verbs in parentheses. Then take the quiz. Guess the answers!*

Travel Quiz
Destination: La Paz, Bolivia

The capital of Bolivia, La Paz, with Illimani mountain in the background

Map of Bolivia

1. In which part of the country _____*is*_____ the capital _____*located*_____?
   (locate)
   - ○ the north
   - ○ the center
   - ● the west

2. When _____ La Paz _____?
   (establish)
   - ○ 1448
   - ○ 1548
   - ○ 1648

3. Which of these items _____ in La Paz?
   (produce)
   - ○ agricultural tools
   - ○ cars
   - ○ electric appliances

4. What _____ the main street in La Paz _____?
   (call)
   - ○ La Rambla
   - ○ El Prado
   - ○ El Alto

5. Which sport _____ the most in La Paz?
   (play)
   - ○ baseball
   - ○ soccer
   - ○ basketball

B | *Complete the answers with the correct form of the verbs in parentheses. Did you guess correctly?*

Answers

1. The highest capital in the world, La Paz _____*was built*_____ in a canyon in the
   (build)

   west of the country. It _____ by mountains, such as the beautiful
   (surround)

   Illimani mountain, which _____ by snow all year.
   (cover)

2. The city _____ in 1548 by Spanish settlers.
   (establish)

3. Agricultural tools along with food products, clothing, and building materials

   _____ in the capital.
   (make)

4. The main street's name changes in different parts of the city, but the tree-lined

   section in downtown La Paz _____ as El Prado.
   (know)

5. Soccer is the favorite sport. The city has several teams. The Strongest, which

   _____ in 1908, has won many tournaments.
   (form)

EXERCISE 4: Questions, Statements, and Short Answers

(*Grammar Note 2*)

Jill Jones is interviewing a Bolivian cultural attaché for an article she's writing. Complete her interview with the passive form of the correct verbs from the boxes and with short answers.

create	grow	~~inhabit~~	spell

JONES: Thanks for giving me some time today. Here is my first question: _____*Was*_____ the

area first _____*inhabited*_____ by the Inca?
1.

ATTACHÉ: _____*No, it wasn't*_____. Long before the Inca, a great civilization _____
2.   **3.**

around Lake Titicaca by the Aymara. The Aymara still live in Bolivia.

JONES: Fascinating. Let's talk about farming. I know potatoes are an important food crop[1] in the

mountains of the Andes. _____ corn _____ there as well?
4.

ATTACHÉ: _____. The climate is too cold. But quinoa grows well there.
5.

JONES: Quinoa? How _____ that _____? With a *k*?
6.

---

[1] *crop:* a plant such as corn or wheat that is grown by a farmer

| eat | mine² | raise | use |

Attaché: No. With a *q*—q-u-i-n-o-a. It's a traditional grain, like corn and wheat in other places.

It _____ by the inhabitants of the Andes for 5,000 years.
       7.

Jones: Everyone connects llamas with Bolivia. What _____ these animals

_____ for?
  8.

Attaché: For many things—clothing, meat, transportation. But they only do well in the Andes. They

_____ in the lowlands of the Oriente, the eastern part of the country.
   9. (negative)

Jones: I see. Now, about other resources. I know that tin is extremely important. Where

_____ it _____?
          10.

| find | produce | see | speak |

Attaché: The richest sources of tin _____ in the Andes.
         11.

Jones: How about the Oriente? What _____ there?
        12.

Attaché: Oil, petroleum, and natural gas. Rice is important, and cattle, for meat and milk.

Jones: What other languages _____ besides Spanish?
        13.

Attaché: Actually, more people speak Native American languages than Spanish.

Jones: Scientists love Bolivia. _____ jaguars still _____ there?
           14.

Attaché: _____. And so are river dolphins and birds like the condor—many, many
   15.

species. In the last decade, our government's mission has been to protect these rare and

beautiful animals.

Jones: Thank you for your time. I'll send you a copy of our publication as soon as the article

comes out.

---

² *mine:* to dig into the ground to get gold, coal, tin, and
other natural resources

Jaguar

A | *Read Jill Jones's article. Her editor found and circled eight factual mistakes.*

A Land of Contrasts
by Jill Jones

Visitors to Bolivia are amazed by the contrasts and charmed by the beauty of this South American country's landscapes—from the breathtaking Andes in the west to the tropical lowlands in the east.

Two-thirds of Bolivia's 10 million people are concentrated in the cool western highlands, or *altiplano*. Today, as in centuries past, corn? and kuinoa *spelling?* are grown in the mountains. Llamas are raised only for transportation? And tin, Bolivia's richest natural resource, is mined in the high Andes.

The Oriente, another name for the eastern lowlands, is mostly tropical. Rice is the major food crop, and llamas? are raised for meat in the lowlands. Rubber? is also found in this region.

Bolivia is home to many fascinating forms of wildlife. The colorful parrot? can be seen flying above the highest mountains. Boa constrictors, jaguars, and many other animals are found in the rain forests.

Hundreds of years before the Inca flourished, a great civilization was created on the shores of the Pacific? probably by ancestors of Bolivia's Aymara people. Their descendants still speak the Aymara language. Today, Native American languages are still widely spoken in Bolivia. Although Portuguese? is spoken in the government, Quechua and Aymara are used more widely by the people. Traditional textiles are woven by hand. Music is played on reed pipes whose tone resembles the sound of the wind blowing over high plains in the Andes.

Lake Titicaca

B | *Rewrite the incorrect sentences with information from Exercise 4.*

1. *Corn isn't grown in the mountains. Potatoes are grown in the mountains.*

2. _____

3. _____

4. _____

5. _____

6. _____

7. _____

8. _____

EXERCISE 6: Including or Deleting the Agent

(Grammar Notes 3–4)

Read Ed Bly's soccer trivia column. Complete the information with the correct form of the verbs in the first set of parentheses. If the agent (in the second set of parentheses) is necessary, include it in your answer. If not, cross it out.

⚽ Soccer is the most popular sport in the world. It ___*is played by more than 20 million people*___ .
   1. (play) (more than 20 million people)

⚽ It ___*is called*___ football _____ in 144 countries.
   2. (call)   ~~(people)~~

⚽ Except for the goalie, players _____ to use their hands. Instead, the
   3. (not allow) (the rules)

   ball _____ .
        4. (control) (the feet, the head, and the body)

⚽ Soccer _____ in the United States very much until 20 years
   5. (not play) (people)

   ago. Since then, the game _____ .
   6. (make popular) (Pelé, Beckham, and other international stars)

⚽ Forms of soccer _____ for thousands of years. A form of
   7. (play) (different cultures)

   soccer _____ in China 2,000 years ago.
   8. (enjoy) (Chinese people)

⚽ It _____ in 1365—his archers spent
   9. (ban) (King Edward III of England)

   too much time playing and too little time practicing archery.

⚽ Medieval games _____ for entire days, over miles of territory.
   10. (play) (players)

⚽ Today, the World Cup games _____ every four years. The best
   11. (hold) (the World Cup Association)

   teams in the world compete.

EXERCISE 7: Editing

*Read this short biography of an internationally famous photojournalist whose photos
have appeared in* National Geographic. *(He took the photo on page 290.) There are eight
mistakes in the use of the passive. The first mistake is already corrected. Find and correct
seven more.*

Seeing the World
by Diana Brodylo

Reza Deghati ~~is~~ *was* born in Tabriz, Iran, in 1952. When he

was only 14 years old, he began teaching himself

photography. At first, he took pictures of his own

country—its people and its architecture. When he was 25,

he was decided to become a professional photographer.

During a demonstration he was asked by a French news

agency to take photos. He only shot one and a half rolls of film (instead of the usual

20 to 40), but his photos was published in *Paris Match* (France), *Stern* (Germany), and

Newsweek (U.S.A.).

Reza, as he is knew professionally, has covered several wars, and he has be

wounded on assignment.[1] Among all his assignments, the project dearest to his heart

is photographing children, who he calls "the real victims of war." He has donated

these photos to humanitarian organizations. Always concerned with the welfare of

children, Reza has made it his life's mission to help them receive an education. His

organization AINA created, in part, to achieve this goal.

When he was interviewed by an interviewer, Reza was asked to give advice to

wannabe[2] photojournalists. He replied, "There is a curtain between the photographer

and the subject unless the photographer is able to break through it. . . . Open your

heart to them so they know you care."

Today Reza Deghati lives in Paris. His photos is widely distributed in more than 50

countries around the world, and his work is published in *National Geographic* as well

as many other internationally famous publications.

---

[1]*wounded on assignment:* injured on the job
[2]*wannabe:* (informal for *want-to-be*) a person who wants to become a member of a specific profession

EXERCISE 8: Listening

A | *Read the statements. Then listen to the conversations. Listen again and check (✓)* **True,** **False,** *or* **?** *(the information isn't in the conversation).*

	True	False	?
1. Ana took the photo of the desert.	☐	☑	☐
2. The hat was made by children.	☐	☐	☐
3. Jill's boss sent her to Morocco.	☐	☐	☐
4. Corn is grown in the mountains.	☐	☐	☐
5. The man's friend wrote an article about Bolivia.	☐	☐	☐
6. You can get *National Geographic* in Korea.	☐	☐	☐

B | *Listen again to the conversations and complete the sentences with the words you hear.*

1. It _____wasn't taken_____ by Ana.

2. It _____ there.

3. She _____ to Morocco to cover a story.

4. Potatoes _____ there.

5. It _____ by a friend of mine.

6. _____ *National Geographic* _____ in Korea?

EXERCISE 9: Pronunciation

A | *Read and listen to the Pronunciation Note.*

Pronunciation Note

When we **correct information**, we usually **stress**:

- the **words we are correcting** (the wrong information)
- the **correction** (the correct information)

EXAMPLES: Corn isn't grown in the **mountains**. It's grown in the **valleys**.

Rice isn't grown in the mountains. **Corn** is grown there.

B | *Listen to the short conversations. Put a dot (•) over the words that are stressed in the responses.*

1. **A:** Where is rice grown. In the north?

   B: No. It isn't grown in the north. It's grown in the south.

2. **A:** That's a great photo. Was it taken in Bolivia?

   B: It wasn't taken in Bolivia. It was taken in Peru.

3. **A:** This article was written by Omar, wasn't it?

   B: No. It wasn't written by him. It was edited by him.

4. **A:** The book I'm reading was written in 1950.

   B: It wasn't written in 1950, it was published then.

5. **A:** It was translated into French.

   B: It wasn't translated into French. It was translated into Spanish.

6. **A:** I heard that John's story was published last month.

   B: No, John's story wasn't published, Tom's was.

C | *Listen again and check your work. Then practice the conversations with a partner.*

EXERCISE 10: Quotable Quotes

Work in small groups. Choose three of these proverbs from around the world and discuss them. What do you think they mean? Are there proverbs from other cultures that mean the same thing?

1. Rome wasn't built in a day. (*English*)

   EXAMPLE: **A:** I think this means that big projects aren't finished quickly.
   B: Yes. They take a lot of time and you have to be patient.
   C: There's a proverb in French that means the same thing: "Paris wasn't built in a day."

2. He who was bitten by a snake avoids tall grass. (*Chinese*)

3. He ran away from the rain and was caught in a hailstorm. (*Turkish*)

4. Never promise a fish until it's caught. (*Irish*)

5. Write the bad things that are done to you in sand, but write the good things that happen to you on a piece of marble. (*Arab*)

6. Skillful sailors weren't made by smooth seas. (*Ethiopian*)

7. From one thing, ten things are known. (*Korean*)

8. What is brought by the wind will be carried away by the wind. (*Iranian*)

EXERCISE 11: Information Gap: The Philippines

The Philippines consist of many islands. The two largest are Luzon in the north and Mindanao in the south. Both islands have many natural resources.

Work in pairs (A and B). **Student B,** *go to page 306 and follow the instructions there.* **Student A,** *follow the instructions on this page.*

1. Look at the map of Luzon. Complete the chart for Luzon. Write *Y* for yes and *N* for no.

2. Student B has the map of Mindanao. Ask Student B questions about Mindanao and complete the chart for Mindanao.

   EXAMPLE: **A:** Is tobacco grown in Mindanao?
   B: No, it isn't.

3. Student B doesn't have the map of Luzon. Answer Student B's questions about Luzon.

   EXAMPLE: **B:** Is tobacco grown in Luzon?
   A: Yes, it is. It's grown in the northern and central part of the island.

			Mindanao	Luzon
G R O W		tobacco	N	Y
		corn		
		bananas		
		coffee		
		pineapples		
		sugar		
R A I S E		cattle		
		pigs		
M I N E		gold		
		manganese		
P R O D U C E		cotton		
		rubber		
		lumber		

When you are done, compare charts. Are they the same?

EXERCISE 12: Game: Trivia Quiz

A | National Geographic Explorer *often has games and puzzles. Work in pairs. Complete this quiz. Then compare answers with your classmates. The answers are on page 306.*

Do you know . . . ?

1. Urdu is spoken in _____.

  a. Ethiopia　　　　**b.** Pakistan　　　　**c.** Uruguay

2. Air-conditioning was invented in _____.

  a. 1902　　　　**b.** 1950　　　　**c.** 1980

3. The X-ray was invented by _____.

  a. Thomas Edison　　**b.** Wilhelm Roentgen　　**c.** Marie Curie

4. The Petronas Towers in Kuala Lumpur were designed by _____.

  a. Minoru Yamasaki　　**b.** César Pelli　　**c.** I. M. Pei

5. The 2010 Olympics were held in _____.

  a. Canada　　　　**b.** Japan　　　　**c.** Norway

6. An ocean route from Portugal to the East was discovered by Portuguese explorer _____.

  a. Hernán Cortés　　**b.** Louis Jolliet　　**c.** Vasco da Gama

7. A baby _____ is called a cub.

  a. cat　　　　**b.** dog　　　　**c.** jaguar

B | *Now, with your partner, make up your own questions with the words in parentheses. For item 11, add your own question. Ask another pair to answer your questions.*

EXAMPLE:

___Guernica___ ___was painted___ by _b_ .
　　　　　　　　　　　(paint)

　a. ___Monet___　**b.** ___Picasso___　**c.** ___El Greco___

8. _____ _____ _____ by ____.
　　　　　　　　　　　(invent)

　a. _____　**b.** _____　**c.** _____

9. _____ _____ _____ by ____.
　　　　　　　　　　　(compose)

　a. _____　**b.** _____　**c.** _____

10. _____ _____ _____ by ____.
　　　　　　　　　　　(write)

　a. _____　**b.** _____　**c.** _____

11. _____ _____ _____ by ____.

　a. _____　**b.** _____　**c.** _____

EXERCISE 13: Writing

A | *Before you write, complete the chart with information about a country you know well.*

Name of country	
Geographical areas	
Crops grown in each area	
Animals raised in each area	
Natural resources found in each area	
Wildlife found in each area	
Languages spoken	
Art, handicrafts, or music created	

B | *Write an essay about the country with the information you have gathered. Use the passive. You can use the article in Exercise 5 as a model (make sure your facts are correct).*

> EXAMPLE: Turkey is both a European and an Asian country. European Turkey is separated from Asian Turkey by the Sea of Marmara, the Bosphorus, and the Dardanelles. Citrus fruits and tobacco are grown in . . .

C | *Check your work. Use the Editing Checklist.*

Editing Checklist

Did you . . . ?
- [ ] use passive sentences to focus on the object
- [ ] form the passive with a form of *be* + **past participle**
- [ ] use *by* if you mentioned the agent
- [ ] only mention the agent when it was important to know who it is

Student B, follow the instructions on this page.

1. Look at the map of Mindanao below. Complete the chart for Mindanao. Write *Y* for yes and *N* for no.

2. Student A doesn't have the map of Mindanao. Answer Student A's questions about Mindanao.

   EXAMPLE: **A:** Is tobacco grown in Mindanao?
   B: No, it isn't.

3. Student A has the map of Luzon. Ask Student A questions about Luzon and complete the chart for Luzon.

   EXAMPLE: **B:** Is tobacco grown in Luzon?
   A: Yes, it is. It's grown in the northern and central part of the island.

		Mindanao	Luzon	
GROW	tobacco	N	Y	Mindanao
	corn			
	bananas			
	coffee			
	pineapples			
	sugar			
RAISE	cattle			
	pigs			
MINE	gold			
	manganese			
PRODUCE	cotton			
	rubber			
	lumber			

When you are done, compare charts. Are they the same?

Answers to Trivia Quiz "Do you know . . . ?" on page 304: **1.** b **2.** a **3.** b **4.** b **5.** a **6.** c **7.** c

UNIT 18 Review

Check your answers on page UR-5.

Do you need to review anything?

A | Complete with active and passive sentences.

Active	Passive
1. They speak Spanish in Bolivia.	_____
2. _____	Soccer is played in Bolivia.
3. _____	The photo was taken by Reza Deghati.
4. They translated the articles into Spanish.	_____
5. They grow quinoa in the mountains.	_____
6. _____	The main street was named El Prado.

B | Complete the sentences with the correct passive form of the verbs in parentheses.

1. Jamaica _____ by Europeans in the 16ᵗʰ century.
              (discover)

2. Today, Creole, a mixture of languages, _____ by many Jamaicans.
                                         (speak)

3. Some of the best coffee in the world _____ on the island.
                                   (grow)

4. Sugar _____ to many countries.
          (export)

5. Many people _____ by the sugar industry.
                 (employ)

6. Reggae music originated in Jamaica. It _____ popular by Bob Marley.
                                 (make)

7. Since the summer of 1992, it _____ at the Sumfest festival on the island.
                             (perform)

8. Every year the festival _____ by music lovers from around the world.
                     (attend)

C | Find and correct six mistakes.

> Photojournalist Alexandra Avakian was born and raise in New York. Since she began her career, she has covered many of the world's most important stories. Her work have been published in many newspapers and magazines including *National Geographic*, and her photographs have being exhibited around the world. Avakian has also written a book, *Window of the Soul: My Journey in the Muslim World*, which was been published in 2008. It has not yet been translated by translators into other languages, but the chapter titles appear in both English and Arabic. Avakian's book have be discussed on international TV, radio, and numerous websites.

UNIT 19

The Passive with Modals and Similar Expressions

THE INTERNATIONAL SPACE STATION

STEP 1 GRAMMAR IN CONTEXT

Before You Read

Look at the article and the photos. Discuss the questions.

1. What does the title of the article mean?
2. What are some problems that can occur when people from different cultures must live and work together?

Read

Read the article about an international space project.

CLOSE QUARTERS

"**Will** decisions **be made** too fast?" the Japanese astronauts wondered. "**Can** they **be made** quickly enough?" the Americans wanted to know. "**Will** dinner **be taken** seriously?" was the question worrying the French and the Dutch, while the Italians were nervous about their personal space: "How **can** privacy **be maintained** in such very close quarters?"

The year was 2000. It was the beginning of the new millennium, and the focus of all these concerns was the International Space Station (ISS), the largest and most complex international project ever. It looked like the ISS **was** finally **going to be launched**[1] that year. But amid the hopes and excitement, many were asking themselves: "**Can** this huge undertaking

Crew members share a meal aboard the ISS.

really **be accomplished** by a multicultural group living in close quarters?" In addition to their other concerns, all the astronauts were worrying about language. English is

---

[1]*launch:* to send into the sky or space, usually with a rocket

the official language on the ISS, and a great number of technical terms **must be learned** by everyone on board. Some members of the first ISS teams also feared that they **might be treated** like outsiders because they didn't know American slang. Another major concern was food. What time **should** meals **be served**? How **should** preparation and cleanup **be handled**? **Can** religious dietary rules **be followed** on board?

Those worries **had to be tested** in space before anyone would know for sure. But by now the answer is clear. For over a decade, ISS astronauts have been proving that great achievements in technology and science **can be made** by an international group working together. Since November 2000, when the first crew boarded the ISS, the station has been operated by astronauts from 16 countries, including Brazil, Canada, Japan, Russia, the United States, and members of the European Union.

Perhaps their greatest challenge so far has been the ISS itself, which **had to be assembled** in space by astronauts floating outside the station. Despite delays, the last major sections of the ISS were attached in February 2010. Now, with the station completed, more focus **can be placed** on scientific goals. Important experiments **will be carried out** in the station's laboratories, and it's possible that more scientists will join the crew.

How has this international group of astronauts managed to cooperate and achieve these goals during long periods in a "trapped environment"? All astronauts receive cross-cultural training, but often sensitivity and tolerance **can't be taught** from a textbook. They**'ve got to be observed** and **experienced** personally.

Two researchers suggested that a model for space station harmony[2] **might be found** in the popular TV series *Star Trek*, in which a multicultural crew has been getting along for eons. However, real-life astronauts have found a more down-to-earth solution: the family dinner. Astronaut Nicolle Stott reports, ". . . we always spend mealtimes together . . . it's a lot like bringing your family together." The dinner table is where the world's (and each other's) problems **can be solved**, and where the astronauts "listen to good music, eat good food, improve our vocabulary in other languages, and laugh a lot."

The International Space Station and Earth seen from space

Astronauts also benefit from their unique perspective of Earth. They like to point out that national borders **can't be seen** from space. As Indian-American astronaut Sunita Williams says, "I consider myself a citizen of the universe. When we go up in space, all we can see is a beautiful Earth where there are no borders of nations and religions." This spirit of cooperation may turn out to be the project's greatest achievement.

---

[2]***harmony:*** a situation in which people are friendly and peaceful together

After You Read

A | Vocabulary: *Complete the sentences with the words from the box.*

assemble	benefit	cooperate	period	perspective	undertaking

1. It took years to _____ the many parts of the Space Station.

2. Astronauts stay on the ISS for a(n) _____ of about three to five months.

3. The ISS is a big _____ and has required a lot of planning.

4. It hasn't been difficult for them to _____ on their missions. Everyone works together very well.

5. We all _____ from the scientific discoveries made in ISS laboratories.

6. Seeing Earth from space changed their _____. They see the world's problems in a different way now.

B | Comprehension: *Check (✓) True, False or ? (the information isn't in the article).*

	True	False	?
1. Japanese and Italian astronauts worried about decision making.	☐	☐	☐
2. All ISS astronauts have to learn technical language in English.	☐	☐	☐
3. Astronauts from seven countries have been operating the ISS.	☐	☐	☐
4. The ISS was completely assembled in less than 10 years.	☐	☐	☐
5. Scientists do medical experiments in ISS laboratories.	☐	☐	☐
6. Astronauts rarely eat meals together.	☐	☐	☐

THE PASSIVE WITH MODALS AND SIMILAR EXPRESSIONS

Statements				
Subject	Modal*	*Be*	Past Participle	
The decision	will (not) should (not) ought (not) to must (not) can (not) had better (not)	be	made	quickly.

*Modals have only one form. They do not have -s in the third person singular.

Statements				
Subject	*Have (got) to / Be going to***	*Be*	Past Participle	
The problem	has (got) to doesn't have to is (not) going to	be	solved	quickly.

**Unlike modals, *have* in *have (got) to* and *be* in *be going to* change for different subjects.
Questions and negatives with *have (got) to* need a form of *do*.

Yes / No Questions				
Modal	Subject	*Be*	Past Participle	
Will				
Should	it	be	made	quickly?
Must				
Can				

Short Answers				
Affirmative			Negative	
Yes,	it	will. should. must. can.	No, it	won't. shouldn't. doesn't have to be. can't.

Yes / No Questions				
Auxiliary Verb	Subject	*Have to / Going to*	*Be*	Past Participle
Does	it	have to	be	solved?
Is		going to		

Short Answers				
Affirmative		Negative	
Yes,	it	does. is.	No, it	doesn't. isn't.

GRAMMAR NOTES

1	**After a modal**, form the **passive** with: *be* + **past participle**.	• The labs *will* **be used** for experiments. • The crew *won't* **be replaced** this month. • Crew members *must* **be trained** very carefully. • Decisions *shouldn't* **be made** too quickly.
2	Use *will* or *be going to* with the passive for the **future**.	• The ISS *will* **be used** for several years. OR • The ISS *is going to* **be used** for several years.
3	Use *can* with the passive for **present ability**. Use *could* with the passive for **past ability**.	• The space station *can* **be seen** from Earth. • It *could* **be seen** very clearly last year too.
4	Use *could*, *may*, *might*, and *can't* with the passive for **future possibility** or **impossibility**.	• The equipment *could* **be repaired** very soon. • Some anxiety *may* **be experienced** on takeoff. • New discoveries *might* **be made**. • The job *can't* **be handled** by just one person.
5	Use *should*, *ought to*, *had better*, *must*, and *have (got) to* with the passive for: a. **advisability** b. **necessity**	 • The crew *should* **be told** to leave now. • They *ought to* **be given** training. • Privacy *had better* **be taken** seriously. • Everyone *must* **be treated** with respect. • Technical language *has (got) to* **be learned**.

REFERENCE NOTES

For a review of **modals and similar expressions**, see Unit 15.
For information about **modals and their functions**, see Appendix 20 on page A-9.

EXERCISE 1: Discover the Grammar

Read the interview with scientist Dr. Bernard Kay (BK) by Comet Magazine (CM). *Underline the passive with modals and similar expressions.*

CM: Some parts of the ISS <u>had to be cancelled</u>, and some parts were delayed. But the whole station has finally been assembled. What an undertaking this has been! When was it completed?

BK: It was finished at the end of 2010. In February of that year, the last major sections—Tranquility[1] and the Cupola[2]—were attached. In Tranquility, oxygen can be produced and waste water can be recycled.[3] Tranquility's equipment will support life on the ISS if communication with Earth can't be maintained for a period of time.

CM: And the Cupola? I understand it was built by the European Space Agency.

BK: Yes, it was. It's amazing. It should be considered one of the most important parts of the station. It's got seven huge windows, and the views of Earth and space are spectacular.

CM: Why the big windows?

BK: Because robots have to be used for maintenance outside the space station. Astronauts can observe and control them more easily from these windows. But I think that the perspective of Earth and space that we gain from these views might be just as important.

[1] *tranquility:* a feeling of calm, peace, and freedom from worry
[2] *cupola:* a small round part on the roof of a building that has the shape of an upside down cup
[3] *recycle:* to clean or treat something such as water or paper so that it can be used again

(continued on next page)

CM: Why is that?

BK: Observing the Earth and space keeps the astronauts in touch with the importance of their mission. Originally the station was going to include sleeping cabins with windows, but that part of the project couldn't be accomplished for a number of reasons. Now the sleeping cabins are windowless, and the Cupola is everyone's favorite hangout.[4]

CM: Now that the station is complete, will more scientific work be done on the ISS?

BK: Yes, it will. The ISS is the first step to further exploration of our solar system. On the ISS, ways to grow food in space can be developed, and new materials can be tested, for example. But most important of all, human interactions have got to be understood better. An international crew from 16 different countries makes the ISS a wonderful laboratory for cross-cultural understanding. This could be one of the great benefits of the ISS.

CM: I guess we don't know what might be discovered, right?

BK: Right. That's what makes it so exciting.

---

[4] *hangout:* a place where people like to spend free time, especially with friends

EXERCISE 2: Affirmative and Negative Statements
(Grammar Notes 1–5)

Complete this article about zero-G (zero gravity or weightlessness) with the correct form of the words in parentheses.

Juggling oranges—it's easy in zero-G

Some tasks _____*can be accomplished*_____ more easily in zero-G. Inside the station,
       1. (can / accomplish)

astronauts _____ from the deadly conditions of space—but life in
       2. (can / protect)

almost zero-G still _____ normal. What's it like to live on the ISS?
       3. (can't / consider)

Getting Rest: Sleeping _____ to floating in water. It's
4. (can / compare)

relaxing, but sleeping bags _____ to the walls of the cabins.
5. (must / attach)

Otherwise, astronauts will drift around as they sleep.

Keeping Clean: Showers _____ because in zero-G water from
6. (can't / use)

a shower flies in all directions and sensitive equipment _____.
7. (might / damage)

Instead, astronauts take sponge baths. Used bath water _____ into
8. (have to / suck)

a container by a vacuum machine. Clothes _____ by putting them into a
9. (could / wash)

bag with water and soap, but astronauts really _____ with laundry. They
10. (not have to / concern)

usually put dirty clothes into a trash container which _____ back toward
11. (can / send)

Earth and _____ in Earth's atmosphere.
12. (burn up)

Dining: From the beginning, ISS planners have known that food _____
13. (should / take)

very seriously. Unlike meals on early space missions, food on the ISS _____
14. (not have to / squeeze)

out of tubes. Frozen, dried, canned, and fresh food _____ and
15. (can / heat)

_____ at a table. Regular utensils are used, but meals are packed
16. (eat)

into containers that _____ to a tray so they don't float away.
17. (must / attach)

Taking It Easy: Not surprisingly, a stressed astronaut is a grouchy astronaut. Free time

_____ for relaxing and enjoying views from the Cupola. All crew
18. (have got to / provide)

members have laptops that _____ for listening to music, reading
19. (can / use)

e-books, and accessing the Internet. In the past, the Internet _____
20. (could / access)

only for work, but now a direct Internet connection is available for astronauts' personal use.

Email _____ easily with friends and family. And blogs, tweets,
21. (can / exchange)

and videos from the astronauts _____ by millions of earthlings.
22. (be going to / enjoy)

Staying Fit: Time also _____ for exercise. In low-gravity
23. (must / allow)

environments, muscle and bone _____ quickly without exercise.
24. (will / lose)

EXERCISE 3: Affirmative and Negative Statements

(Grammar Notes 1–5)

Some scientists who are going to join the space station have just completed a simulation[1] of life on the station. Complete their conversations using the modals in parentheses and correct verbs from the boxes.

accept	do	~~keep~~	reject	send	train

CESAR: This simulation was great, but it was too warm in there. I think the temperature on the ISS

_____ should be kept _____ at 68 degrees—no warmer than that.
       1. (should)

GINA: Shorts and T-shirts _____ to the station for you. That's what most
                              2. (can)

astronauts ask for.

CESAR: That new space visitor _____ on our mission. They're considering
                                  3. (might not)

her application now. Her company wants her to do a space walk, and so far only astronauts

have done that.

GINA: Her application _____ just for that. But she ought to complete a
                         4. (shouldn't)

simulation first.

LYLE: Of course she'll have to do a simulation. She _____ to work while
                                                       5. (have got to)

wearing a space suit. That _____ except underwater in one of the
                           6. (can't)

space labs.

approve	do	send	share	surprise

HANS: Did you fill in your food preference forms? They _____ to the Food
                                                         7. (should)

Systems Lab today.

HISA: I did. I'm glad the new dishes _____ by everyone. We all benefit
                                         8. (have to)

from the variety. I really liked some of the Japanese and Russian meals.

HANS: You'll find that the food _____ by everyone too. Everyone enjoys
                                   9. (will)

trying different things.

LUIS: Shaving in zero-G is weird. The whisker dust from my beard and mustache kept flying back

into my face. I wonder if something _____ about that.
                                     10. (could)

HANS: I have a feeling we _____ by a lot of unexpected problems.
                             11. (be going to)

---

[1] **simulation:** something you do in order to practice what you would do in a real situation

EXERCISE 4: Editing

Read an astronaut's journal notes. There are eight mistakes in the use of the passive with modals and similar expressions. The first mistake is already corrected. Find and correct seven more.

October 4

6:15 A.M. I used the sleeping restraints last night, so my feet and hands didn't float around as much. I slept a lot better. I'm going to suggest some changes in the restraints, though—I think they ought to
be ~~make~~ *made* more comfortable. I felt really trapped. And maybe these sleeping quarters could designed differently. They're too small.

10:45 A.M. My face is puffy, and my eyes are red. Exercise helps a little—I'd better be gotten on the exercise bike right away. I can be misunderstanding very easily when I look like this. Sometimes people think I've been crying. And yesterday Max thought I was angry when he turned on *Star Trek*. Actually, I love that show.

1:00 P.M. Lunch was pretty good. Chicken teriyaki. It's nice and spicy, and the sauce can actually been tasted, even at zero gravity. They'd better fly in some more of it for us pretty soon. It's the most popular dish in the freezer.

4:40 P.M. I'm worried about my daughter. Just before I left on this mission, she said she was planning to quit school at the end of the semester. That's only a month away. I want to call her and discuss it. But I worry that I might get angry and yell. I might overheard by the others. They really should figure out some way to give us a little more privacy.

10:30 P.M. The view of Earth is unbelievably breathtaking! Tonight I spent a long time just looking out the window and watching Earth pass below. At night a halo of light surrounds the horizon. It's so bright that the tops of the clouds can see. It can't be described. It simply have to be experienced. I think it's even given me a better perspective on my problems with my daughter.

EXERCISE 5: Listening

🎧 **A** | *Some crew members aboard the ISS are watching a science fiction movie. Listen to the conversations from the movie. Listen again and check (✓) **True** or **False** about each statement. Correct the false statements.*

	True	False
1. A meteorite hit ~~Earth~~. *the spaceship*	☐	☑
2. Picarra wants the people on CX5 to understand *Endeavor*'s messages.	☐	☐
3. Picarra thinks both Lon and Torsha should be sent to CX5.	☐	☐
4. Lon thinks that oxygen may be necessary on the planet.	☐	☐
5. Picarra thinks that Lon and Torsha's equipment might not work.	☐	☐
6. The plants will grow well in space.	☐	☐
7. The spaceship crew can't fix the spaceship alone.	☐	☐

🎧 **B** | *Listen again to the conversations. Circle the underlined words that you hear.*

1. It can / (can't) be repaired out here.

2. Our messages <u>could / should</u> be misunderstood.

3. We know that Lon <u>will / won't</u> be taken seriously down there.

4. Oxygen <u>must / mustn't</u> be used in this situation.

5. They'll <u>pick up / be picked up by</u> the radar.

6. They <u>can / can't</u> be grown in space.

7. As you know, we have to <u>help / be helped</u> with the repairs.

EXERCISE 6: Pronunciation

🎧 **A** | *Read and listen to the Pronunciation Note.*

Pronunciation Note

In conversation, we often **drop the final "t"** in *must be*, *mustn't be*, *couldn't be*, and *shouldn't be*.

EXAMPLES: The project **must be** finished soon. → "The **project mus'** be finished soon."
Oxygen **couldn't be** used. → "Oxygen **couldn'** be used."
The captain **shouldn't be** told. → "The captain **shouldn'** be told."

---

1. **A:** Could you see Tokyo or was it too cloudy?

    B: Too cloudy. Tokyo _____ seen at all.

2. **A:** Should I tell Commander Kotov about the problem?

    B: No. He _____ disturbed right now.

3. **A:** Did they decide on the new crew yesterday?

    B: No. It _____ decided then.

4. **A:** They haven't fixed our Internet connection yet.

    B: I know. But it _____ fixed by tomorrow.

5. **A:** When should we eat dinner?

    B: It probably _____ served before 6:00.

6. **A:** Mikel's working late on that experiment.

    B: Yeah. He says it _____ finished by next week.

🎧 **C** | *Listen again to the conversations and repeat the responses. Then practice the conversations with a partner. Use the short forms.*

EXERCISE 7: Reaching Agreement

A | *Work in small groups. Imagine that in preparation for a space mission, your group is going to spend a week together in a one-room apartment. Discuss the rules that should be made for living in close quarters.*

Some issues to consider:

- food
- clothes
- room temperature
- noise
- neatness

- cleanliness
- privacy
- language
- entertainment
- *Other:* _____

> **EXAMPLE:** **A:** I think dinner should be served at 6:00 every night.
> **B:** Do meals have to be eaten together? Some people might not want to eat that early.
> **C:** Neatness has to be taken seriously. We'd better . . .

B | *Make a list of rules that you've agreed on. Use the passive with modals and similar expressions. Compare your list with another group's list.*

> **EXAMPLE:** Dinner will be served at 6:00 P.M.
> The dishes must be washed after each meal.
> Noise has to be . . .

EXERCISE 8: Problem Solving

Work in groups. Look at the picture of a student lounge. You are responsible for getting it in order, but you have limited time and money. Agree on five things that should be done.

EXAMPLE: **A:** The window has to be replaced.
B: No. That'll cost too much. It can just be taped.
C: That'll look terrible. It's really got to be replaced.
D: OK. What else should be done?

EXERCISE 9: For or Against

Sending people to the International Space Station costs millions of dollars. Should money be spent for these space projects, or could it be spent better on Earth? If so, how should it be spent? Discuss these questions with your classmates.

EXAMPLE: **A:** I think space projects are useful. A lot of new products are going to be developed in space.
B: I don't agree. Some of that money should be spent on public housing.

EXERCISE 10: Writing

A | *Write two paragraphs about your neighborhood, your school, or your workplace. In your first paragraph, write about what might be done to improve it. In your second paragraph, write about what shouldn't be changed. Use the passive with modals and similar expressions.*

> EXAMPLE: I enjoy attending this school, but I believe some things could be improved. First, I think that more software ought to be purchased for the language lab . . .

B | *Check your work. Use the Editing Checklist.*

Editing Checklist

Did you use . . . ?

☐ *be* + **past participle** to form the passive after modals

☐ *will* or *be going to* for the future

☐ *can* for present ability

☐ *could* for past ability and future possibility

☐ *may*, *might*, and *can't* for future possibility or impossibility

☐ *should*, *ought to*, and *had better* for advisability

☐ *must* and *have (got) to* for necessity

UNIT 19 Review

Check your answers on page UR-5.

Do you need to review anything?

A | *Circle the correct words to complete the sentences.*

1. What should be <u>did / done</u> about the student lounge?

2. I think the furniture should <u>be replaced / replace</u>.

3. Maybe some computer workstations <u>could / have</u> be provided.

4. The air conditioning <u>has / had</u> better be repaired.

5. It might not <u>be / being</u> fixed by the summer.

6. The lounge <u>don't / won't</u> be used by students while it's being painted.

7. The school office <u>has / had</u> got to be told about these problems.

8. In the future, problems <u>will / are</u> going to be handled faster.

B | *Complete the sentences with the correct form of the verbs in parentheses.*

1. Astronauts _____ in zero gravity.
     (should / train)

2. They _____ the chance to work in those conditions.
     (have to / give)

3. Equipment _____ also _____ in conditions similar to space.
     (must / test)

4. Zero gravity _____ underwater as well as on the ISS.
     (can / experience)

5. Underwater living space _____ by Aquatics Laboratory.
     (will / provide)

6. A lot more astronauts _____ there for training.
     (may / send)

7. Skills for Moon missions _____ also _____ underwater.
     (could / develop)

C | *Find and correct five mistakes.*

The new spacesuits are going to be testing underwater today. They've got to been improved before they can be used on the Moon or Mars. Two astronauts are going to be wearing them while they're working, and they'll watched by the engineers. This morning communication was lost with the Earth's surface, and all decisions had to be make by the astronauts themselves. It was a very realistic situation. This crew will got to be very well prepared for space travel. They're going to the Moon in a few years.

STEP 1 GRAMMAR IN CONTEXT

Before You Read

Look at the photos on this page and the next. Discuss the questions.

1. Which forms of body art do you think are attractive?
2. Does body art have any disadvantages? What are they?

Read

Read the article from a fashion magazine.

Each culture has a different ideal of beauty, and throughout the ages,[1] men and women have done amazing things to achieve the ideal. They have **had *their hair* shaved**, **cut**, **colored**, **straightened**, and **curled**; and they have **had *their bodies* decorated** with painting and tattoos. Here are some of today's many options:

HAIR

Getting *your hair* done is the easiest way to change your appearance. Today, both men and women **have *their hair* permed**. This chemical procedure[2] can curl hair or just give it more body.[3] If your hair is long, you can, of course, **get *it* cut**. But did you know that you can also **have *short hair* lengthened** with hair extensions[4]? Of course you can **have *your hair* colored** and become a blonde, brunette, or redhead. But you can also **have *it* bleached** white or **get *it* dyed** blue, green, or orange!

(continued on next page)

---

[1]***throughout the ages:*** during different periods of time
[2]***chemical procedure:*** a technique that uses chemicals (for example, hydrogen peroxide) to change the appearance or texture of something
[3]***body:*** hair thickness
[4]***hair extensions:*** pieces of hair (natural or synthetic) that people have attached to their own hair to make it longer

Body Art

TATTOOS

This form of body art was created many thousands of years ago. Today, tattoos have again become popular. More and more people are **having _them_ done**. However, caution is necessary. Although nowadays you can **get _a tattoo_ removed** with less pain and scarring[5] than before, **having _one_ applied** is still a big decision.

BODY PAINT

If a tattoo is not for you, you can **have _ornaments_ painted** on your skin instead. Some people **have _necklaces and bracelets_ painted** on their neck and arms or **get _a butterfly mask_ applied** to their face for a special event. Sports fans often get their face painted with their team's colors or the name of their favorite player. Body paintings can be large, but unlike tattoos, they can be washed off.

PIERCING

Pierced ears are an old favorite, but lately the practice of piercing has expanded.[6] Many people now **are getting _their noses_, _lips_, _or other parts of the body_ pierced** for jewelry. Piercing requires even more caution than tattooing, and aftercare is very important to avoid infection.

COSMETIC SURGERY

You can **get _your nose_ shortened**, or **have _your chin_ lengthened**. You can even **have _the shape of your body_ changed**. There is always some risk involved, so the decision to have cosmetic surgery requires a lot of thought.

Some of the ways of changing your appearance may be cheap and temporary. However, others are expensive and permanent. So, think before you act, and don't let today's choice become tomorrow's regret.

—By Debra Santana

---

[5]**scarring:** the creation of a permanent mark on the skin as a result of an accident, or a cosmetic or medical procedure

[6]**expand:** to become larger

After You Read

A | Vocabulary: *Complete the sentences with the words from the box.*

appearance	event	option	permanent	remove	risk

1. Dana and Nasir's wedding was a wonderful _____. The whole town attended.

2. Getting a tattoo isn't (an) _____ if you're under 16. It's illegal at that age.

3. Piercing can be attractive, but there's always the _____ of infection.

4. You won't recognize Elsa! She's completely changed her _____.

5. Carly hates her new hair color. It's a good thing it isn't _____.

6. Can a dry cleaner _____ this stain? Coffee is hard get out.

B | Comprehension: *Check (✓)* **True, False,** *or* **?** *(the information isn't in the article).*

	True	False	?
1. Most people have the same idea about beauty.	☐	☐	☐
2. There are many ways people can change their hair.	☐	☐	☐
3. Many men change their hair color.	☐	☐	☐
4. Tattoos are a modern invention.	☐	☐	☐
5. Tattoos are permanent.	☐	☐	☐
6. Body paint is a temporary alternative to tattoos.	☐	☐	☐
7. Body piercing has more risks than tattooing.	☐	☐	☐
8. You can have cosmetic surgery to lengthen your nose.	☐	☐	☐
9. It's always easy to change back to the way you looked before.	☐	☐	☐

THE PASSIVE CAUSATIVE

Statements					
Subject	*Have / Get*	Object	Past Participle	(*By* + Agent)	
She	has	*her hair*	cut	*by André*	every month.
He	has had	*his beard*	trimmed		before.
I	get	*my nails*	done		at André's.
They	are going to get	*their ears*	pierced.		

Yes / No Questions						
Auxiliary Verb	Subject	*Have / Get*	Object	Past Participle	(*By* + Agent)	
Does	she	have	*her hair*	cut	*by André*?	
Has	he	had	*his beard*	trimmed		before?
Do	you	get	*your nails*	done		at André's?
Are	they	going to get	*their ears*	pierced?		

Wh- Questions							
Wh- Word	Auxiliary Verb	Subject	*Have / Get*	Object	Past Participle	(*By* + Agent)	
How often	does	she	have	*her hair*	cut	*by André*?	
Where	did	he	get	*his beard*	trimmed		before?
When	do	you	get	*your nails*	done		at André's?
Why	are	they	going to get	*their ears*	pierced?		

GRAMMAR NOTES

1	Form the **passive causative** with the appropriate form of *have* or *get* + **object** + **past participle**. *Have* and *get* have the same meaning.	• I **have** *my hair* **cut** by André. OR • I **get** *my hair* **cut** by André.
	You can use the **passive causative** with: • **all verb tenses** • **modals** • **gerunds** • **infinitives**	• I **had** *the car* **washed** yesterday. • You **should get** *the oil* **changed**. • I love **having** *my hair* **done**. • I want **to get** *it* **colored**.
2	Use the **passive causative** to talk about **services** that you arrange for someone to do for you.	• I used to color my own hair, but I've started to **have** *it* **colored**. • André is going to **get** *his hair salon* **remodeled** by a local architect.
	BE CAREFUL! Do **NOT confuse** the **passive causative** with *had* with the **past perfect**.	**PASSIVE CAUSATIVE WITH *HAD*:** • I **had** *it* **colored** last week. *(Someone did it for me.)* **PAST PERFECT:** • I **had colored** it before. *(I did it myself.)*
3	Use *by* when it is necessary to mention the **agent** (the person doing the service). Do **NOT use** *by* when it is clear who is doing the service.	• This week Lynne **is getting her hair done** *by a new stylist*. NOT: Where does Lynne get her hair done ~~by a hair stylist~~?

REFERENCE NOTE

For information on when to include the **agent**, see Unit 18, page 293.

EXERCISE 1: Discover the Grammar

Read the conversations. Decide if the statement that follows each conversation is **True (T)** *or* **False (F).**

1. **JAKE:** Have you finished writing your article on body art?

   DEBRA: Yes. I'm going to get it copied and then take it to the post office.

   _F_ Debra is going to copy the article herself.

2. **DEBRA:** I'm glad that's done. Now I can start planning for our party.

   JAKE: Me too. I'm going to get my hair cut tomorrow for the big event.

   _____ Jake cuts his own hair.

3. **JAKE:** Speaking about hair—Amber, *your* hair's getting awfully long.

   AMBER: I know, Dad. I'm cutting it tomorrow.

   _____ Amber cuts her own hair.

4. **AMBER:** Mom, why didn't you get your nails done last time you went to the hairdresser?

   DEBRA: Because I did them just before my appointment.

   _____ Debra did her own nails.

5. **AMBER:** I was thinking of painting a butterfly on my forehead for the party.

   DEBRA: A butterfly! Well, OK. As long as it's not permanent.

   _____ Someone is going to paint a butterfly on Amber's forehead for her.

6. **DEBRA:** Jake, do you think we should get the floors waxed before the party?

   JAKE: I think they look OK. We'll get them done afterward.

   _____ Debra and Jake are going to hire someone to wax their floors after the party.

7. **DEBRA:** I'm going to watch some TV and then go to bed. What's on the agenda for tomorrow?

   JAKE: I have to get up early. I'm getting the car washed before work.

   _____ Jake is going to wash the car himself.

8. **DEBRA:** You know, I think it's time to change the oil too.

   JAKE: You're right. I'll do it this weekend.

   _____ Jake is going to change the oil himself.

EXERCISE 2: Statements

(Grammar Notes 1–2)

Today is February 15. Look at the Santanas' calendar and write sentences about when they **had/got things done,** *and when they are* **going to have/get things done.** *Use the correct form of the words in parentheses.*

FEBRUARY

SUNDAY	MONDAY	TUESDAY	WEDNESDAY	THURSDAY	FRIDAY	SATURDAY
1	2	3	4	5	6	7 Deb– hairdresser
8	9	10	11	12 Jake– barber	13 carpets	14 dog groomer
15 TODAY'S DATE	16 windows	17	18	19	20 food and drinks	21 party!! family pictures
22	23	24	25 Amber– ears pierced	26	27	28

1. (The Santanas / have / family pictures / take)

   The Santanas are going to have family pictures taken on the 21st.

2. (Debra / get / her hair / perm)

   _____

3. (Amber / have / the dog / groom)

   _____

4. (They / get / the windows / wash)

   _____

5. (They / have / the carpets / clean)

   _____

6. (Amber / have / her ears / pierce)

   _____

7. (Jake / get / his hair / cut)

   _____

8. (They / have / food and drinks / deliver)

   _____

EXERCISE 3: Statements and Questions

(Grammar Notes 1–3)

Debra and Jake are going to have a party. Complete the conversations with the passive causative of the appropriate verbs in the box.

color	cut	dry clean	paint	remove	repair	~~shorten~~	wash

1. **AMBER:** I bought a new dress for the party, Mom. What do you think?

   DEBRA: It's pretty, but it's a little long. Why don't you _____*get it shortened*_____?

   AMBER: OK. They do alterations at the cleaners. I'll take it in tomorrow.

2. **AMBER:** By the way, what are *you* planning to wear?

   DEBRA: My white silk suit. I'm glad you reminded me. I'd better _____.

   It has a stain on the sleeve.

   AMBER: I can drop it off at the cleaners with my dress.

3. **JAKE:** The house is ready, except for the windows. They look pretty dirty.

   DEBRA: Don't worry. We _____ tomorrow.

4. **DEBRA:** Amber, your hair is getting really long. I thought you were going to cut it.

   AMBER: I decided not to do it myself this time. I _____ by André.

5. **DEBRA:** My hair's getting a lot of gray in it. Should I _____?

   JAKE: Well, I guess that's an option. But it looks fine to me the way it is.

6. **AMBER:** Mom, I've been thinking about getting a butterfly tattoo instead of having one painted.

   I can always _____ if I decide I don't like it.

   DEBRA: No! That's *not* an option! There are too many risks involved in the procedure.

7. **AMBER** Someone's at the door, and it's only 12 o'clock!

   DEBRA: No, it's not. The clock stopped again.

   JAKE: Oh no, not again. I don't believe it! I _____ already

   _____ twice this year, and it's only February!

8. **GUEST:** The house looks beautiful, Jake. I love the color. _____ you

   _____?

   JAKE: No, actually we did it ourselves last summer.

EXERCISE 4: Editing

*Read Amber's Facebook post. There are seven mistakes in the use of the passive causative.
The first mistake is already corrected. Find and correct six more.*

February 21: The party was tonight. It went really well! The house looked great.

Last week, Mom and Dad had the floors waxed and all the windows ~~clean~~ *cleaned* professionally so everything

sparkled. And of course we had the whole house painted ourselves last summer. (I'll never forget that.

It took us two weeks!) I wore my pink dress that I have

shortened by Bo, and my best friend, Alicia, wore her new

black gown. Right before the party, I got cut my hair by André.

He did a great job. There were a lot of guests at the party. We

had almost 50 people invited, and they almost all showed up

for our family event! The food was great too. Mom made most

of the main dishes herself, but she had the rest of the food

prepare by a caterer. Mom and Dad had hired a professional

photographer, so at the end of the party we took our pictures.

As you can see, they look great!

EXERCISE 5: Listening

A | *Amber has just gone to college. Read the statements. Then listen to her conversation with her father. Listen again and circle the words to complete each statement.*

1. Amber walks / (drives) / takes the bus to school.

2. Amber does not have a new car / apartment / roommate.

3. Her neighborhood is old / safe / noisy.

4. Her apartment needed cleaning / carpeting / painting.

5. Amber didn't have to buy a computer / a computer desk / lamps.

6. Amber didn't change the appearance of her hair / face / hands.

B | *Listen again to the conversation. Check (✓) the correct column.*

Amber . . .	Did the job herself	Hired someone to do the job
1. change the oil in her car	☐	☑
2. change the locks	☐	☐
3. paint the apartment	☐	☐
4. put up bookshelves	☐	☐
5. bring new furniture to the apartment	☐	☐
6. paint her hands	☐	☐
7. cut her hair	☐	☐
8. color her hair	☐	☐

EXERCISE 6: Pronunciation

A | *Read and listen to the Pronunciation Note.*

Pronunciation Note

We often **contract *have*** in sentences in the **present perfect**.

EXAMPLES: She **has cut** her hair. → "She**'s cut** her hair."
  She **has had** her hair cut. → "She**'s had** her hair cut."

But we do **NOT contract *have*** in sentences that use the **passive causative** in the **simple present**.

EXAMPLES: She **has** her hair **cut**. Not: "~~She's~~ her hair cut."
  They **have** their taxes **done**. Not: "~~They've~~ their taxes done."

---

    1. A: Marta's hair looks great.

        B: Yes. She _____.

    2. A: Do you do your own taxes or do you have them done?

        B: I _____.

    3. A: Is Anton's car OK now?

        B: Yes. He _____.

    4. A: Does Amy wash her own car?

        B: She _____ once a month.

    5. A: What color is your new apartment?

        B: I _____ green.

    6. A: Your hair looks different!

        B: Yes. I _____.

🎧 **C |** *Listen again to the conversations and repeat the answers. Then practice the conversations with a partner.*

EXERCISE 7: Making Plans

A | *Work in small groups. Imagine that you are taking a car trip together to another country. You'll be gone for several weeks. Decide where you're going. Then make a list of things you have to do and arrange before the trip. Use the ideas below and ideas of your own.*

- passport and visa
- car (oil, gas, tires, brake fluid)
- home (pets, plants, mail, newspaper delivery)
- personal (clothing, hair)
- medical (teeth, eyes, prescriptions)
- *Other:* _____

    EXAMPLE: **A:** I have to get my passport renewed.
                  B: Me too. And we should apply for visas right away.

B | *Now compare your list with that of another group. Did you forget anything?*

EXERCISE 8: Compare and Contrast

A | *Work in pairs. Look at the Before and After pictures of a fashion model. You have five minutes to find and write down all the things she had done to change her appearance.*

Before

After

> EXAMPLE: She had her nose shortened.

B | *When the five minutes are up, compare your list with that of another pair. Then look at the pictures again to check your answers.*

C | *Do you think the woman looks better? Why or why not?*

> EXAMPLE: A: I don't know why she had her nose fixed.
> B: Neither do I. I think it looked fine before.

EXERCISE 9: Cross-Cultural Comparison

Work in small groups. Think about other cultures. Discuss the types of things people do or get done in order to change their appearance. Report back to your class.

Some procedures to think about:

- **eyes:** lengthening eyelashes, coloring eyebrows
- **teeth:** straightening, whitening
- **face:** shortening nose, plumping lips
- **hair:** coloring, lengthening, styling, curling, straightening, braiding
- **skin:** whitening, tanning, tattooing, painting
- **hands / feet:** painting nails, painting hands or soles of feet

> EXAMPLE: A: In India, women get their hands painted for special occasions. I think it looks nice.
> B: In Japan, . . .

Hand painting in India

EXERCISE 10: Writing

A | *Write an email to someone you know. Describe your activities. Include things that you have recently done or have had done. Also talk about things you are going to do or are going to have done. Use the passive causative.*

EXAMPLE:　　Hi Sara,

I've just moved into a new apartment. I've already had it painted, but there are still so many things that I have to get done! . . .

B | *Check your work. Use the Editing Checklist.*

Editing Checklist

Did you . . . ?

☐ form the passive causative with the appropriate form of
　have or *get* + **object** + **past participle**

☐ use *by* when it was necessary to mention the agent

Check your answers on page UR-5.

Do you need to review anything?

A | *Circle the correct words to complete the sentences.*

1. I don't cut my own hair. I <u>have it cut</u> / have cut it.

2. My friend has her hair <u>did</u> / <u>done</u> every week.

3. We should <u>get</u> / <u>gotten</u> the house painted again this year.

4. Did you have <u>painted your house</u> / <u>your house painted</u>?

5. I want to have the job done <u>by</u> / <u>from</u> a professional.

B | *Complete each sentence with the correct passive causative form of the verb in parentheses and a pronoun.*

1. My computer stopped working. I have to _____.
   (repair)

2. I don't clean the windows myself. I _____ once a year.
   (clean)

3. Your pants are too long. You should _____.
   (shorten)

4. Does Monica color her own hair or does she _____?
   (color)

5. I can't fix this vacuum cleaner myself. I'll have to _____.
   (fix)

6. Todd used to have a tattoo, but he _____ last year.
   (remove)

7. My passport is going to expire soon. I need to _____.
   (renew)

8. The car has been making a strange noise. I _____ tomorrow.
   (check)

C | *Find and correct seven mistakes.*

I'm going on vacation next week. I'd like to have done some work in my office, and this seems like a good time for it. Please have my carpet clean while I'm gone. And could you have my computer and printer looked at? It's been quite a while since they've been serviced. Ted wants to have my office painted by a painter while I'm gone. Please tell him any color is fine except pink! Last week, I had designed some new brochures by Perfect Print. Please call the printer and have them delivered directly to the sales reps. And could you get made up more business cards too? When I get back, it'll be time to plan the holiday party. I think we should have it catered this year from a professional. While I'm gone, why don't you call around and get some estimates from caterers? Has the estimates sent to Ted. Thanks.

PART VIII

From Grammar to Writing
CHANGING THE FOCUS WITH THE PASSIVE

Reports often **focus on the results of an action** rather than the people who performed the action. Use the **passive** to focus on the results.

> **EXAMPLE:** Artists **carved** many wooden statues for the temple. (*active*)
> Many wooden statues **were carved** for the temple. (*passive*)

1 | *Read about a famous building in Korea. Underline the passive forms and their subjects.*

Two Buddhist monks built Haeinsa Temple in the year 802. The king gave them the money to build the temple after the two monks saved his queen's life. Haeinsa burned down in 1817, but the Main Hall was rebuilt in 1818 on its original foundations. Today, Haeinsa is composed of several large, beautiful buildings. It contains many paintings and statues. Someone carved three of the statues from a single ancient tree. Behind the Main Hall is a steep flight of stone stairs that leads to the Storage Buildings. These buildings, which escaped the fire, were constructed in 1488 in order to store wooden printing blocks of Buddhist texts. It was believed that these printing blocks could protect the country against invaders. Monks carved the 81,258 wooden blocks in the 13th century. A century later, nuns carried them to Haeinsa for safekeeping. Architects designed the Storage Buildings to preserve the wooden blocks. For more than 500 years, the blocks have been kept in perfect condition because of the design of these buildings. Haeinsa, which means *reflection on a smooth sea*, is also known as the Temple of Teaching because it houses the ancient printing blocks.

2 | *Find five sentences in Exercise 1 that would be better expressed in the passive. Rewrite them.*

1. *Haeinsa Temple was built by two Buddhist monks in the year 802.*

2. _____

3. _____

4. _____

5. _____

3 | *Answer these questions about Haeinsa Temple.*

    1. When was it built?

    _____

    2. Who built it?

    _____

    3. Why was it built?

    _____

    4. What are some of its features?

    _____

    5. What is it famous for?

    _____

4 | *Before you write . . .*

    1. Choose a famous building to write about. Do some research in the library or on the Internet. Answer the questions in Exercise 3.

    2. Work with a partner. Ask and answer questions about your topic.

5 | *Write a research report about the building you researched. Use the passive where appropriate. If possible, include a photograph or drawing of the building.*

6 | *Exchange paragraphs with a different partner. Answer the following questions.*

    1. Did the writer answer all the questions in Exercise 3?_____

    2. What interested you the most about the building?_____

    3. What would you like to know more about?_____

    4. Did the writer use the passive appropriately?_____

    5. Are the past participles correct?_____

7 | *Work with your partner. Discuss each other's editing questions from Exercise 6. Then rewrite your report and make any necessary corrections.*

CONDITIONALS

Present Real Conditionals
SHOPPING

Before You Read

Look at the title of the article and the picture on this page. Discuss the questions.

1. What is a cyber mall?
2. Have you ever purchased something online?
3. What are some steps people should take to shop safely online?

Read

Read the article about cyber malls.

Pick and Click Shopping @ Home
By E. Buyer

Where is the largest mall[1] in the world? **If you think it's in Alberta, Canada, you're wrong!** It's in cyberspace![2] And you can get there from home on your very own computer.

Cyber shopping is fast, convenient, and often less expensive. **It doesn't matter if it's a book or a diamond necklace**—with just a click of your mouse, you can buy anything without getting up from your chair. **If you're looking for the best price, you can easily compare prices and read other buyers' reviews of products.** Shopping online can save you time and money—but you need to surf[3] and shop safely. Here are some tips to make your trip to the cyber mall a good one:

🔒 **You are less likely to have a problem if you shop with well-known companies.**

🔒 **If you don't know the company, ask them to send you information.** What is their address? Their phone number?

🔒 **Always pay by credit card if you can. If you are unhappy with the product (or if you don't receive it), then you can dispute the charge.**

---

[1]***mall:*** a very large building or outdoor area with a lot of stores in it
[2]***cyberspace:*** all the connections between computers in different places (people think of it as a real place where information, messages, pictures, etc. exist)
[3]***surf:*** to go quickly from one website to another in order to find information that interests you

Pick and Click Shopping @ Home

🔒 Only enter your credit card information on a secure site. **If you see a closed lock (🔒) or complete key (🔑) symbol at the bottom of your screen, the site is secure.** Also, the web address will change from http://www to https://www. This means that your credit card number will be encrypted (changed so that others can't read it). **If the site isn't secure, don't enter your credit card information.**

🔒 **If you have kids, don't let them give out personal information.**

🔒 **If you have any doubts about a site's security, contact the store by phone or email.**

🔒 Find out the return policy. **What happens if you don't like the product?**

🔒 Print out and save a record of your purchase. **If there is a problem, the receipt gives you proof of purchase.**

🔒 **If you change your mind about an order, contact the company immediately.**

As you can see, many of these steps are similar to the ones you follow in a "store with doors." Just use common sense. **If you take some basic precautions, you shouldn't have any problems.**

Internet shopping has literally[4] brought a world of opportunity to consumers. Today we can shop 24 hours a day, 7 days a week in stores that are halfway around the globe without ever having to leave home or stand in line. As with many things in life, there are some risks. Just remember that online or off, **if an offer seems too good to be true, it probably is.** Happy cyber shopping!

SHOPPING ON LINE IS CONVENIENT... BUT I MISS PUSHING AND SHOVING AND GRABBING SALE ITEMS FROM OTHER SHOPPER'S HANDS!

McLemore 5-04

---

[4]**literally:** (used to emphasize that something is actually true)

After You Read

A | **Vocabulary:** *Complete the statements with the words from the box.*

| consumer | dispute | policy | precaution | secure | site |

1. You should ask about a store's return _____.

2. A smart _____ always compares prices before making a purchase.

3. As a safety _____, you should never give your password to anyone.

4. My friend never shops online. He doesn't think it's _____ enough.

5. I don't like that store's online _____. It's very confusing.

6. I need to _____ that charge. I ordered one sweater, but they charged me for two.

B | Comprehension: *Circle the letter of the word or phrase that best completes each statement.*

1. The largest mall in the world is in _____.

    a. Canada

    b. the United States

    c. cyberspace

2. Cyber shopping is often _____ than shopping in a store with walls.

    a. slower

    b. cheaper

    c. more dangerous

3. It's a good idea to shop with a company that has _____.

    a. a nice website

    b. a name you know

    c. products for children

4. If possible, you should pay for Internet purchases _____.

    a. by credit card

    b. by check

    c. with cash

5. A closed lock at the bottom of the computer screen means _____.

    a. you can't make a purchase

    b. it's safe to enter your credit card information

    c. the site doesn't have the product you want

6. In some ways, shopping online is _____ shopping in a "store with doors."

    a. exactly the same as

    b. totally different from

    c. similar to

7. One of the biggest advantages of shopping online is _____.

    a. convenience

    b. quality

    c. safety

PRESENT REAL CONDITIONALS

Statements	
If Clause	**Result** Clause
If I **shop** online,	I **save** time.
If the mall **is** closed,	I **can shop** online.

Statements	
Result Clause	**If** Clause
I **save** time	**if** I **shop** online.
I **can shop** online	**if** the mall **is** closed.

Yes / No Questions	
Result Clause	**If** Clause
Do you **save** time	**if** you **shop** online?
Can you **shop** online	**if** the mall **is** closed?

Short Answers			
Affirmative		**Negative**	
Yes,	I **do**.	No,	I **don't**.
	I **can**.		I **can't**.

Wh- Questions	
Result Clause	**If** Clause
What **happens**	**if** I **don't like** it?

GRAMMAR NOTES

1 Use **present real conditional** sentences for **general truths**.

The **if clause** talks about the **condition**, and the **result clause** talks about **what happens** if the condition occurs.

Use the **simple present** in both clauses.

USAGE NOTE: We often use **even if** when the **result is surprising**.

- IF CLAUSE   RESULT CLAUSE
- **If** it**'s** a holiday, the store **is** closed.

- PRESENT   PRESENT
- **If** you **use** a credit card, it**'s** faster.

- **Even if** it's a holiday, this store stays open.

2 You can also use **real conditional** sentences for **habits** and things that happen again and again.

Use the **simple present** or **present progressive** in the **if clause**. Use the **simple present** in the **result clause**.

- **If** Bill **shops** online, he **uses** a credit card.

- PRESENT   PRESENT
- **If** I **surf** the Web, I **use** Google.

- PRESENT PROGRESSIVE   PRESENT
- **If** I**'m surfing** the Web, I **use** Google.

(continued on next page)

3	You can use **modals** (*can, should, might, must . . .*) in the **result clause**.	• If you don't like the product, you *can* **return** it. • If you have children, you *shouldn't* **let** them shop online.
	USAGE NOTE: We sometimes use ***then*** to **emphasize the result** in real conditional sentences with modals.	• If you don't like the product, ***then*** you **can return** it. • If you have children, ***then*** you **shouldn't let** them shop online.

4	Use the **imperative** in the **result clause** to give **instructions**, **commands**, and **invitations** that depend on a certain condition.	IMPERATIVE • If you change your mind, **call** the company. • If a site isn't secure, **don't enter** your credit card information.
	USAGE NOTE: We sometimes use ***then*** to **emphasize the result** in real conditional sentences with imperatives.	• If you change your mind, ***then* call** the company. • If a site isn't secure, ***then* don't enter** your credit card information.

5	You can **begin conditional sentences** with the ***if* clause** or **the result clause**. The meaning is the same.	• ***If* I shop online,** I save time. OR • I save time ***if* I shop online**.
	BE CAREFUL! Use a **comma** between the two clauses only when the ***if* clause comes first**.	Not: I save time, if I shop online.

6	A **conditional sentence** does not always have ***if***. You can often use ***when*** instead of ***if***.	• ***When*** Bill **shops** online, he **uses** a credit card. • I **use** Google ***when*** I'm **surfing** the Web.
	Notice that both clauses can use the **present progressive** to describe actions that happen at the same time.	• ***When*** stores **are opening** in Los Angeles, they **are closing** in Johannesburg.

EXERCISE 1: Discover the Grammar

Read these shopping tips. In each real conditional sentence, underline once the result clause. Underline twice the clause that talks about the condition.

SHOP SMART

You're shopping in a foreign city. Should you pay full price, or should you bargain? <u><u>If you don't know the answer,</u></u> <u>you can pay too much or miss a fun experience</u>. Bargaining is one of the greatest shopping pleasures if you know how to do it. The strategies are different in different places. Check out these tips before you go.

Hong Kong

Hong Kong is one of the world's greatest shopping cities. If you like to bargain, you can do it anywhere except the larger department stores. The trick is not to look too interested. If you see something you want, pick it up along with some other items and ask the prices. Then make an offer below what you are willing to pay. If the seller's offer is close to the price you want, then you should be able to reach an agreement quickly.

Italy

Bargaining in Italy is appropriate at outdoor markets and with street vendors. In stores, you can politely ask for a discount if you want to bargain. Take your time. Make conversation if you speak Italian. Show your admiration for the object by picking it up and pointing out its wonderful features. When you hear the price, look sad. Make your own offer. Then end the bargaining politely if you can't agree.

Mexico

In Mexico, people truly enjoy bargaining. There are some clear rules, though. You should bargain only if you really are interested in buying the object. If the vendor's price is far more than you want to pay, then politely stop the negotiation. If you know your price is truly reasonable, walking away will often bring a lower offer.

Remember, bargaining is always a social interaction, not an argument. And it can still be fun even if you don't get the item you want at the price you want to pay.

EXERCISE 2: Conditional Statements: Modals and Imperatives   (Grammar Notes 1–4)

Read this Q and A about shopping around the world. Write conditional sentences to summarize the advice. Start with the **if** clause and use appropriate punctuation.

1. **Hong Kong**

   Q: I want to buy some traditional crafts. Any ideas?

   A: You ought to visit the Western District on Hong Kong Island. It's famous for its crafts.

   If you want to buy some traditional crafts, (then) you ought to visit the Western District on Hong Kong Island.

2. **Barcelona**

   Q: I'd like to buy some nice but inexpensive clothes. Where can I go?

   A: Take the train to outdoor markets in towns *outside* of the city. They have great stuff.

   _____

3. **Istanbul**

   Q: I want to go shopping in the Grand Bazaar. Is it open on Sunday?

   A: You have to go during the week. It's closed on Sunday.

   _____

4. **Bangkok**

   Q: My son wants to buy computer games. Where should he go?

   A: He should try the Panthip Plaza. The selection is huge.

   _____

5. **Mexico City**

   Q: I plan to buy some silver jewelry in Mexico. Any tips?

   A: Try bargaining. That way, you'll be able to get something nice at a very good price.

   _____

6. **London**

   Q: I'd like to find some nice secondhand clothing shops. Can you help me?

   A: Try the Portobello market on the weekend. Happy shopping!

   _____

EXERCISE 3: Conditional Statements

(Grammar Notes 1–3, 5)

*Complete the interview with Claudia Leggett, a fashion buyer. Combine the two sentences in parentheses to make a real conditional sentence. Keep the same order and decide which clause begins with **if**. Make necessary changes in capitalization and punctuation.*

INTERVIEWER: Is understanding fashion the most important thing for a career as a buyer?

LEGGETT: It is. *If you don't understand fashion, you don't belong in this field.*

                1. (You don't understand fashion. You don't belong in this field.)

But buyers need other skills too.

INTERVIEWER: Such as?

LEGGETT: _____

                2. (You can make better decisions. You have good business skills.)

INTERVIEWER: "People skills" must be important too.

LEGGETT: True. _____

                3. (A buyer needs great interpersonal skills. She's negotiating prices.)

INTERVIEWER: Do you travel in your business?

LEGGETT: A lot! _____

                4. (There's a big international fashion fair. I'm usually there.)

INTERVIEWER: Why fashion fairs?

LEGGETT: Thousands of professionals attend. _____

                5. (I go to a fair. I can see hundreds of products in a few days.)

INTERVIEWER: You just got back from the Leipzig fair, didn't you?

LEGGETT: Yes, and I went to Paris and Madrid too. _____

                6. (I usually stay two weeks. I'm traveling to Europe.)

INTERVIEWER: Does your family ever go with you?

LEGGETT: Often. _____

                7. (My husband can come. He and our son, Pietro, do things together.)

                8. (Pietro comes to the fair with me. My husband can't get away.)

Next week, we're all going to Hong Kong.

INTERVIEWER: What do you do when you're not at a fashion fair?

LEGGETT: _____

                9. (I always go shopping. I have free time.)

EXERCISE 4: Conditional Statements with *When* (Grammar Note 6)

Look at the map. Write sentences about the cities with clocks. Use the words in parentheses and **when***. Note: The light clocks show daylight hours; the shaded clocks show evening or nighttime hours.*

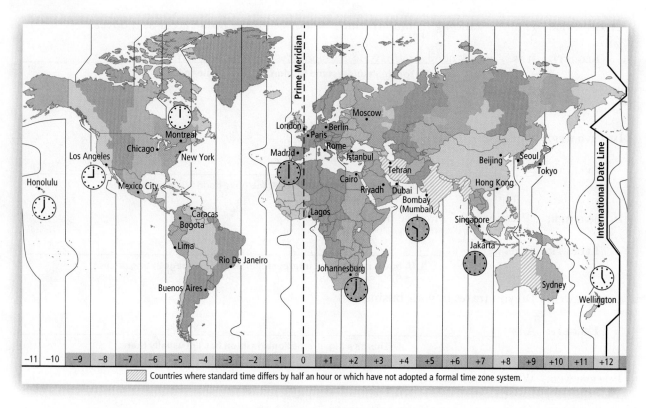

Countries where standard time differs by half an hour or which have not adopted a formal time zone system.

1. _When it's noon in Montreal, it's midnight in Jakarta._
   (be noon / be midnight)

2. _When stores are opening in Los Angeles, they're closing in Johannesburg._
   (stores open / stores close)

3. _____
   (people watch the sun rise / people watch the sun set)

4. _____
   (be midnight / be 6:00 P.M.)

5. _____
   (people eat lunch / people eat dinner)

6. _____
   (people get up / people go to bed)

7. _____
   (be 7:00 A.M. / be 7:00 P.M.)

8. _____
   (be 5:00 A.M. / be 9:00 A.M.)

EXERCISE 5: Editing

Read Claudia's email message. There are eight mistakes in the use of present real conditionals. The first mistake is already corrected. Find and correct seven more. Don't forget to check punctuation.

Tomorrow I'm flying to Hong Kong for a fashion show! My son, Pietro, is flying with me, and

                                                        like

my husband is already there. Whenever Pietro's off from school, I ~~liked~~ to take him on trips with

me. If my husband comes too, they are going sightseeing during the day. Our plane leaves Los

Angeles around midnight. If we flew at night, we can sleep on the plane. (At least that's the plan!)

I love Hong Kong. We always have a great time, when we will go there. The shopping is really

fantastic. When I'm not working I'm shopping.

I'll call you when I arrive at the hotel (around 7:00 A.M.). When it will be 7:00 A.M. in Hong

Kong, it's midnight in London. Is that too late to call? If you want to talk, just calling.

And, of course you can always email me.

STEP 4 COMMUNICATION PRACTICE

EXERCISE 6: Listening

A | *Claudia and her 10-year-old son, Pietro, are flying from Los Angeles to Hong Kong by way of Taipei. Read the statements. Then listen to each announcement. Listen again and circle the correct words to complete each statement.*

1. The airline's policy allows passengers to take **one** / two / no piece(s) of luggage on the plane.

2. Flight 398 makes <u>one / two / no</u> stop(s) before Taipei.

3. Passengers need to show their <u>boarding passes / passports / boarding passes and passports</u>

   before getting on the plane.

4. The plane has six <u>flight attendants / emergency exits / captains</u>.

5. The plane will probably arrive <u>early / on time / late</u>.

6. The temperature in Taipei is <u>cool / warm / very hot</u>.

B | *Read the statements. Then listen to each announcement and check (✓)* **True** *or* **False** *for the statement with the same number.*

	True	False
1. Claudia has two pieces of carry-on luggage, and Pietro has one. They can take them on the plane.	☐	☑
2. Look at their boarding passes. They can board now.	☐	☐

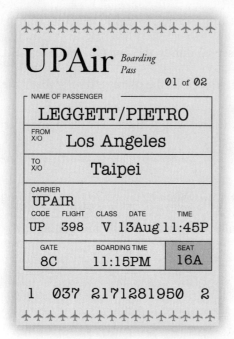

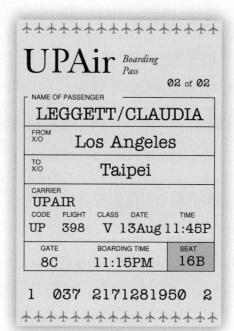

	True	False
3. Look at their boarding passes again. They can board now.	☐	☐
4. Pietro is only 10 years old. Claudia should put his oxygen mask on first.	☐	☐
5. Claudia is sitting in a left-hand window seat. She can see the lights of Tokyo.	☐	☐
6. Claudia needs information about their connecting flight. She can get this information on the plane.	☐	☐

Passengers on Flight 398 to Taipei

EXERCISE 7: Pronunciation

A | *Read and listen to the Pronunciation Note.*

Pronunciation Note

In **conditional statements**, we use **intonation** at the **end of the first clause** to show that the sentence **isn't finished**.

When the **clause with *if* or *when*** is **first**, the voice **falls** and then **rises a little** at the end of the clause.

EXAMPLE: *If* I shop online, I pay by credit card.

When the **main clause** is **first**, the voice **falls just a little** at the end of the clause.

EXAMPLE: I return the item *if* I don't like it.

The voice always **falls lower** at the **end of the second clause** to show that the sentence **is finished**.

When the clause with *if* or *when* is **first**, we usually **pause** briefly at the **end of the clause** (where the comma is in written sentences).

EXAMPLE: *If* **I shop online**, I pay by credit card. →
"*If* **I shop online** [PAUSE] I pay by credit card."

B | *Listen to each sentence and add a comma where you hear the pause.*

1. If I have time I like to go to the mall.

2. I pay by cash if my purchase isn't expensive.

3. If I like something I sometimes buy two.

4. When I shop online I only use secure sites.

5. I usually read reviews when I shop online.

6. I always check the return policy when I buy something.

7. If I don't like something I return it.

8. When I shop with friends I always buy more.

9. If the mall is crowded I don't stay long.

10. I often stop at the food court when I'm at the mall.

C | *Listen again to each sentence and repeat. Notice the intonation and the pause (if any).*

EXERCISE 8: Reaching Agreement

A | *Work with a partner. You are going to buy some T-shirts for a friend—an 18-year-old male or female. Look at part of a store's website, and discuss the selections. Agree on a purchase. Think about these issues:*

- color
- size
- style
- quantity
- price
- shipping

NEW! UNISEX T-SHIRTS

| short-sleeves, crew neck $15.00 | short-sleeves, V-neck $15.00 | long-sleeves, crew neck $18.00 | long-sleeves, V-neck $18.00 |

Available in:

☐ tangerine ☐ hot pink ☐ cherry red ☐ ivory ☐ ebony ☐ ink blue ☐ turquoise

All T-shirts available in Small, Medium, Large
Buy 1, get the second at 50% off! Buy today, take another 10% off!

Return/Exchange Policy: Return by mail (within 45 days of purchase): $6.00 fee
Exchange by mail (within 45 days of purchase): free

EXAMPLE:
A: Let's get a cherry red T-shirt.
B: What if she doesn't like red?
A: Well, if she doesn't like it, she can always exchange it for another color.
B: OK. If we decide today, ...

B | *With your partner, complete the order form for the item(s) you decided on.*

	Quantity	Color	Size
short-sleeved, crew neck T	☐	☐	○ S ○ M ○ L
short-sleeved, V-neck T	☐	☐	○ S ○ M ○ L
long-sleeved, crew neck T	☐	☐	○ S ○ M ○ L
long-sleeved, V-neck T	☐	☐	○ S ○ M ○ L

| **Shipping Method** | ○ Standard: | 5–9 business days | $5.00 |
| | ○ Express: | 2 business days | $10.00 |

EXERCISE 9: Cross-Cultural Comparison

Work with a partner. Compare shopping in a place you've lived in or one you have visited. Choose two different places and consider these questions:

- What days and hours are stores open?
- What kinds of stores are there: malls? small stores? indoor or outdoor markets?
- Do people bargain?
- How do people pay?
- What are some special products sold in that country?
- Is there a sales tax for clothing? If yes, how much is it?
- Do stores allow refunds or exchanges?

EXAMPLE: **A:** If you're in a small city or town in Mexico, stores are usually open from Monday to Friday between 9:00 A.M. and 2:00 or 4:00 P.M.
B: In South Korean cities, stores usually stay open until 10:00 P.M. And if you want to go shopping after that, you can find many stores that are open 24 hours.

EXERCISE 10: Discussion

Work in small groups. Discuss what you do when you want to make an important purchase (a gift, a camera, a car).

EXAMPLE: **A:** If I want to buy a camera, I check prices online.
B: When I buy a camera, I always ask friends for recommendations.
C: I always . . .

EXERCISE 11: For or Against

Look at the cartoon. What are some of the differences between shopping in a "store with doors" and shopping online? What are the advantages and disadvantages of each? Discuss these questions with your classmates.

EXAMPLE: **A:** If you shop for clothes in a store, you can try them on first.
B: And you can feel the material. That's important.
C: But you have a lot more choices if you shop online.

EXERCISE 12: Writing

A | *Work with a partner. Imagine that you are preparing an information sheet for tourists about your city or town. Write a list of tips for visitors. Include information on shopping. Use present real conditional sentences.*

> EXAMPLE: • If you like to shop, Caterville has the biggest mall in this part of the country.
> • If you enjoy swimming or boating, you should visit Ocean Park.

B | *Compare your list with another pair's.*

> EXAMPLE: **A:** If you're interested in history, there's a lot to see in Caterville.
> **B:** If golf is your sport, Ames has several beautiful golf courses.

C | *Check your work. Use the Editing Checklist.*

Editing Checklist

Did you use . . . ?

☐ the simple present in both clauses for general truths

☐ the simple present or present progressive in the *if / when* clause for habits and things that happen again and again

☐ a comma between the two clauses when the *if / when* clause comes first

Check your answers on page UR-6.
Do you need to review anything?

A | *Complete the present real conditional sentences in the conversation with the correct form of the verbs in parentheses.*

A: What _____ you _____ when you _____ too busy to shop?
　　　　　　　　　　1. (do)　　　　　　　　　　　　　　　**2. (be)**

B: It depends. If a store _____ open late, I _____ in the evening.
　　　　　　　　　　　　　3. (be)　　　　　　　　　　　**4. (shop)**

A: What _____ if a store _____ open late?
　　　　5. (happen)　　　　　　　　　　**6. (not stay)**

B: If it _____ early, I _____ to its website. It's really easy.
　　　　　7. (close)　　　　　　　　**8. (go)**

A: Great idea! When I _____ rushed, I never _____ of that.
　　　　　　　　　　9. (feel)　　　　　　　　　　　**10. (think)**

B | *Combine each pair of sentences to make a present real conditional sentence. Keep the same order.*

1. It's 7:00 A.M. in Honolulu. What time is it in Mumbai?

　　_____.

2. You love jewelry. You should visit an international jewelry show.

　　_____.

3. A tourist might have more fun. She tries bargaining.

　　_____.

4. You're shopping at an outdoor market. You can always bargain for a good price.

　　_____.

5. But don't try to bargain. You're shopping in a big department store.

　　_____.

C | *Find and correct five mistakes. Remember to check punctuation.*

1. If I don't like something I bought online, then I returned it.

2. Don't buy from an online site, if you don't know anything about the company.

3. When he'll shops online, Frank always saves a lot of time.

4. I always fell asleep if I fly at night. It happens every time.

5. Isabel always has a wonderful time, when she visits Istanbul.

Before You Read

Look at the pictures. Discuss the questions.

1. What is a superstition? Can you give an example of one?
2. Do you believe in any superstitions?
3. Do you wear or carry things that make you feel lucky?

Read

Read the magazine article about superstitions.

KNOCK ON WOOD!

🍀 **If you knock on wood, you'll keep bad luck away.**

🍀 **You'll get a good grade on the test if you wear your shirt inside out.**

🍀 **You'll get a bad grade unless you use your lucky pen.**

Superstitions may sound silly to some, but millions of people all over the world believe in their power to bring good luck or prevent bad luck. Different cultures share many similar superstitions:

🍀 **If you break a mirror, you'll have seven years of bad luck.**

🍀 **If the palm of your hand itches, you're going to get some money.**

🍀 **If it rains when you move to a new house, you'll get rich.**

All superstitions are based on a cause and effect relationship: **If X happens, then Y will also happen**. However, in superstitions, the cause is magical and unrelated to the effect. In our scientific age, why are these beliefs so powerful and widespread? The Luck Project, an online survey of superstitious behaviors, gives us some fascinating insight. Read some of their findings on the next page.

🍀 Emotions can influence superstitions, especially in uncertain situations where people do not have control. **People will react more superstitiously if they are worried. They will feel less superstitious if they aren't feeling a strong need for control.**

🍀 We make our own luck. **If you believe you're lucky, you will carry out superstitions that make you feel good** (crossing your fingers for luck, for example). As a result, you probably won't fear bad luck superstitions, and you might perform better in stressful situations. In contrast, **if you think you're unlucky, you will anticipate the worst and look for bad luck superstitions that confirm your belief.** Your attitude makes a difference.

🍀 More people than you might think believe in superstitions. Of the 4,000 people surveyed, 84 percent knocked on wood for good luck. Almost half feared walking under a ladder. And 15 percent of the people who studied or worked in the sciences feared the number 13.

Clearly, education doesn't eliminate superstition—college students are among the most superstitious people. Other superstitious groups are performers, athletes, gamblers,[1] and stock traders. People in these groups often have lucky charms[2] or personal good luck rituals.[3]

Deanna McBrearty, a New York City Ballet member, has lucky hair bands. **"If I have a good performance when I'm wearing one, I'll keep wearing it,"** she says. Baseball player Wade Boggs would only eat chicken before a game. Brett Gallagher, a stock trader, believes **he'll be more successful if he owns pet fish.** "I had fish for a while, and after they died, the market didn't do so well," he points out.

Will you do better on the test if you use your lucky pen? Maybe. **If the pen makes you feel more confident, you might improve your score.** So go ahead and use it. But don't forget: **Your lucky pen will be powerless unless you study.** The harder you work, the luckier you'll get.

---
[1] **gambler:** someone who risks money in a game or race (cards, horse race) because he or she might win more money
[2] **lucky charm:** a very small object worn on a chain that will bring good luck (horseshoe, four-leaf clover, etc.)
[3] **ritual:** a set of actions always done in the same way

After You Read

A | Vocabulary: *Match the words with their definitions.*

_____ 1. widespread	**a.** to expect that something will happen
_____ 2. insight	**b.** sure
_____ 3. percent	**c.** a way of thinking about something
_____ 4. confident	**d.** the ability to understand something clearly
_____ 5. anticipate	**e.** happening in many places
_____ 6. attitude	**f.** equal to a certain amount in every hundred

B | Comprehension: *Check (✓)* **True** *or* **False**. *Correct the false sentences. Use information from the article.*

	True	False
1. Not many people are superstitious.	☐	☐
2. If you are worrying about something, you might act less superstitiously.	☐	☐
3. If you feel lucky, you'll have more good luck superstitions.	☐	☐
4. If you study science, you won't be superstitious.	☐	☐
5. If you don't study, your good luck pen won't work.	☐	☐

STEP 2 GRAMMAR PRESENTATION

FUTURE REAL CONDITIONALS

Statements	
If **Clause: Present**	**Result Clause: Future**
If she **studies,**	she **won't fail** the test. she **'s going to pass** the test.
If she **doesn't study,**	she **'ll fail** the test. she **isn't going to pass** the test.

Yes / No Questions	
Result Clause: Future	*If* **Clause: Present**
Will she **pass** the test **Is** she **going to pass** the test	*if* she **studies?**

Short Answers			
Affirmative		**Negative**	
Yes,	she **will.** she **is.**	No,	she **won't.** she **isn't.**

Wh- Questions	
Result Clause: Future	*If* **Clause: Present**
What **will** she **do** What **is** she **going to do**	*if* she **passes** the test?

GRAMMAR NOTES

1

Use **future real conditional** sentences to talk about what **will happen under certain conditions**.

The **if clause** gives the **condition**. The **result clause** gives the **probable or certain result**.

Use the **simple present** in the *if* **clause**. Use the **future** with *will* or *be going to* in the **result clause**.

BE CAREFUL! Even though the *if* **clause** refers to the future, use the **simple present**.

IF CLAUSE   RESULT CLAUSE
- *If* I **use** this pen, I**'ll pass** the test.
  (It's a real possibility that I will use this pen.)

    SIMPLE PRESENT   FUTURE
- *If* you **feel** lucky, you**'ll expect** good things.
- *If* you **feel** unlucky, you**'re going to expect** bad things to happen.

- *If* she **gets** an A on her test, she will stop worrying.
  NOT: If she ~~will get~~ an A on her test, she will stop worrying.

2

You can also use **modals** (*can, should, might, must*...) in the **result clause**.

USAGE NOTE: We sometimes use *then* to **emphasize the result** in future real conditionals with **modals** or *will*.

- If she studies hard, she *might* **get** an A.
- If she has questions, she *should* **ask** her teacher.

- If she studies hard, *then* she **might get** an A.
- If she studies hard, *then* she**'ll get** an A.

3

You can **begin conditional sentences** with the *if* **clause or the result clause**. The meaning is the same.

BE CAREFUL! Use a **comma** between the two clauses only when the *if* **clause comes first**.

- *If* **she uses that pen,** she'll feel lucky.
  OR
- She'll feel lucky *if* **she uses that pen.**

4

You can use *if* and *unless* in conditional sentences, but their <u>meanings are very different</u>.

Use *unless* to state a **negative condition**.

Unless often means *if . . . not*.

- *If* he studies, he will pass the test.

- *Unless* he studies, he will fail the test.
  (If he doesn't study, he will fail the test.)

- *Unless* you're superstitious, you won't be afraid of black cats.
  OR
- *If* you are**n't** superstitious, you won't be afraid of black cats.

Future Real Conditionals   **359**

EXERCISE 1: Discover the Grammar

A | *Match the conditions with the results.*

Condition

_d_	**1.**	If I lend someone my baseball bat,
____	**2.**	If it rains,
____	**3.**	If I give my boyfriend a new pair of shoes,
____	**4.**	If the palm of your hand itches,
____	**5.**	If I use my lucky pen,
____	**6.**	If you wear your sweater backwards,

Result

a. you could have an allergy.

b. people might laugh at you.

c. I'll get 100 percent on the test.

d. I won't hit a home run.

e. I'm going to get wet.

f. he'll walk out of the relationship.

B | *Now write the sentences that are superstitions.*

1. *If I lend someone my baseball bat, I won't hit a home run.* _____

2. _____

3. _____

EXERCISE 2: *If* or *Unless*

(Grammar Note 4)

*Two students are talking about a test. Complete their conversations with **if** or **unless**.*

🍀 YUKI: It's midnight. _____Unless_____ we get some sleep, we won't do well tomorrow.
    1.

EVA: But I won't be able to sleep _____ I stop worrying about the test.
    2.

YUKI: Here's my lucky charm. _____ you wear it, you'll do fine!
    3.

🍀 EVA: I found my blue shirt! _____ I wear my blue shirt today, I'm confident
    4.
    that I'll pass!

YUKI: Great. Now _____ we just clean up the room, we can leave for school.
    5.

EVA: We can't clean up! There's a Russian superstition that says _____ you
    6.
    clean your room, you'll get a bad test grade!

🍀 YUKI: _____ we finish the test by noon, we can go to the job fair.
    7.

EVA: I want to get a job, but nobody is going to hire me _____ I pass this test.
    8.

🍀 EVA: I'm looking for my lucky pen. _____ I find it, I won't pass the test!
    9.

YUKI: Don't worry. _____ you use the same pen that you used to study with,
    10.
    you'll do great! The pen will remember the answers.

Eva: I was so nervous without my lucky pen. It'll be a miracle[1] _____ I pass.
11.

Yuki: That's the wrong attitude! There aren't any miracles. _____ you study,
12.

you'll do well. It's that simple.

Eva: Do you think a company like ZY3, Inc. will offer me a job _____ I fill out
13.

an application?

Yuki: Only _____ you use your lucky pen. I'm kidding! You won't know
14.

_____ you try!
15.

---

[1] *miracle:* something lucky that happens when you didn't think it was possible

EXERCISE 3: Simple Present or Future

(Grammar Note 1)

Complete these superstitions from all over the world. Use the correct form of the verbs in parentheses.

Russia: If you _____*spill*_____ salt at the table, you _____*'ll have*_____ an argument.
1. (spill)   2. (have)

England: If a cat _____ behind its ears, it _____.
3. (wash)   4. (rain)

Canada: If you _____ under a ladder, you _____ bad luck.
5. (walk)   6. (have)

China: If you _____ the dirt and dust out of your house through the front door,
7. (sweep)

you _____ away your family's good luck.
8. (sweep)

Greece: If your right hand _____ itchy, you _____ money. If your left
9. (be)   10. (get)

hand _____, you _____ someone money.
11. (itch)   12. (give)

Iceland: If somebody _____ away a dead mouse, the wind _____ to
13. (throw)   14. (start)

blow from that direction.

Slovakia: If you _____ at the corner of the table, you _____ married.
15. (sit)   16. (not get)

Mexico: If you _____ red beans at a newly married couple, they _____
17. (throw)   18. (have)

good luck.

Turkey: If you _____ food on your clothing while you're eating, you
19. (drop)

_____ guests that day.
20. (have)

Brazil: If you _____ a broom behind the front door, you _____
21. (put)   22. (keep away)

bad visits.

Japan: If you _____ a snake skin in your wallet, you _____ rich.
23. (put)   24. (become)

Korea: If you _____ your hair, you _____ taller.
25. (cut)   26. (grow)

EXERCISE 4: Statements

(Grammar Notes 1, 3)

Eva is thinking of working for a company called ZY3, Inc. Her friend Don, who used to work there, thinks it's a terrible idea and is explaining the consequences. Write his responses. Use the words in parentheses and future real conditional sentences.

1. **Eva:** If I work for ZY3, I'm going to be happy. I'm sure of it.

   Don: *If you work for ZY3, you're not going to be happy. You're going to be miserable.*
   (miserable)

2. **Eva:** You have such a pessimistic attitude! I'll have the chance to travel a lot if I take this job.

   Don: Not true. _____
   (never leave the office)

3. **Eva:** But I'll get a raise every year if I stay at ZY3.

   Don: _____
   (every two years)

4. **Eva:** Well, if I join ZY3, I'm going to have wonderful health care benefits.

   Don: Stay healthy!_____
   (terrible health care benefits)

5. **Eva:** I don't believe you! If I accept ZY3's offer, it'll be the best career move of my life.

   Don: Believe me, _____
   (the worst)

EXERCISE 5: Statements

(Grammar Notes 1–2)

*Yuki Tamari is not sure whether to go to law school. She made a decision tree to help her decide. In the tree, arrows connect the conditions and the results. Write future real conditional sentences about her decision. Use **may, might,** or **could** if the result is uncertain. Remember to use commas where necessary.*

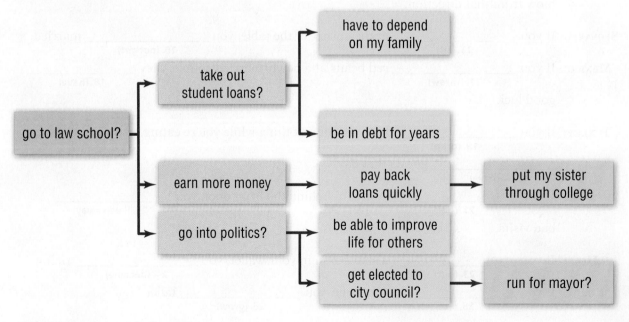

1. _If I go to law school, I might take out student loans._
2. _I'll be in debt for years if I take out student loans._
3. _____
4. _____
5. _____
6. _____
7. _____
8. _____
9. _____
10. _____

EXERCISE 6: Editing

Read Yuki's journal entry. There are seven mistakes in the use of future real conditionals. The first mistake is already corrected. Find and correct six more. Don't forget to check punctuation.

October 1

    Should I campaign for student council president? I'll have to decide
soon if I ~~wanted~~ *want* to run. If I'll be busy campaigning, I won't have much
time to study. That's a problem because I'm not going to get into law
school if I get good grades this year. On the other hand, the problems in
this school are widespread, and nothing is getting done if Todd Laker
becomes president again. I'm 100 percent certain of that, and most
people agree with me. But will <u>I</u> know what to do if I'll get the job?
Never mind. I shouldn't anticipate difficulties. I really need to have a
better attitude. I'll deal with that problem, if I win. I know what I'll do.
If I become president, I cut my hair. That always brings me good luck!

EXERCISE 7: Listening

A | *Yuki is talking about her campaign platform. Read the list of issues. Then listen to the interview. Listen again and check (✓) the things that Yuki promises to work for if she is elected.*

☑ **1.** have contact with a lot of students

☐ **2.** improve the student council's newsletter

☐ **3.** publish teacher evaluations on the student council's website

☐ **4.** get the college to provide a bus service between the airport and the college

☐ **5.** get the college to offer a major in environmental science

☐ **6.** reduce tuition costs

B | *Read the statements. Then listen again to the interview and check (✓)* **True** *or* **False**. *Correct the false statements.*

	True	False
1. If Yuki gets elected, she'll have ~~formal~~ *informal* meetings with students.	☐	☑
2. Yuki wants to improve the student council's website.	☐	☐
3. She thinks student council representatives should have their phone numbers on the website.	☐	☐
4. She believes the college should have free bus service between the airport and the college at the beginning and end of every semester.	☐	☐
5. She wants the college to offer more majors.	☐	☐
6. She wants to meet with students to discuss college costs.	☐	☐
7. Yuki wears a lucky charm for good luck.	☐	☐
8. She anticipates winning the election.	☐	☐

EXERCISE 8: Pronunciation

A | *Read and listen to the Pronunciation Note.*

Pronunciation Note

As with other questions, in **conditional questions**:

The voice usually **rises** at the **end of *yes* / *no* questions**.

EXAMPLES: If you win the election, will you work with the president?

Will you work with the president if you win the election?

The voice usually **falls** at the **end of *wh-* questions**.

EXAMPLES: What will you do if you win the election?

If you win the election, what will you do?

B | *Listen to the short conversations. Draw a rising arrow (⤴) or a falling arrow (⤵) over the end of each question to show if the voice rises or falls.*

1. **A:** What will you do if you win the election?
   B: I'll go out and celebrate.

2. **A:** Will you take out a loan if you go to law school?
   B: Yes, I'll have to.

3. **A:** If you can't get a loan, what will you do?
   B: I'll get a part-time job.

4. **A:** Will you buy a new car if you get a raise?
   B: No, I'll get a used car.

5. **A:** If your computer stops working, will you buy a new one?
   B: Yes. It's too old to repair.

6. **A:** Where will you go if you have to find a new apartment?
   B: I'll move back to my parent's house.

C | *Listen again to the conversations and repeat the questions. Then practice the conversations with a partner.*

EXERCISE 9: Problem Solving

Work in small groups. Read these problems and discuss possible solutions. Use **if,** **if . . . not,** *or* **unless.**

1. Your neighbors are always playing music so loudly that you can't fall asleep.

   EXAMPLE: **A:** What will you do if they don't stop?
   B: If they don't stop, I'll call the police.
   C: Unless they stop, I'll call the landlord.
   D: I'll consider moving if they continue to bother me.

2. You've had a headache every day for a week. You can't concentrate.

3. You keep phoning your parents, but there's no answer. It's now midnight.

4. You like your job, but you just found out that other workers are making much more money than you are.

5. You live in an apartment building. It's winter, and the building hasn't had any heat for a week. You're freezing.

6. You're 10 pounds overweight. You've been trying for months to lose weight, but so far you haven't lost a single pound.

7. You bought a radio at a local store. It doesn't work, but when you tried to return it, the salesperson refused to take it back.

8. Your roommates don't clean up after they cook. You've already reminded them several times, but they always "forget."

9. You paid for a parking space near school or work. For the past week the same car has taken your space.

EXERCISE 10: Cross-Cultural Comparison

Here are some superstitions about luck. Work in small groups and discuss similar superstitions that you know about.

- If you cross your fingers, you'll have good luck.

  EXAMPLE: **A:** In Germany, people believe that if you press your thumbs together, you will have good luck.
  B: In Mexico, . . .
  C: In Russia, . . .

- If you touch blue, your dreams will come true.

- If you break a mirror, you will have seven years of bad luck.

- If you put a piece of clothing on inside out, you will have good luck.

- If your palm itches, you're going to find some money soon.

EXERCISE 11: Writing

A | *Imagine you are running for class or school president. Write a short speech. Include five campaign promises with **will** or **be going to**. List problems that **may, might,** or **could** happen if you are not elected. In small groups, give your speeches and elect a candidate. Then hold a general class election.*

EXAMPLE: If I become school president, I will ask for 10 new computers . . .
If I'm not elected, classroom conditions might . . .

B | *Check your work. Use the Editing Checklist.*

Editing Checklist

Did you use . . . ?
☐ the simple present in the *if* clause
☐ the future with **will** or **be going to** in the result clause for probable results
☐ **may**, **might**, or **could** in the result clause for possible results
☐ **unless** to state a negative condition
☐ a comma between the two clauses when the *if* or **unless** clause comes first

Check your answers on page UR-6.

Do you need to review anything?

A | Match the cause and effect.

Cause	Effect
_____ **1.** If it rains,	**a.** I'll answer it.
_____ **2.** Unless you study,	**b.** I'll pay you back tomorrow.
_____ **3.** If the phone rings,	**c.** you should ask the teacher.
_____ **4.** If you have questions,	**d.** I'll take an umbrella.
_____ **5.** If you lend me $10,	**e.** you can't drive.
_____ **6.** If you don't have a license,	**f.** you won't pass.

B | Complete the future real conditional sentences in these conversations with the correct form of the verbs in parentheses.

- **A:** Are you going to take the bus?

  B: No. If I _____ the bus, I _____ late.

  1. (take)   2. (be)

- **A:** What _____ you _____ if you _____ the job?

  3. (do)   4. (not get)

  B: I _____ in school unless I _____ the job.

  5. (stay)   6. (get)

- **A:** If I _____ the test, I _____.

  7. (pass)   8. (celebrate)

  B: Good luck, but I'm sure you'll pass. You've studied really hard for it.

  A: Thanks!

C | Find and correct six mistakes. Remember to check punctuation.

It's been a hard week, and I'm looking forward to the weekend. If the weather will be nice tomorrow Marco and I are going to go to the beach. The ocean is usually too cold for swimming at this time of year, so I probably don't go in the water unless it's really hot outside. But I love walking along the beach and breathing in the fresh sea air.

If Marco has time, he might makes some sandwiches to bring along. Otherwise, we'll just get some pizza. I hope it'll be a nice day. I just listened to the weather report, and there may be some rain in the afternoon. Unless it rains, we probably go to the movies instead. That's our Plan B. But I really want to go to the beach, so I'm keeping my fingers crossed!

Before You Read

Read the first sentence of the story and look at the picture. Discuss these questions.

1. Is this a true story? What makes you think so?
2. How do fairy tales begin in your culture?

Read

🎧 *Read this version of a famous fairy tale.*

The Fisherman and His Wife

Once upon a time there was a poor fisherman and his wife who lived in a pigpen[1] near the sea. Every day the man went to fish. One day, after waiting a very long time, he caught a very big fish. To his surprise, the fish spoke and said, "Please let me live. I'm not a regular[2] fish. **If you knew my real identity, you wouldn't kill me.** I'm an enchanted prince."

"Don't worry. I won't kill you," responded the kind-hearted fisherman. With these words, he threw the fish back into the clear water and went home to his wife.

"Husband," said the wife, "didn't you catch anything today?"

"I caught a fish, but it said it was an enchanted prince, so I let it go."

"You mean you didn't wish for anything?" asked the wife.

"No," said the fisherman. "What do I need to wish for?"

"Just look around you," said the wife. "We live in a pigpen. **I wish we had a nice little cottage.[3] If we had a cottage, I would be a lot happier.** You saved the prince's life. He's sure to grant your wish. Go back and ask him."

(continued on next page)

[1]*pigpen:* a small building where pigs are kept
[2]*regular:* ordinary
[3]*cottage:* a small house, usually in the country

"I'm not going to ask for a cottage! **If I asked for a cottage, the fish might get angry**." But in the end, he consented because he was much more afraid of his wife's anger.

When he got to the sea, it was all green and yellow. "**My wife wishes we had a cottage**," said the fisherman. "Just go on back," said the fish. "She already has it."

When he returned home, the fisherman found his wife sitting outside a lovely little cottage. The kitchen was filled with food and all types of cooking utensils.[4] Outside was a little garden with vegetables, fruit trees, hens, and ducks.

Things were fine for a week or two. Then the wife said, "This cottage is much too crowded. **I wish we lived in a bigger house. If we lived in a big stone castle, I would be much happier**. Go and ask the fish for it."

The fisherman didn't want to go, but he did. When he got to the sea, it was dark blue and gray. "**My wife wishes we lived in a big stone castle**," he said to the fish.

"Just go on back. She's standing in front of the door," said the fish.

When he returned home, the fisherman found his wife on the steps of a great big stone castle. The inside was filled with beautiful gold furniture, chandeliers,[5] and carpets. There were servants everywhere.

The next morning the wife woke up and said, "**I wish I were King of all this land**."

"**What would you do if you were King?**" asked her husband. "**If I were King, I would own all this land**. Go on back and ask the fish for it."

This time, the sea was all blackish gray, and the water was rough and smelled terrible. "What does she want now?" asked the fish.

"She wants to be King," said the embarrassed fisherman.

"Just go on back. She already is."

When the fisherman returned home, he found an enormous palace.[6] Everything inside was made of marble and pure gold, and it was surrounded by soldiers with drums and trumpets. His wife was seated on a throne, and he said to her, "How nice for you that you are King. Now we won't need to wish for anything else."

But his wife was not satisfied. "I'm only King of *this* country," she said. "**I wish I were Emperor of the whole world. If I were Emperor, I would be the most powerful ruler on Earth**."

"Wife, now be satisfied," responded the fisherman. "You're King. You can't be anything more."

The wife, however, wasn't convinced. She kept thinking and thinking about what more she could be. "**If I were Emperor, I could have anything—and you wouldn't have to ask the fish for anything more**. Go right now and tell the fish that I want to be Emperor of the whole world."

"Oh, no," said the fisherman. "The fish can't do that. **If I were you, I wouldn't ask for anything else**." But his wife got so furious that the poor fisherman ran back to the fish. There was a terrible storm, and the sea was pitch black[7] with waves as high as mountains. "Well, what does she want now?" asked the fish.

"**She wishes she were Emperor of the whole world**," said the fisherman.

"Just go on back. She's sitting in the pigpen again."

And they are still sitting there today.

---

[4]*utensil:* a tool used for cooking or preparing food
[5]*chandelier:* a large structure that hangs from the ceiling and holds many lights or candles
[6]*palace:* a very large house where the ruler of a country lives
[7]*pitch black:* the color of coal or tar; very dark black

After You Read

A | Vocabulary: *Circle the letter of the word or phrase that best completes each sentence.*

1. If something is **enchanted**, it has been _____.

   a. changed by magic

   b. broken

   c. stolen

2. When you **consent**, you _____ to do something.

   a. refuse

   b. agree

   c. like

3. Someone who is **furious**, is very _____.

   a. kind-hearted

   b. poor

   c. angry

4. Someone who is **embarrassed** feels _____.

   a. uncomfortable

   b. powerful

   c. frightened

5. If you **grant** something, you _____ to do it.

   a. want

   b. refuse

   c. agree

6. When you **respond**, you _____ a question.

   a. ask

   b. answer

   c. forget

B | Comprehension: *Check (✓)* **True** *or* **False**. *Correct the false statements.*

	True	False
1. Before the man caught the fish, he and his wife lived in a nice little cottage.	☐	☐
2. At first, the fish believed that the man was going to kill him.	☐	☐
3. The man didn't want to ask for the first wish because he didn't want to make the fish angry.	☐	☐
4. The wife was satisfied with the stone castle.	☐	☐
5. The man advised his wife not to ask to be Emperor of the whole world.	☐	☐
6. The fish granted the wife's wish to be the most powerful ruler on Earth.	☐	☐

PRESENT AND FUTURE UNREAL CONDITIONALS

Statements		Contractions		
If Clause: Simple Past	**Result Clause: Would (not) + Base Form**	I would	=	**I'd**
If Mia **had** money,	she **would live** in a palace.	you would	=	**you'd**
If she **were*** rich,	she **wouldn't live** in a cottage.	he would	=	**he'd**
If Mia **didn't have** money,	she **wouldn't live** in a palace.	she would	=	**she'd**
If she **weren't** rich,	she **would live** in a cottage.	we would	=	**we'd**
		they would	=	**they'd**
		would not	=	**wouldn't**

*With the verb be, use were for all subjects.

Yes / No Questions		Short Answers	
Result Clause	**If Clause**	**Affirmative**	**Negative**
Would she **live** here	**if** she **had** money?	**Yes**, she **would**.	**No**, she **wouldn't**.
	if she **were** rich?		

Wh- Questions	
Result Clause	**If Clause**
What **would** she **do**	**if** she **had** money?
	if she **were** rich?

GRAMMAR NOTES

1 Use **present and future unreal conditional** sentences to talk about **unreal conditions and their results**. A condition and its result may be untrue, imagined, or impossible.

The **if clause** gives the **unreal condition**, and the **result clause** gives the **unreal result** of that condition.

The sentence can be about:
- the **present**

- the **future**

IF CLAUSE   RESULT CLAUSE
- If I **had** more time, I **would read** fairy tales.
  (But I don't have time, so I don't read fairy tales.)

IF CLAUSE   RESULT CLAUSE
- If I **lived** in a palace *now*, I **would give** parties.
  (I don't live in a palace. I don't give parties.)

IF CLAUSE   RESULT CLAUSE
- If I **moved** *next month*, I **would buy** a car.
  (I won't move. I won't buy a car.)

		SIMPLE PAST	WOULD + BASE FORM

2 Use the **simple past** in the *if* clause.
Use *would* + **base form** in the **result clause**.

- *If* he **had** a nice house, he **wouldn't move**.

BE CAREFUL!
- The *if* clause uses the simple past, but the **meaning is NOT past**.
- Do **NOT** use *would* in the *if* clause.

- *If* I **had** more money *now*, I would take a trip around the world.
- *If* she **knew** the answer, she would tell you.
  Nᴏᴛ: If she ~~would know~~ the answer . . .

- Use *were* for **all subjects** when the verb in the *if* clause is a form of *be*.

- *If* she **were** prime minister, she would deal with this problem.

  Nᴏᴛ: If she ~~was~~ prime minister . . .

USAGE NOTE: Some people use *was* with *I*, *he*, *she*, and *it*. However, this is usually considered incorrect, especially in formal or written English.

3 You can also use *might* or *could* in the **result clause**, but the meaning is different from *would*.

a. Use *would* if the result is **certain**.
Do NOT use *will* in unreal conditional sentences.

- They love to travel. If they had time, they *would* **take** a trip next summer.
  Nᴏᴛ: If they had time, they ~~will~~ take a trip . . .

b. Use *might* or *could* if the result is **not certain**.
Do NOT use *may* or *can*.

- If they took a trip, they *might* **go** to Japan.
  Nᴏᴛ: If they took a trip, they ~~may~~ go to Japan.
- If they took a trip, they *could* **go** to Japan.
  Nᴏᴛ: If they took a trip, they ~~can~~ go to Japan.

You can also use *could* in the result clause to express **ability**.

- You don't know Japanese. If you knew Japanese, you *could* **translate** this article for them.

4 You can **begin conditional sentences** with the *if* **clause** or **the result clause**. The meaning is the same.

- *If* **I had more money,** I would move.
  ᴏʀ
- I would move *if* **I had more money**.

BE CAREFUL! Use a **comma** between the two clauses only when the *if* **clause comes first**.

- Nᴏᴛ: I would move if I had more money.

5 Use *If I were you*, . . . to give **advice**.

- *If I were you,* I wouldn't ask for anything else.

6 Use *wish* + **simple past** to talk about things that you **want to be true** now, but that are **not true**.

- I *wish* I **lived** in a castle.
  (I don't live in a castle now, but I want to.)

BE CAREFUL!
- Use *were* instead of *was* after *wish*.

- I **wish** I *were* a child again.
  Nᴏᴛ: I wish I ~~was~~ a child again.
- Use *could* or *would* after *wish*.
  Do NOT use *can* or *will*.

- I **wish** I *could* **buy** a car.
  Nᴏᴛ: I wish I ~~can~~ buy a car.
- I **wish** she *would* **call** tomorrow.
  Nᴏᴛ: I wish she ~~will~~ call tomorrow.

EXERCISE 1: Discover the Grammar

Read the numbered statements. Decide if the sentences that follow are **True (T)** *or* **False (F)**.

1. If I had time, I would read fairy tales in English.

   ___F___ **a.** I have time.

   ___F___ **b.** I'm going to read fairy tales in English.

2. If it weren't so cold, I would go fishing.

   _____ **a.** It's cold.

   _____ **b.** I'm going fishing.

3. If I caught an enchanted fish, I would make three wishes.

   _____ **a.** I believe I'm going to catch an enchanted fish.

   _____ **b.** I'm going to make three wishes.

4. If I had three wishes, I wouldn't ask for a palace.

   _____ **a.** I have three wishes.

   _____ **b.** I don't want a palace.

5. If my house were too small, I would try to find a bigger one.

   _____ **a.** My house is big enough.

   _____ **b.** I'm not looking for a bigger house right now.

6. If I got a raise, I could buy a new car.

   _____ **a.** I recently got a raise.

   _____ **b.** I want a new car.

7. If we didn't earn enough money, I might train for a better job.

   _____ **a.** We don't earn enough money.

   _____ **b.** I'm training for a better job.

8. Your friend tells you, "If I were you, I wouldn't change jobs."

   _____ **a.** Your friend is giving you advice.

   _____ **b.** Your friend thinks you shouldn't change jobs.

9. I wish I were a princess.

   _____ **a.** I'm a princess.

   _____ **b.** I want to be a princess.

10. I wish I lived in a big house.

    _____ **a.** I want to live in a big house.

    _____ **b.** I don't live in a big house.

EXERCISE 2: *If* and Result Clauses: Verb Forms

(Grammar Notes 1–4, 6)

Complete this article from a popular psychology magazine. Use the correct form of the verbs in parentheses to form unreal conditional sentences.

Marty Hijab has always wanted to invite his whole family over for the holidays, but his apartment is small, his family is very large, and he doesn't want to feel embarrassed. "If I _____invited_____ them all for
1. (invite)
dinner, there _____wouldn't be_____ enough room for everyone to sit
2. (not be)
down," he told a friend. If Marty _____ a complainer,
3. (be)
he _____ about the size of his apartment and spend
4. (moan)
the holiday at his parents' house. But Marty is a problem solver.

This year he is hosting an open house. People can drop in at different times during the day, and there will be room for everyone.

"If life _____ a fairy tale, we _____ problems away," noted
5. (be)   6. (can / wish)
therapist Joel Grimes. "What complainers are really saying is, 'If I _____ a magical
7. (have)
solution, I _____ with this myself.' I wish it _____ that
8. (not have to deal)   9. (be)
easy," says Grimes. He gives an example of a very wealthy client who is convinced that he has almost no time for his family. "He's waiting for a miracle to give him the time he needs. But he _____ the time if he _____ about the problem creatively,"
10. (can / find)   11. (think)
says Grimes.

Even the rich have limited time, money, and space. If complainers _____ this,
12. (realize)
then they _____ that there will always be problems. Then they
13. (understand)
could stop complaining and try to find possible solutions. Marty, who is still in college,

_____ for years before inviting his family over if he _____
14. (may / have to wait)   15. (insist)
on a bigger apartment for his party. Instead, he is creatively solving his problems right now.

There's an old saying: "If wishes _____ horses, then beggars _____."
16. (be)   17. (can / ride)
But wishes aren't horses. We have to learn to create our own good fortune and not wait for a genie with three wishes to come along and solve our problems.

EXERCISE 3: Statements

(Grammar Notes 1–4)

Psychologist Joel Grimes hears all types of excuses from his clients. Rewrite each excuse as a present unreal conditional sentence. Keep the same order and decide which clause begins with **if**. *Use commas where necessary.*

1. I'm so busy. That's why I don't read bedtime stories to my little girl.

   If I weren't so busy, I would read bedtime stories to my little girl.

2. My husband won't ask for a raise. It's because he's not ambitious.

   _____

3. I don't play sports. But only because I'm not in shape.

   _____

4. I don't have enough time. That's why I'm not planning to study for the exam.

   _____

5. I'm too old. That's why I'm not going back to school.

   _____

6. I can't do my job. The reason is, my boss doesn't explain things properly.

   _____

7. I'm not good at math. That's why I don't balance my checkbook.

   _____

8. I can't stop smoking. The problem is, I feel nervous all the time.

   _____

9. I'm so tired. That's why I get up so late.

   _____

EXERCISE 4: Wishes About the Present

(Grammar Note 6)

Remember the fish from the fairy tale on pages 369–370? Read the things the fish would like to change. Then write sentences with **wish**.

1. I'm a fish. *I wish I weren't a fish.*

2. I'm not a handsome prince. _____

3. I live in the sea. _____

4. I don't live in a castle. _____

5. I'm not married to a princess. _____

6. The fisherman comes here every day. _____

7. His wife always wants more. _____

8. She isn't satisfied. _____

9. They don't leave me alone. _____

10. I can't grant my own wishes. _____

EXERCISE 5: Questions

(Grammar Notes 1–4)

Marty is having his open-house holiday party. His nieces and nephews are playing a fantasy question game. Write questions using the words in parentheses and the present unreal conditional. Use commas where necessary. Keep the same order.

1. (what / you / do / if / you / be a millionaire)

   What would you do if you were a millionaire? _____

2. (if / you / be the leader of this country / what / you / do)

   _____

3. (how / you / feel / if / you / never need to sleep)

   _____

4. (what / you / do / if / you / have more free time)

   _____

5. (if / you / have three wishes / what / you / ask for)

   _____

6. (what / you / do / if / you / not have to work)

   _____

7. (if / you / have a ticket for anywhere in the world / where / you / travel)

   _____

8. (if / you / can build anything / what / it / be)

   _____

9. (if / you / can meet a famous person / who / you / want to meet)

   _____

10. (who / you / have dinner with / if / you can invite three famous people)

   _____

EXERCISE 6: Editing

Read part of a book report that Marty's niece wrote. There are eight mistakes in the use of the present unreal conditional. The first mistake is already corrected. Find and correct seven more.

NAME: Laila Hijab   CLASS: English 4

The Disappearance

                                                                    disappeared
What would happen to the women if all the men in the world ~~would disappear~~? What would happen to the men when there were no women in the world? Philip Wylie's 1951 science-fiction novel, *The Disappearance*, addresses these fascinating questions. The answers show us how society has changed since the 1950s.

According to Wylie, if men and women live in different worlds, the results would be a disaster. In Wylie's vision, men are too aggressive to survive on their own, and women are too helpless. If women didn't control them, men will start more wars. If men aren't there to pump gas and run the businesses, women wouldn't be able to manage.

If Wylie is alive today, would he write the same novel? Today, a lot of men take care of their children, and a lot of women run businesses. In 1951, Wylie couldn't imagine these changes because of his opinions about men and women. I wish that Wylie was here today. If he were, then he might learns that men are not more warlike than women, and women are not more helpless than men. His story might be very different.

EXERCISE 7: Listening

A | *Read the sentences. Then listen to a modern fairy tale about Cindy, a clever young girl, and a toad. Listen again and circle the correct answers.*

1. Cindy loses her soccer (ball) / game.

2. A toad wants to <u>marry / play soccer with</u> Cindy.

3. The toad tells Cindy about his amazing <u>modern laboratory / magic powers</u>.

4. The toad agrees to turn Cindy into a <u>princess / scientist</u>.

5. Cindy <u>went to a lot of ceremonies / worked in her laboratory</u>.

6. The toad became a good <u>king / magician</u>.

B | *Read the statements. Listen again to the fairy tale, and check (✓)* **True** *or* **False**. *Correct the false statements.*

	True	False
1. Cindy wishes she ~~had a new~~ soccer ball. *could find her*	☐	☑
2. The toad wishes Cindy would marry him.	☐	☐
3. If Cindy married the toad, he would become a prince again.	☐	☐
4. Cindy wishes she could become a beautiful princess.	☐	☐
5. If Cindy became a princess, she'd have plenty of time to study science.	☐	☐
6. The toad doesn't know how to use his powers to help himself.	☐	☐
7. Cindy wants to become a scientist and help the prince.	☐	☐
8. Cindy and the prince get married and live happily ever after.	☐	☐

EXERCISE 8: Pronunciation

🎧 **A** | *Read and listen to the Pronunciation Note.*

Pronunciation Note

In **conversation**, we usually pronounce *would* "d" after pronouns in **conditional sentences** and after *wish*.

    EXAMPLES: If you came, we **would** drive you.   →   "If you came, we**'d** drive you."
                    I wish you **would** come.   →   "I wish you**'d** come."

We usually **drop the final "t"** in ***wouldn't*** before words beginning with a **consonant** sound.

    EXAMPLES: I wish they **wouldn't** call so late. →   "I wish they **wouldn'** call so late."
                    If I were you, I **wouldn't** pick it up. →   "If I were you, I **wouldn'** pick it up."

But do NOT use *wouldn'* in **writing**. Use ***wouldn't***.

🎧 **B** | *Listen to these short conversations. Circle the words you hear.*

    1. A: I want to give one big party this year.

        B: If I were you, I <u>'d / wouldn't</u> give it during the holidays.

    2. A: Karen's soccer team has a big game today.

        B: I know. I wish she <u>'d / wouldn't</u> play.

    3. A: Is Don coming over?

        B: Probably not. If he came, he <u>'d / wouldn't</u> stay for dinner.

    4. A: She always looks upset. Does she tell you what's wrong?

        B: No. But if she told me, I <u>'d / wouldn't</u> be able to help.

    5. A: I hate to keep reminding Debra about her homework.

        B: If you didn't remind her, she <u>'d / wouldn't</u> remember by herself.

    6. A: The kids don't read enough.

        B: If I were you, I <u>'d / wouldn't</u> read to them.

🎧 **C** | *Listen again to the conversations and repeat the responses. Then practice the conversations with a partner. Use the short forms.*

EXERCISE 9: What About You?

Work in small groups. Answer the questions in Exercise 5. Discuss your answers with the whole class.

EXAMPLE: **A:** What would you do if you were a millionaire?
B: If I were a millionaire, I'd donate half my money to charity.
C: With half the money, you could . . .

EXERCISE 10: Problem Solving

Work in small groups. One person describes a problem. Group members give advice with
If I were you, I would / wouldn't . . . *Use the problems below and write three more.*

1. You need $500 to pay this month's rent. You only have $300.

    EXAMPLE: **A:** I can't pay the rent this month. I only have $300, and I need $500. I wish I knew what to do.
    B: If I were you, I'd try to borrow the money.
    C: If I were you, I'd call the landlord right away.

2. You're lonely. You work at home and never meet new people.

3. You never have an opportunity to practice English outside of class.

4. You've been invited to dinner. The main dish is going to be shrimp. You hate shrimp.

5. _____

6. _____

7. _____

EXERCISE 11: Discussion

A | *In fairy tales, people are often given three wishes. Imagine that you had just three wishes. What would they be? Write them down.*

EXAMPLE: **1.** I wish I were famous.
2. I wish I spoke perfect English.
3. I wish I knew how to fly a plane.

B | *Discuss your wishes with a partner.*

EXAMPLE: **A:** I wish I were famous.
B: What would you do if you were famous?
A: I would. . . .

C | *There is an old saying: "Be careful what you wish for; it may come true." Look at your wishes again. Discuss the results—negative as well as positive—that might happen if they came true.*

EXAMPLE: **A:** If I were famous, I might not have enough free time. I wouldn't have a private life because . . .
B: Yes, but if you were famous, maybe you could travel a lot and meet a lot of interesting people.

EXERCISE 12: Writing

A | *If you had one wish, what would you wish for your own life or for society? Write two paragraphs. In the first paragraph, explain your wish with examples. In the second paragraph, describe the changes that might occur if your wish came true.*

EXAMPLE: In Philip Wylie's book, men and women live in separate societies. I don't wish that men and women lived separately, but sometimes I think that boys and girls would learn better if they went to separate schools. For example, when I was in middle school, boys and girls were embarrassed to make mistakes in front of each other . . .

If boys and girls went to separate schools, they might feel more comfortable about speaking in class. They could . . .

B | *Check your work. Use the Editing Checklist.*

Editing Checklist

Did you use . . . ?

☐ present and future unreal conditional sentences

☐ simple present in the *if* clause

☐ *would* + **base form** of the verb in the result clause if the result is certain

☐ *might* or *could* + **base form** of the verb in the result clause if the result is possible

☐ *wish* + **simple past**, *could*, or *would* for wishes about the present

☐ *were* for all subjects in *if* clauses and after *wish*

UNIT 23 Review

Check your answers on page UR-6.
Do you need to review anything?

A | Circle the correct words to complete the conversation.

A: If I lived in another city, I <u>'d feel / 'm feeling</u> much happier.

1.

B: Then if I <u>am / were</u> you, I'd move.

2.

A: I wish I <u>can / could</u> move, but that's just impossible right now.

3.

B: Would it be impossible if you <u>found / 'll find</u> a job somewhere else?

4.

A: No, I think Harry <u>can / could</u> help me find a job if I asked him. But I hate to ask.

5.

B: If he <u>isn't / weren't</u> an old friend, he might not want to help. But he's been your friend for ages.

6.

A: That's true. You know, I thought that if I talked to you, I <u>'ll / 'd</u> get some good ideas.

7.

B | Complete the present and future unreal conditional sentences in this paragraph with the correct form of the verbs in parentheses.

What _____ you _____ if you _____ a wallet in

1. (do)   2. (find)
the street? _____ you _____ the money if you _____

3. (take)   4. (know)
no one would ever find out? When Lara faced that situation, she first said to herself, "Our life
_____ a lot easier if I just _____ this money in my

5. (become)   6. (put)
pocket." Then she brought the wallet to the police. Her family needed the money, but she's not
sorry. "If we _____ bad choices, our kids _____ the

7. (make)   8. (learn)
wrong lessons," she told reporters. "So we always try to do the right thing."

C | Find and correct five mistakes.

1. Pablo wishes he can speak German.

2. If he had the time, he'll study in Germany. But he doesn't have the time right now.

3. He could get a promotion when he spoke another language.

4. His company may pay the tuition if he took a course.

5. What would you do if you are in Pablo's situation?

Past Unreal Conditionals
ALTERNATE HISTORIES

Before You Read

Look at the first cartoon and the title of the article. Discuss the questions.

1. What in the cartoon is different from reality? Describe it.
2. Do you ever ask *What if* questions?
3. Do you think *What if* questions are useful?

Read

Read the article on alternate history.

What would have happened if I had stayed in my own country? What would have happened if I had never met my husband? It's human nature to wonder how **life would have been different if certain events had (or had not) occurred.** There's even a name for the stories we create to answer these *What if* questions—alternate histories. Scientists, historians, fiction writers, and everyday people are always asking *What if* questions. Here are some examples.

Science

More than 65 million years ago, dinosaurs roamed[1] our planet. Then, a meteor[2] hit the Earth, changing the climate, causing the complete extinction[3] of most types of dinosaurs and making the development of other kinds of animals possible. But **what if the meteor had missed?** Phil Currie, a scientist from the University of Alberta, Canada, believes that **if the meteor had not struck the Earth, some types of dinosaurs would have continued to develop and would have become more intelligent.** They **would have gone on to dominate[4] the world** the way humans do today. **Would humans have been able to develop alongside these "supersaurs"?** If yes, **what would our lives have been like if most types of dinosaurs had survived?**

JUST THINK IF THAT METEOR HAD NEVER HIT PLANET EARTH 65 MILLION YEARS AGO...

POLLY WANTS A CRACKER!

2935   OLSEN

A dinosaur* and his pet human

*Today most scientists believe that birds are really a type of dinosaur.

---
[1]***roam:*** to travel freely over a wide area
[2]***meteor:*** a rock that falls from space into the Earth's atmosphere
[3]***extinction:*** the disappearance of a whole group of animals so that no more animals of that kind exist any more
[4]***dominate:*** to have power and control over other people, animals, or things

What if . . . ?

History

Many alternate history questions are about wars. One of the most common is, **What would have happened if Adolph Hitler had never been born or if the assassination[5] attempt on his life had been successful?** Many people believe that **World War II could have been avoided or at least might have been shortened**.

But **there are many other famous events that would have had different outcomes if just one fact had been different**. Take the case of the *Titanic*, for example. The largest luxury ship in the world, the *Titanic* hit an iceberg and sank on April 15, 1912, taking with it the lives of more than 1,500 people. **Could the event have been avoided or could more lives have been saved?** Yes, say historians. **If the *Titanic's* lookout had seen the iceberg earlier, the ship wouldn't have hit it.** Or, **if the *Titanic* had had more lifeboats, more people would have been saved**.

Everyday Life

A woman rushes to catch a subway train. Just as she gets there, the doors close. The train pulls away, leaving her on the platform. What would have happened if she had gotten on the train? The film *Sliding Doors* explores this question by showing us two parallel stories: the life of the woman **if she had gotten on the train**, and the life of the same woman **if she had missed the train**. In one version of the story, the woman meets a man on the train, and the two end up falling in love. In the other, she gets mugged[6] while running to catch a taxi and has to go to the hospital. The results of this everyday occurrence—catching or

missing a train—show us how a single ordinary moment can change the direction of our lives.

Some people argue that there is no way of ever really knowing **what would have happened if a single event had been different**. To those people, speculating about the past is just a game, an amusing way to pass the time. Yet to others it is obvious that alternate histories have a lot to offer. To them, while we can never know exactly how **a small change could have affected an outcome**, exploring the results of an alternate past—in books, movies, or our own lives—can teach us important lessons.

Big or small—the choices we make and the accidents that occur can change the course of history—for the whole world or for us as individuals.

---

[5]***assassination:*** the murder of an important person, usually for political reasons
[6]***get mugged:*** to be attacked and robbed in a public place

After You Read

A | Vocabulary: *Match the words with their definitions.*

_____ 1. alternate   **a.** to happen

_____ 2. intelligent   **b.** one person's description of an event

_____ 3. occur   **c.** smart

_____ 4. outcome   **d.** happening at the same time

_____ 5. parallel   **e.** different

_____ 6. version   **f.** a result

B | Comprehension: *Circle the words or phrases that complete the sentences.*

1. Alternate histories answer *What if* questions about the <u>present / past / future</u>.

2. Most types of dinosaurs became extinct as a result of <u>an accident / a decision / a human plan</u>.

3. Alternative histories are often about <u>the weather / military events / movies</u>.

4. Many people believe that avoiding World War II was <u>possible / impossible / dangerous</u>.

5. Historians think that the *Titanic* disaster was NOT <u>avoidable / necessary / major</u>.

6. In *Sliding Doors*, a woman's life changes because of a <u>missed train / train crash / bad choice</u>.

STEP 2 GRAMMAR PRESENTATION

PAST UNREAL CONDITIONALS

Statements

If Clause: Past Perfect	Result Clause: *Would (not) have* + Past Participle
If I **had missed** the train,	I **would have been** late. I **wouldn't have come** on time.
If I **had not gotten** that job,	I **would have felt** very bad. I **wouldn't have met** my wife.

Yes / No Questions

Result Clause	*If* Clause
Would you **have walked**	if you **had had** the time?

Short Answers

Affirmative	Negative
Yes, I **would have**.	**No**, I **wouldn't have**.

Wh- Questions

Result Clause	*If* Clause
What **would** you **have done**	if you **had missed** the train?

Contractions

would have = **would've**
would not have = **wouldn't have**

GRAMMAR NOTES

1 Use **past unreal conditional** sentences to talk about **past unreal conditions and their results**. A condition and its result may be untrue, imagined, or impossible.

The *if* **clause** gives the **unreal condition**, and the **result clause** gives the **unreal result** of that condition.

IF CLAUSE	RESULT CLAUSE

- *If* he **had missed** the train, he **would have been** late.
  (But he didn't miss the train, so he wasn't late.)
- *If* he **hadn't taken** that job, he **wouldn't have met** his wife.
  (But he took the job, so he met his wife.)

2 Use the **past perfect** in the *if* **clause**. Use *would have* + **past participle** in the **result clause**.

USAGE NOTE: Sometimes speakers use *would have* in the *if* clause. However, this is often considered incorrect, especially in formal or written English.

PAST PERFECT	WOULD HAVE + PAST PARTICIPLE

- *If* it **had won** an award, it **would have become** a famous movie.
- *If* I **had owned** a DVD player, I **would have watched** the movie.
  Not: If I would have owned . . .

3 You can also use *might have* or *could have* in the **result clause**, but the meaning is different from *would have*.

   a. Use *would have* if the result is **certain**. Do NOT use *will* in unreal conditional sentences.

- If Glen had gone to college, he *would have* **studied** hard.
  Not: . . . he will have studied hard.

   b. Use *might have* or *could have* if the result is **not certain**. Do NOT use *may* or *can*.

- If Glen had gone to college, he *might have* **become** a history teacher.
  Not: . . . he may have become . . .
- If Glen had gone to college, he *could have* **become** a history teacher.
  Not: . . . he can have become . . .

You can also use *could have* in the result clause to express **ability**.

- If Glen had become a history teacher, he *could have* **taught** here.

4 You can **begin conditional sentences** with the *if* **clause or the result clause**. The meaning is the same.

BE CAREFUL! Use a **comma** between the two clauses only when the *if* **clause comes first**.

- *If* he **had won a million dollars,** he would have traveled around the world. OR
- He would have traveled around the world *if* **he had won a million dollars**.

5 **Past unreal conditionals** are often used to **express regret** about what really **happened in the past**.

- *If* I **had been** free, I **would have gone** to the movies with you.
  (I regret that I didn't go to the movies.)

6 Use *wish* + **past perfect** to express **regret or sadness** about things in the past that you **wanted to happen but didn't**.

- Glen *wishes* he **had studied** history.
  (He didn't study history, and now he thinks that was a mistake.)

EXERCISE 1: Discover the Grammar

*Read the numbered statements. Decide if the sentences that follow are **True (T)** or **False (F)**.*

1. If a girl hadn't stepped in front of her, Helen wouldn't have missed her train.

   _T_ **a.** A girl stepped in front of Helen.

   _T_ **b.** Helen missed her train.

2. If she had gotten on the train, she would've met James.

   _____ **a.** She met James.

   _____ **b.** She got on the train.

3. She wouldn't have gotten her new job if James hadn't told her about it.

   _____ **a.** She got a new job.

   _____ **b.** James didn't tell her about it.

4. If I had gotten home before 10:00, I could've watched the movie *Sliding Doors*.

   _____ **a.** I got home before 10:00.

   _____ **b.** I didn't watch the movie.

5. I would have recorded the movie if my DVD player hadn't stopped working.

   _____ **a.** I recorded the movie.

   _____ **b.** My DVD recorder broke.

6. If I hadn't had a history test the next day, I wouldn't have gone to bed so late.

   _____ **a.** I had a history test the next day.

   _____ **b.** I went to bed late.

7. I wish I had studied hard for the test.

   _____ **a.** I studied hard for the test.

   _____ **b.** I feel bad about not studying hard.

8. Ana would've helped me if I had asked.

   _____ **a.** Ana helped me.

   _____ **b.** I asked Ana for help.

9. If I had studied more, I might have gotten a good grade.

   _____ **a.** I definitely would have gotten a good grade.

   _____ **b.** I possibly would have gotten a good grade.

10. If I had gotten a good grade, I would've been happy.

    _____ **a.** I didn't get a good grade.

    _____ **b.** I wasn't happy.

EXERCISE 2: *If* and Result Clauses: Verb Forms

(Grammar Notes 1–3)

George is a character from the movie It's a Wonderful Life. *Complete his thoughts about the past. Use the correct form of the verbs in parentheses.*

1. I didn't go into business with my friend Sam. If I _____*had gone*_____ into business
   with him, I _____*might have become*_____ a success.
                    (may / become)

2. I couldn't go into the army because I was deaf in one ear. I _____ into
                                                                          (go)
   the army if I _____ the hearing in that ear.
                        (not lose)

3. Mary and I weren't able to go on a honeymoon. We _____ away if my
                                                              (can / go)
   father _____ sick.
               (not get)

4. My uncle lost $8,000 of the company's money. I _____ so desperate if
                                                              (not feel)
   he _____ the money.
              (find)

5. I'm so unhappy about losing my father's business. I wish I _____

   never _____ born.
               (be)

6. Clarence showed me how the world would look without me.

   I _____ that I was so important if
           (not know)
   he _____ me.
              (not show)

7. If I _____ my little brother, Harry,
            (not rescue)
   he _____ all those lives, later on,
              (not save)
   when he was a soldier.

8. My old boss once almost made a terrible mistake in his

   shop. If I _____ him, my old boss
                  (not help)
   _____ to jail.
          (may / go)

George with his angel, Clarence

9. Mary _____ happy if she _____ me.
              (not be)   (not meet)

10. Life here really _____ worse if I _____ born.
                            (be)   (not be)

EXERCISE 3: Affirmative and Negative Statements   *(Grammar Notes 1–3)*

A | *The movie* The Curious Case of Benjamin Button *explores how simple actions can change lives. Read the information below.*

Events that occurred

Daisy

- someone's shoelace broke
- a delivery truck moved
- a package wasn't wrapped on time
- a girl broke up with her boyfriend
- a man forgot to set his alarm clock and got up five minutes late
- a taxi driver stopped for a cup of coffee
- a woman forgot her coat and took a later taxicab
- Daisy and her friend didn't cross the street
- the taxi didn't drive by
- Daisy was hit by the taxi

B | *Daisy, a dancer and the love of Benjamin Button's life, was in a serious accident. Look at the information in Part A. Complete Benjamin's story from the movie. Use the correct form of the verbs in parentheses. Choose between affirmative and negative.*

"Sometimes we're on a collision course,[1] and we just don't know it. Whether it's by accident or by design,[2] there's not a thing we can do about it. . . . And if only one thing

_____ *had happened* _____ differently: If that shoelace _____;
      1. (happen)   **2. (not break)**

or that delivery truck _____ moments earlier; or that package
                               3. (not move)

_____ wrapped and ready because the girl _____
         4. (be)   **5. (not break up)**

with her boyfriend; or that man _____ his alarm and
                               6. (set)

_____ five minutes earlier; or that taxi driver _____
       7. (get up)   **8. (not stop)**

for a cup of coffee; or that woman _____ her coat, and
                               9. (remember)

_____ into an earlier cab, Daisy and her friend _____
     10. (get)   **11. (cross)**

the street, and the taxi _____ by. But life being what it is—a series
                       12. (drive)

of intersecting lives[3] and incidents, out of anyone's control—that taxi did not go by, and that

driver was momentarily distracted, and that taxi hit Daisy, and her leg was crushed."

---
[1] *collision course:* a direction that leads to a crash
[2] *by design:* according to a plan
[3] *intersecting lives:* lives that cross each other

EXERCISE 4: Regrets About the Past

(Grammar Note 6)

These characters from the movie Sliding Doors *feel bad about things that happened. Read their regrets. Then write their wishes.*

1. **HELEN:** I took supplies from my office. My boss fired me.

   I wish I hadn't taken supplies from my office. I wish my boss hadn't fired me.

2. **HELEN:** I didn't catch my train. I had to find a taxi.

   _____

3. **TAXI DRIVER:** She got mugged near my taxi. She needed to go to the hospital.

   _____

4. **GERRY** *(Helen's old boyfriend)*: Helen saw me with Lydia. Helen left me.

   _____

5. **LYDIA** *(Gerry's old girlfriend)*: I started seeing Gerry again. I didn't break up with him.

   _____

6. **JAMES** *(Helen's new boyfriend)*: I didn't tell Helen about my wife. I lost her trust.

   _____

7. **HELEN:** James didn't call me. I got so depressed.

   _____

8. **ANNA** *(Helen's best friend)*: James lied to Helen. He hurt her.

   _____

Helen and James after their first meeting

EXERCISE 5: Negative and Affirmative Statements

(Grammar Notes 1–4)

Read these stories from an Internet message board about how people met their wives, husbands, boyfriends, or girlfriends. Using the words in parentheses, combine each pair of sentences to make one past unreal conditional sentence.

1. **My temp became permanent.** I'd already planned this great vacation to Jamaica when my boss cancelled my time off. "Sorry," she told me, "I'm going to be away, but I'll hire a temp to help you out." I was so furious that I almost quit right on the spot. I thought,

   If she had planned ahead, we wouldn't have needed that temp .
   _____
   a. She didn't plan ahead. We needed that temp. (would)

   Now I know that _____ .
   b. She didn't plan ahead. I met the love of my life. (might)

   When Vlad, the temp, walked in that first morning, I nearly ran into her office to thank her.

   _____ .
   c. She was so disorganized. My next trip to Jamaica was for my honeymoon. (would)

2. **She knocked me off my feet.**[1] I was skiing with some friends in Colorado. I met my wife when she knocked me down on a ski slope. It's a good thing I was OK because

   _____ .
   a. I didn't break my leg. I accepted her dinner invitation. (could)

   Actually, I only accepted because she felt so bad about the accident. But after the first few minutes, I knew I had to see her again. She was pretty, funny, and really intelligent.

   _____ .
   b. I went skiing that day. She knocked me over. (would)

   And _____ !
   c. She knocked me over. We got married. (would)

3. **Best in the universe.** I met my boyfriend online. We write stories on a *Star Trek* fan site.

   _____ .
   a. He was such a good writer. I thought about contacting him. (would)

   because I'm very careful about online privacy. In fact, I didn't even know he was a guy!

   _____ .
   b. I didn't know. I was brave enough to write to him. (might)

   But I thought he was another Isaac Asimov,[2] so I wanted to discuss his writing. We just emailed for a long time. Then we decided to meet at a Star Trek conference. I'm really glad we waited. He isn't the most handsome Klingon[3] in the universe, but to me he's Mr. Right.

   _____ .
   c. We didn't meet right away. I realized that. (might)

   _____

[1] *knock someone off his/her feet:* to make a very big impression on someone
[2] *Isaac Asimov:* a famous science fiction writer
[3] *Klingon:* in *Star Trek* stories, a race of people from another planet

EXERCISE 6: Editing

Read the student's book report. There are eleven mistakes in the use of the past unreal conditional. The first mistake is already corrected. Find and correct ten more.

Have you ever had a small accident that made a big difference in your life? If it ~~haven't~~ *hadn't*
happened, would your life have been much different? A lot of people think so. They wish they were
avoided a mistake. Or they worry that today's good luck *was* just a mistake. Isaac Asimov's short
story, *What If* – suggests another way to look at life. Norman and Livvy are traveling to New York
to celebrate their fifth wedding anniversary. The two met on a streetcar when Livvy accidentally
fell into Norman's lap. Although they're happy, Livvy always thinks about other possible outcomes
of their lives. Now, on the train to New York, she asks her favorite question: "Norman, what if you
would have been one minute later on the streetcar corner and had taken the next car? What do you
suppose would had happened?" Minutes later, a man carrying a box sits in the seat across from
them. He takes out a piece of glass that looks like a TV screen and shows them the answers to
Livvy's question.

Sadly, the couple sees that if Livvy hadn't fallen, the two wouldn't connected that day. Then
the screen shows Norman's marriage—to Livvy's friend Georgette. Upset, Livvy now thinks
Norman only married her because she fell into his lap. "If I hadn't, you would have married
Georgette. If she hasn't wanted you, you would have married somebody else. You would have
marry *anybody*." However, the couple next sees a New Year's Eve party with a very unhappily
married Norman and Georgette. The truth is clear: Norman could never have forgotten Livvy, even
if they did not married. But will Norman and Georgette have stayed together? Now *Norman* needs
to know! What would they be doing right now, he wonders: "This very minute! If I have married
Georgette." In the final scene, the couple sees themselves, married (after Norman and Georgette's
divorce), and traveling on the same train, at the same time, headed for their honeymoon in New
York. If Livvy hadn't fallen into Norman's lap, nothing would have changes! At the end, Livvy
sees that her *What if* questions have caused pain, and that ". . . all the possibles are none of our
business. The real is enough."

EXERCISE 7: Listening

A | *Read the sentences. Then listen to the conversations. Listen again and circle the words that complete the sentences.*

1. The man is describing why he was (late)/ injured.

2. The woman is explaining how she <u>got sick / became a teacher</u>.

3. The man is telling how he found a(n) <u>bookstore / apartment</u>.

4. The <u>man / woman</u> is expressing regret.

5. The man <u>lost / found</u> a wallet on the train.

6. The man and his wife opened a <u>bank / café</u>.

B | *Read the statements. Then listen again to the conversations and check (✓) **True** or **False**. Correct the false statements.*

	True	False
1. The man ~~was~~ *wasn't* injured in a train accident.	☐	☑
2. The woman became a teacher as a result of her friend's illness.	☐	☐
3. The man found an apartment when he was lost.	☐	☐
4. The woman enjoyed the movie.	☐	☐
5. The man had definitely planned on calling the police.	☐	☐
6. The man doesn't regret losing his job.	☐	☐

EXERCISE 8: Pronunciation

A | *Read and listen to the Pronunciation Note.*

> ### Pronunciation Note
>
> In **conversation** when we use the **past unreal conditional**,
>
> - we usually pronounce *have* like the word "**of**"
> - we use the **contractions** "'**d**" for *had* and "**hadn't**" for *had not*
> - we use the **contractions** "**wouldn't**" for *would not* and "**couldn't**" for *could not*
>
> **EXAMPLES:**
>
> | If **I had** been on the train, I **could have** been injured. | → | "If **I'd** been on the train, I **could of** been injured." |
> | If I **had not** caught it, I **would not have** arrived on time. | → | "If I **hadn't** caught it, I **wouldn't of** arrived on time." |
> | If he **had been** injured, he **could not have** called you. | → | "If **he'd** been injured, he **couldn't of** called you." |
>
> In **writing**, use *would have*, *wouldn't have*, *could have*, and *couldn't have*,
> NOT would ~~of~~, wouldn't ~~of~~, could ~~of~~, and couldn't ~~of~~.

B | *Listen to the short conversations. Circle the words you hear in each response.*

1. **A:** Did Mike go to the movie with you?

   B: No, but if his cousin <u>had / hadn't</u> been in town, he would've gone.

2. **A:** Did you get to the theater by 8:00?

   B: Well, if I'd taken a different train, I <u>could've / couldn't have</u> done it.

3. **A:** What's the matter? You look upset.

   B: I wish <u>I'd / I hadn't</u> invited Jason to go with us.

4. **A:** Did you like the movie?

   B: Not really. If I'd understood more of the English, I <u>could've / would've</u> enjoyed it.

5. **A:** I called you at 11:00, but there was no answer.

   B: Well, I would've been home if <u>I'd / I hadn't</u> walked.

6. **A:** What would you have done instead?

   B: I <u>would've / wouldn't have</u> taken a taxi.

C | *Listen again to the conversations and check your answers. Then practice the conversations with a partner.*

EXERCISE 9: What About You?

Work in small groups. Tell your classmates how a single decision or event changed your life or the life of someone you know. What would have happened if that decision or event hadn't occurred?

EXAMPLE: I had just moved to a new town. I didn't know anyone, and I was lonely and depressed. One day, I *forced* myself to go out for a walk. (All I really wanted to do was stay in my room and read). I was sitting near the lake when this guy came over and asked me if I had a watch. We started to talk. He was funny, handsome, and seemed really intelligent. If I hadn't gone for that walk, I never would've met him. Six months later we were married!

EXERCISE 10: Problem Solving

Work in small groups. Read the following situations. Did the person make the right decision? What would you have done in each situation? Why? What might have or could have happened as a result?

1. Zeke started his business making and selling energy bars[1] when he was a teenager. Ten years later, a large company offered to buy the business. Zeke turned the offer down because he wanted to make sure Zeke's Bars were always very high quality. If he had accepted, he could have retired rich by age 35. What would you have done?

   EXAMPLE: **A:** I wouldn't have rejected the offer. I would've sold the business.
   B: If he'd sold the business, he could've started a new one.
   C: He might've . . .

2. A man was walking down the street when he found ten $100 bills lying on the ground. There was no one else around. He picked them up and put them in his pocket.

3. A woman came home late and found her apartment door unlocked. She was sure she had locked it. No one else had the keys. She went inside.

---

[1] *energy bar:* food that gives you energy and that is in the shape of a candy bar

EXERCISE 11: Discussion

With a partner, discuss a situation in your life that you regret. Describe the situation and talk about what you wish had happened and why.

EXAMPLE: **A:** Someone asked me to go to a party the night before a test. I didn't like the course, and I didn't feel like studying, so I decided to go.
B: What happened? Did you do OK on the test?
A: No. I failed it.
B: Oh, that's too bad.
A: It's even worse than that. I had to repeat the course! I wish I hadn't gone to the party. If I'd stayed home, I'd have studied for the test. If I'd been prepared, I would've passed.

EXERCISE 12: Writing

A | *Write one or two paragraphs about an event that changed your life or the life of someone you know. If the event hadn't happened, what would have been different?*

EXAMPLE: Two years ago, I was in a serious car accident that changed my life. I was in the hospital for a long time, and my friends and family were always there for me. If I hadn't been so badly injured, I might never have realized what good friends and family I had. . . .

B | *Check your work. Use the Editing Checklist.*

Editing Checklist

Did you use . . . ?
- ☐ the past perfect in the *if* clause
- ☐ *would have*, *might have*, or *could have* + **past participle** in the result clause
- ☐ a comma between the two clauses when the *if* clause comes first
- ☐ *wish* + **past perfect** to express a regret

Check your answers on page UR-6.

Do you need to review anything?

A | *Circle the correct words to complete the sentences.*

1. If you <u>didn't tell / hadn't told</u> us about the movie, we wouldn't have seen it.

2. I wish I <u>had / hadn't</u> gone to the movie too. I hear it's great.

3. We <u>had been / would have been</u> late if we had taken the bus.

4. <u>If / When</u> you had called me, I might have driven you there.

5. I would've <u>gone / went</u> to the movies if I had had the time.

B | *Complete the past unreal conditional sentences in these conversations with the correct form of the verbs in parentheses.*

- **A:** Sorry I'm late. I _____ on time if I _____ my train.

　　　　　　　　　　　　1. (be)　　　　　　　　　　　　2. (not miss)

  B: Well, if you _____ on time, I _____ that great café.

　　　　　　　　　3. (be)　　　　　　　　4. (not discover)

- **A:** I wish I _____ this job offer.

　　　　　4. (not accept)　[5. (not accept)]

  B: But, if you _____ another job instead, we _____!

　　　　　　　　6. (take)　　　　　　　　　7. (not meet)

- **A:** It's hard to believe that birds are a type of dinosaur!

  B: I know. If I _____ that science program on TV, I _____ it.

　　　　　　8. (not see)　　　　　　　　　9. (not believe)

C | *Find and correct six mistakes.*

　　Tonight we watched the movie *Back to the Future* starring Michael J. Fox. I might never had seen it if I hadn't read his autobiography, *Lucky Man*. His book was so good that I wanted to see his most famous movie. Now I wish I saw it in the theater when it first came out, but I hadn't even been born yet! It would have been better if we would have watched it on a big screen. Fox was great. He looked really young—just like a teenager. But I would have recognized him even when I hadn't known he was in the film.

　　In real life, when Fox was a teenager, he was too small to become a professional hockey player. But if he hadn't looked so young, he can't have gotten his role in the TV hit series *Family Ties*. In Hollywood, he had to sell his furniture to pay his bills, but he kept trying to find an acting job. If he wouldn't have, he might never have become a star.

From Grammar to Writing
SHOWING CAUSE AND EFFECT

One way to develop a topic is to discuss its causes and effects. **To show cause and effect**, you can

- **connect sentences** with *as a result* and *therefore*
- **connect clauses** with *so*, *because*, or *if*

                 CAUSE   EFFECT

EXAMPLE: *I was shy*   *I didn't talk in class.* ➔

            I was shy. **As a result**, I didn't talk in class.

            I was shy. **Therefore**, I didn't talk in class.

            I was shy, **so** I didn't talk in class.

            Because I was shy, I didn't talk in class.

            If I hadn't been shy, I would have talked in class.

Notice the use of a **comma**: 1) after *as a result* and *therefore*, 2) before *so*, 3) after a clause beginning with *because* or *if* when it comes before the main clause.

1 | *Read this essay. Underline once sentences or clauses that show a cause.*
     Underline twice sentences or clauses that show an effect. Circle the connecting words.

(Almost) No More Fear of Talking

My biggest problem in school is my fear of talking in class. <u>My hands always shake</u> (if) <u>I answer a question or present a paper.</u> If it is a big assignment, I even feel sick to my stomach.

There are several reasons for my problem, but my family's attitude is the most important. My family motto is, "Children should be seen, but not heard." Because my parents never ask for our opinions, we never give them. I can feel my mother's disapproval if a talkative friend visits. In addition, my parents classify their children. My older brother is the "Smart One." I am the "Creative One." I think I would do better in school if they expected more, but they don't expect much. Therefore, I have not tried very hard.

Recently I decided to do something about my problem. I discovered that I feel less nervous about giving a speech in class if I role-play my presentation with a friend. I have also joined a discussion club. As a result, I get a lot of practice talking. My problem has causes, so it must have solutions!

2 | *Connect the pairs of sentences. Use the word(s) in parentheses.*

1. Mr. Stewart didn't help me. I never spoke in class. (if)

   If Mr. Stewart hadn't helped me, I never would have spoken in class.

2. He believed in me. I became more courageous. (because)

   _____

3. We worked in groups. I got used to talking about ideas with classmates. (so)

   _____

4. I have gotten a lot of practice. I feel more confident. (as a result)

   _____

5. Sena didn't understand the question. She didn't raise her hand. (therefore)

   _____

3 | *Before you write . . .*

1. Work with a partner. Discuss the causes of a strong feeling that you have.

   EXAMPLE: I usually feel excited at the beginning of the school year.

2. Complete this outline for a cause and effect essay.

   Paragraph I The feeling you are going to write about: _____

   One or two examples: _____

   Paragraph II The causes and effects of the feeling:

   A. _____

   B. _____

   C. _____

   Paragraph III How you deal with the feeling:

   A. _____

   B. _____

4 | *Write a three-paragraph essay about the causes and effects of a feeling that you have. Use your outline to organize your writing.*

5 | *Exchange essays with a different partner. Outline your partner's essay. Write questions about anything that is not clear.*

6 | *Work with your partner. Discuss each other's questions from Exercise 5. Then rewrite your own essay and make any necessary corrections.*

PART X

INDIRECT SPEECH
AND EMBEDDED QUESTIONS

UNIT	GRAMMAR FOCUS	THEME
25	Direct and Indirect Speech	Truth and Lies
26	Indirect Speech: Tense Changes	Extreme Weather
27	Indirect Instructions, Commands, Requests, and Invitations	Health Problems and Remedies
28	Indirect Questions	Job Interviews
29	Embedded Questions	Travel Tips

Direct and Indirect Speech
TRUTH AND LIES

Before You Read

Look at the title of the article and the photo, and read what the woman is saying. Discuss the questions.

1. Do you think the woman's hair looks great?
2. Is it ever all right to tell a lie?
3. If so, in what situations?

Read

Read the magazine article about lying.

THE TRUTH ABOUT LYING

BY JENNIFER MORALES

At 9:00, a supervisor from Rick Spivak's bank called and **said Rick's credit card payment was late.** **"The check is in the mail,"** Rick **replied** quickly. At 11:45, Rick left for a 12 o'clock meeting across town. Arriving late, Rick **told his client that traffic had been bad**. That evening, Rick's fiancée, Ann, came home with a new haircut. Rick hated it. **"It looks great,"** he **said**.

Three lies in one day! Does Rick have a problem? Or is he just an ordinary guy? Each time, he **told himself that sometimes the truth causes too many problems**. Like Rick, most of us tell white lies—harmless untruths that help us avoid trouble. In fact, one social psychologist[1] estimates that the average American tells about 200 lies a day! He **says that lying is a habit**, and we are often not even aware that we are doing it. When we do notice, we justify the lie by **telling ourselves it was for a good purpose**.

> He **said my hair looked great this way!**

These are our six most common excuses:

◆ To be polite: **"I'd love to go to your party, but I have to work."**

◆ To protect someone else's feelings: **"Your hair looks great that way!"**

◆ To feel better about yourself: **"I'm looking better these days."**

◆ To appear more interesting to others: **"I run a mile every day."**

◆ To get something more quickly: **"I have to have that report today."**

◆ To avoid uncomfortable situations: **"I tried to call you, but your cell phone was turned off."**

---

[1]*social psychologist:* a psychologist who studies how social groups affect the way people behave

How do we get away with all those white lies? First of all, it's difficult to recognize a lie because body language usually doesn't reveal dishonesty. But even when we suspect[2] someone is lying, we often don't want to know the truth. If an acquaintance **says she's fine**, but she clearly isn't, a lot of people find it easier to take her statement at face value.[3] And when someone **tells you, "You did a great job!"** you probably don't want to question the compliment!

Is telling lies a new trend? In one survey, the majority of people who answered **said that people were more honest in the past.** Nevertheless, lying wasn't really born yesterday. In the 18th century, the French philosopher[4] Vauvenargues told the truth about lying when he **wrote, "All men are born truthful and die liars."**

---

[2]***suspect:*** to think that something is probably true
[3]***take something at face value:*** to accept the obvious meaning of words and not look for hidden meanings
[4]***philosopher:*** someone who thinks a lot and questions the meaning of life and ideas about the world

After You Read

A | Vocabulary: *Circle the letter of the word or phrase that best completes each sentence.*

1. I was an **average** student. I _____ every semester.
   a. got B's and C's
   b. failed a couple of courses
   c. was at the top of my class

2. Ed was **aware** that Sid lost his job. He _____ it.
   a. suspected
   b. didn't know about
   c. knew about

3. Some people **justify** lying. They _____ it.
   a. always avoid
   b. find good reasons for
   c. never recognize

4. The **majority** of people are honest. _____ of them don't tell lies.
   a. None
   b. All
   c. Most

5. Hamid **revealed** his plans yesterday. He _____ about them.
   a. refused to say anything
   b. told his friends and family
   c. didn't tell the truth

B | Comprehension: *Find the situations in the article. Check (✓) the person's exact words.*

1. The supervisor at Rick's bank (to Rick):
   ☐ "His credit card payment was late."
   ☐ "Your credit card payment is late."

2. Rick (to his client):
   ☐ "Traffic had been bad."
   ☐ "Traffic was bad."

3. You (to a new friend):
   ☐ "You run a mile every day."
   ☐ "I run a mile every day."

4. An acquaintance (to you):
   ☐ "She's fine."
   ☐ "I'm fine."

5. People answering a survey question:
   ☐ "That people were more honest 10 years ago."
   ☐ "People were more honest 10 years ago."

STEP 2 GRAMMAR PRESENTATION

DIRECT AND INDIRECT SPEECH

Direct Speech			
Direct Statement	**Subject**	**Reporting Verb**	**Noun / Pronoun**
"The check **is** in the mail," "The haircut **looks** great," "The traffic **was** bad,"	he	**told**	the bank. Ann. her.
		said.	

Indirect Speech				
Subject	**Reporting Verb**	**Noun / Pronoun**	**Indirect Statement**	
He	**told**	the bank Ann her	**(that)**	the check **was** in the mail. the haircut **looked** great. the traffic **had been** bad.
	said			

GRAMMAR NOTES

1

Direct speech states the <u>exact words</u> that a speaker used.

In **writing**, put **quotation marks** before and after the speech you are quoting. That speech (called the **quotation**) can go at the **beginning** or at the **end** of the sentence.

Use a **comma** to separate the quotation from the rest of the sentence.

- **"The check is in the mail,"** he said.
- **"I like that tie,"** she told him.

- **"The traffic is bad,"** he said. OR
- He said, **"The traffic is bad."**

2

Indirect speech (also called *reported speech*) reports what a speaker said <u>without using the exact words</u>.

The word **that** can introduce indirect speech.

BE CAREFUL! Do **NOT** use quotation marks when writing indirect speech.

- He said **the check was in the mail**.
- She told him **she liked that tie**.

- He said **that the check was in the mail**.
- She told him **that she liked that tie**.

- She said **that she had to work**.
  Not: She said that "she had to work."

3

Reporting verbs (such as **say** and **tell**) are usually in the **simple past** for both direct and indirect speech.

Use **say** when you **do not mention the listener**.

Use **tell** when you **mention the listener**.

BE CAREFUL! Do **NOT** use **tell** when you don't mention the listener.

DIRECT SPEECH:
- "It's a great haircut," he **said**.
- "I'm sorry to be late," Rick **told** Ann.

INDIRECT SPEECH:
- He **said** it was a great haircut.
- Rick **told** Ann that he was sorry to be late.

- "It's a great haircut," he **said**.
- He **said** it was a great haircut.

- "It's a great haircut," he **told Ann**.
- He **told her** that it was a great haircut.

- He **said** he had been sick.
  Not: He told he had been sick.

4

When the **reporting verb** is in the **simple past** (*said, told*), we often **change the verb tense** in the indirect speech statement.

The **simple present** in direct speech becomes the **simple past** in indirect speech.

The **simple past** in direct speech becomes the **past perfect** in indirect speech.

- "I only **buy** shoes on sale," she **said**.
- She **said** she only **bought** shoes on sale.

- "I **found** a great store," she **said**.
- She **said** she **had found** a great store.

(continued on next page)

5	You do **NOT have to change the tense** when you report:	
	a. something that was **just said**	**A:** I**'m** tired from all this shopping. **B:** What did you say? **A:** I **said** I**'m** tired. OR I **said** I **was** tired.
	b. something that is **still true**	• Rick **said** the bank **wants** a check. OR • Rick **said** the bank **wanted** a check.
	c. a **general truth** or **scientific law**	• Mrs. Smith **told** her students that water **freezes** at 0° Celsius. OR • Mrs. Smith **told** her students that water **froze** at 0° Celsius.
6	When the **reporting verb** is in the **simple present**, do **NOT change the verb tense** in the indirect speech statement. **USAGE NOTE:** In newspapers, magazines, and on the TV and radio news, **reporting verbs** are often in the **simple present**.	• "I **run** a mile every day," **says** Ann. • Ann **says** that she **runs** a mile every day. NOT: Ann says that she ~~ran~~ a mile every day. • The majority of women **say** that they never **lie**.
7	In **indirect speech**, make necessary changes in **pronouns** and **possessives** to keep the speaker's <u>original meaning</u>.	• Rick told Ann, "**I** like **your** haircut." • Rick told Ann that **he** liked **her** haircut.

REFERENCE NOTES

For **punctuation rules for direct speech**, see Appendix 27 on page A-13.
For additional **tense changes in indirect speech**, see Unit 26, page 420.
For a list of **reporting verbs**, see Appendix 14 on page A-5.

EXERCISE 1: Discover the Grammar

Read the magazine article about lying on the job. Circle the reporting verbs. Underline once the examples of direct speech. Underline twice the examples of indirect speech. Go to Appendix 14 on page A-5 for help with reporting verbs.

"Lying during a job interview is risky business," says Martha Toledo, director of the management consulting firm Maxwell. "The truth has a funny way of coming out." Toledo tells the story of one woman applying for a job as an office manager. The woman told the interviewer that she had a B.A. degree. Actually, she was eight credits short. She also said that she had made $50,000 at her last job. The truth was $10,000 less. "Many firms really do check facts," warns Toledo. In this case, a call to the applicant's company revealed the truth. "She was a strong applicant," says Toledo, "and most of the information on the resume was true. Nevertheless, those details cost her the job."

Toledo relates a story about another job applicant, George. During an interview, George reported that he had quit his last job. George landed the new job and was doing well until the company hired another employee, Pete. George and Pete had worked at the same company. Pete later told his boss that his old company had fired George. After George's supervisor became aware of the lie, he stopped trusting George, and their relationship became difficult. Eventually, George quit.

EXERCISE 2: *Said* and *Told*; Verb and Pronoun Changes   *(Grammar Notes 2–5, 7)*

Complete the student's essay with the correct words.

Once when I was a teenager, I went to my Aunt Leah's house. Aunt Leah collected pottery,

and as soon as I got there, she _____*told*_____ me she _____ to show me
                                1. (said / told)   2. (wants / wanted)

_____ lovely new bowl. She _____ she _____ just
3. (my / her)   4. (said / told)   5. (has / had)

bought it. When Aunt Leah left the room, she handed me the bowl. As I was looking at it, it

slipped and broke on the floor. When she came back, I _____ the cat had broken
                                                       6. (said / told)

_____ bowl. She _____ me that it _____ important.
7. (her / your)   8. (said / told)   9. (isn't / wasn't)

   I didn't sleep at all that night, and the next morning I called my aunt and _____
                                                                              10. (said / told)

her that I had broken the bowl. I apologized and _____ that I _____
                                                 11. (said / told)   12. (feel / felt)

terrible. She laughed and said _____ had known all along. We still laugh about it.
                              13. (I / she)

EXERCISE 3: Indirect Speech

(Grammar Notes 2–4, 7)

*Look at the pictures. Rewrite the statements as indirect speech. Use **said** as the reporting verb and make all necessary changes in the verbs and pronouns.*

1.

a. *She said it was her own recipe.*

b. *He said it looked great.*

2.

a. _____

b. _____

3.

a. _____

b. _____

4.

a. _____

b. _____

5.

a. _____

b. _____

6.

a. _____

b. _____

EXERCISE 4: Indirect Speech

(Grammar Notes 3–7)

Rewrite Lisa and Ben's conversation using indirect speech. Use the reporting verbs in parentheses. Make necessary changes in the verbs and pronouns.

1. **LISA:** I just heard about a job at a scientific research company.

   (tell) _She told him she had just heard about a job at a scientific research company._

2. **BEN:** Oh, I majored in science at Florida State.

   (say) _He said that he had majored in science at Florida State._

3. **LISA:** They didn't mention the starting salary.

   (say) _____

4. **BEN:** I need a lot of money to pay off my student loans.

   (say) _____

5. **LISA:** They want someone with some experience as a programmer.

   (say) _____

6. **BEN:** Well, I work as a programmer for Data Systems.

   (tell) _____

7. **LISA:** Oh—they need a college graduate.

   (say) _____

8. **BEN:** Well, I graduated from Florida State.

   (tell) _____

9. **LISA:** But they don't want a recent graduate.

   (say) _____

10. **BEN:** I got my degree four years ago.

    (tell) _____

11. **LISA:** Great—I wasn't aware of that.

    (tell) _____

12. **BEN:** I really appreciate the information.

    (say) _____

13. **LISA:** My boss just came in, and I have to go.

    (tell) _____

EXERCISE 5: Editing

Read the article. There are nine mistakes in the use of direct and indirect speech. The first mistake is already corrected. Find and correct eight more.

WARNING!!!! THIS MESSAGE IS A HOAX!!!!!

Everyone gets urgent email messages. They tell you that Bill Gates now ~~wanted~~ *wants* to give away his money—to YOU! They say you that a popular floor cleaner kills family pets. They report that your computer monitor had taken photographs of you. Before I became aware of Internet hoaxes, I used to forward these emails to all my friends. Not long ago, a very annoyed friend explains that the story about killer bananas was a hoax (an untrue story). He said me "that the majority of those scary emails were hoaxes." He told me about these common telltale signs of hoaxes:

! The email always says that it was very urgent. It has lots of exclamation points.

! It tells that it is not a hoax and quotes important people. (The quotations are false.)

! It urges you to send the email to everyone you know.

He also told that a lot of Internet sites reveal information about Internet hoaxes. With this information, you can avoid the embarrassment of forwarding all your friends a false warning. So, before *you* announce that sunscreen had made people blind, check out the story on a reliable website.

EXERCISE 6: Listening

A | *Read the sentences. Then listen to Lisa's conversations. Listen again and circle the correct word or phrase to complete each sentence.*

1. **a.** Alex told Lisa that he'd found a new <u>Armenian /</u> <u>(vegetarian)</u> restaurant.

   b. He probably thinks that Lisa is going to go out with <u>her parents / Ben</u> on Saturday.

2. **a.** Lisa told Ben that she loves to <u>work / work out</u> too.

   b. Ben probably thinks that Lisa will <u>miss / attend</u> her next aerobics class.

3. **a.** Lisa told Mark that she needed the report on <u>Monday / Tuesday</u>.

   b. Mark thought the staff meeting was on <u>Monday / Tuesday</u>.

4. **a.** Chris said she wanted Lisa's <u>opinion of / recipe for</u> the sauce.

   b. She probably thinks that Lisa <u>will / won't</u> cook the sauce in the future.

B | *Now read Lisa's weekly planner. Lisa wasn't always honest in her conversations. Listen to the conversations again and notice the differences between what Lisa said and the truth. Then write sentences about Lisa's white lies.*

SATURDAY		MONDAY
Morning		Morning
Afternoon		Afternoon
Evening *6:00 date with Ben!*	*6:00 Vegetarian Society meeting*	Evening
	7:30 dinner with Chris	
SUNDAY *sleep late!*		TUESDAY
Morning *9:00* ~~*aerobics class*~~		Morning
Afternoon	*4:00 weekly staff meeting – present sales report*	Afternoon
Evening		Evening

1. *She said her parents were in town, but she actually has a date with Ben.*

2. _____

3. _____

4. _____

EXERCISE 7: Pronunciation

A | *Read and listen to the Pronunciation Note.*

Pronunciation Note

As you learned in Unit 9, the **way we say something** can express our **feelings** about it. For example:

We can say *He said he had to work late.* and mean that we **believe** that he had to work late. But we can also say *He said he had to work late.* and mean that we **don't believe** he had to work late.

When we **don't believe** what the person said, we usually **give extra stress** to the **reporting verb** and our **voice falls** when we say it.

EXAMPLE: He said he had to work.

When we **believe** what the person said, we usually **don't give extra stress** to the **reporting verb** and our **voice doesn't fall** when we say it.

EXAMPLE: He said he had to work.

B | *Listen to the short conversations. Notice the stress and intonation. Decide if the speaker* **believes** *or* **doesn't believe** *what he is reporting. Check (✓) the correct box.*

The speaker . . .	Believes	Doesn't believe
1. A: We haven't received Bob Miller's rent check yet.		
B: He said he mailed it last week.	☐	☐
2. A: Didn't you go out with Lisa Saturday night?		
B: No, she said her parents were in town this weekend.	☐	☐
3. A: Anton went skiing this weekend.		
B: And he said he had to work all weekend.	☐	☐
4. A: I saw Karen in the Chinese takeout place last night.		
B: She told us she'd cooked everything herself.	☐	☐
5. A: Ben looks very fit.		
B: He told me he exercises every day.	☐	☐
6. A: Guess how old Kellan is.		
B: Well, he says he's twenty-two.	☐	☐

EXERCISE 8: Discussion

Review the six excuses for lying described in "The Truth About Lying" *on page 402. Work in small groups. Is it OK to lie in these circumstances? Give examples from your own experience to support your ideas.*

EXAMPLE: **A:** Once my friend told me that my haircut looked great, but it really looked awful. I know she wanted to protect my feelings, but I think she should have told me the truth. Now it's hard for me to believe anything she says.
B: I think at times it's OK to lie to protect someone's feelings. Once I told my friend that . . .
C: I think . . .

EXERCISE 9: Questionnaire: Honesty

A | *Complete the questionnaire. Check (✓) your answers.*

	Always	Usually	Sometimes	Rarely	Never
1. I tell the truth to my friends.					
2. I tell the truth to my family.					
3. It's OK to lie on the job.					
4. "White lies" protect people's feelings.					
5. Most people are honest.					
6. It's best to tell the truth.					
7. I tell people my real age.					
8. My friends are honest with me.					
9. It's difficult to tell a convincing lie.					
10. Politicians are honest.					
11. Doctors tell patients the whole truth.					
12. I answer questionnaires honestly.					

B | *Work in small groups and compare your answers. Summarize your group's results and report them to the rest of the class.*

EXAMPLE: **A:** Five of us said that we usually told the truth.
B: Only one of us said it was always best to tell the truth.
C: Everyone in our group said that they tell people their real age.

EXERCISE 10: Game: To Tell the Truth

A | *Work in groups of three. Each student tells an interesting fact about his or her life. Each fact is <u>true for only one student</u>. The group chooses one of the facts to tell the class.*

> EXAMPLE: **ALICIA:** Once I climbed a mountain that was 7,000 meters high.
> **BERNARDO:** I speak four languages.
> **CHEN:** I scored the winning point for my soccer team at a big tournament.

B | *The group goes to the front of the class. Each student states the same fact, but <u>only one</u> student is telling the truth.*

> EXAMPLE:

C | *The class asks the three students questions to find out who is telling the truth.*

> EXAMPLES: **A:** Alicia, how long did it take you?
> **B:** Bernardo, who did you climb the mountain with?
> **C:** Chen, did you train for a long time?

D | *As a class, decide who was telling the truth. Explain your reasons.*

> EXAMPLES: **A:** I didn't believe Alicia. She said it had taken two weeks to climb the mountain.
> **B:** I think Bernardo was lying. He told us he'd climbed the mountain alone.
> **C:** I think Chen was telling the truth. She said that she'd trained for several months.

EXERCISE 11: Quotable Quotes

Work in small groups. Discuss these famous quotations about lying. Do you agree with them? Give examples to support your opinion. Use **says** *to report the proverbs and* **said** *to report the ideas of individuals.*

1. All men are born truthful and die liars.
   —*Vauvenargues (French philosopher, 1715–1747)*

> EXAMPLE: **A:** Vauvenargues said that all men are born truthful and die liars.
> **B:** I agree because babies don't lie, but children and adults do.
> **C:** I don't believe that *everyone* lies . . .

2. A half truth is a whole lie.
   —*Jewish proverb*

3. A little inaccuracy saves tons of explanation.
   —*Saki (British short story writer, 1870–1916)*

4. A liar needs a good memory.
   —*Quintilian (first-century Roman orator)*

5. The man who speaks the truth is always at ease.
   —*Persian proverb*

6. The cruelest lies are often told in silence.
   —*Robert Louis Stevenson (Scottish novelist, 1850–1894)*

EXERCISE 12: Writing

A | *Read the conversation between Rick and Ann. Then write a paragraph reporting what they said. Use direct and indirect speech. At the end of your paragraph, say who you think is lying and why.*

> **RICK:** Hi, honey. Sorry I'm late.
>
> **ANN:** That's all right. I made liver and onions. It's almost ready.
>
> **RICK:** *(looking upset)* It smells great, honey. It's one of my favorites.
>
> **ANN:** You look upset!
>
> **RICK:** I'm OK. I had a rough day at work. Oh, I stopped and bought some frog legs for dinner tomorrow. It's my turn to cook.
>
> **ANN:** *(looking upset)* That's interesting. I look forward to trying them.

EXAMPLE: Rick came home and said he was sorry he was late. Ann said that was all right.

B | *Check your work. Use the Editing Checklist.*

Editing Checklist

Did you use . . . ?
- ☐ quotation marks before and after direct speech
- ☐ a comma to separate direct speech from the rest of the sentence
- ☐ *say* when you didn't mention the listener
- ☐ *tell* when you mentioned the listener
- ☐ the correct verb tenses and pronouns in indirect speech

Check your answers on page UR-7.

Do you need to review anything?

A | *Circle the correct words to complete the sentences.*

1. My friend Bill always <u>says / tells</u> that white lies are OK.

2. When Trish invited him to dinner, he said, <u>"I'd love to." / "That he'd love to."</u>

3. Then Trish told him that she <u>plans / planned</u> to cook a Chinese meal.

4. Bill said that <u>he / I</u> loved Chinese food. That was a white lie—he really dislikes it.

5. Trish served a wonderful meal. She told Bill that she <u>'d / 'll</u> cooked it all herself.

6. Bill really liked it! When he finished dinner, he <u>told / said</u> Trish, "That was great."

7. After they got married, Trish told Bill that the Chinese meal <u>is / had been</u> takeout.

8. Today, Bill always says it was the best meal of <u>my / his</u> life—and that's the truth.

B | *Rewrite each direct statement as an indirect statement. Keep the original meaning. (The direct statement was said <u>one week ago</u>.)*

Direct Speech	Indirect Speech
1. "I always get up early."	She said _____.
2. "Water boils at 100 degrees Celsius. "	He told them _____.
3. "I like your haircut."	He told me _____.
4. "I loved the pasta."	She said _____.
5. "It's my own recipe."	He said _____.
6. "I mailed you the check."	She told him _____.
7. "My boss liked my work."	He said _____.

C | *Find and correct five mistakes.*

1. A psychologist I know often tells me "that people today tell hundreds of lies every day."

2. Yesterday Marcia's boyfriend said her that he liked her new dress.

3. When she heard that, Marcia said she didn't really believe you.

4. I didn't think that was so bad. I said that her boyfriend tells her a little white lie.

5. But Marcia hates lying. She said that to me, all lies were wrong.

STEP 1 GRAMMAR IN CONTEXT

Before You Read

Look at the map and the photos on this page and the next. Discuss the questions.

1. What was happening and where?
2. What do you think the title of the article means?

Read

Read the news article about a flood.

THE FLOOD OF THE CENTURY

Central Europe

July was hot and dry. Then, in August, the skies opened. Writing from Berlin on August 13, 2002, journalist John Hooper reported **that it had been raining for more than 24 hours straight**. A huge weather system was dumping rain on eastern and central Europe. Berliners worried not only about their own city but also about Prague and Dresden, the homes of priceless treasures of art and architecture.[1] The journalist noted **that people were already evacuating Prague and were just beginning to leave Dresden**.

As Hooper wrote his story, about 50,000 residents were streaming[2] out of Prague.

[1]**architecture:** the style of buildings in a particular country or at a particular time in history
[2]**stream:** to move in a continuous flow in the same direction, like water in a river

(continued on next page)

THE FLOOD OF THE CENTURY

The city's 16th century Charles Bridge was in danger of collapsing. Still, Mayor Igor Nemec told reporters **that the historic Old Town should remain safe**. Dr. Irena Kopencova wasn't that optimistic. She was sloshing[3] through the National Library of the Czech Republic in big rubber boots, grabbing old manuscripts.[4] She told Hooper sadly **that many original copies of the most treasured poems in the Czech language had been lost**.

A few days later, Dresden was battling its worst flood since 1501. All over the city, museum employees rushed items to the top floors. Egyptian stone tablets lay mixed together with some Roman statues, and masterpieces[5] by Rembrandt were piled on top of paintings by Rubens. The museum director, Martin Rohl, was still worried. He told reporter Julian Coman of the *News Telegraph* **that with another few feet of water, nothing would be safe**.

Heiko Ringel stopped stacking sandbags to talk to Coman. Ringel didn't live in Dresden anymore, but he said **he was back in his hometown that summer to help**. Why? He couldn't stand seeing all that history swept away.[6] He said **it would have been too cruel to bear**. "Dresden and Prague are the twin jewels of Central Europe."

The danger didn't stop tourism. "Flood tourists" moved from city to city gaping[7] at the flood of the century. One speculated **that it might even be the flood of the millennium**. John Hooper didn't agree. He thought climate change was causing these events, and believed that they would get worse. His headline announced **that the summer of 2002 would go down in history as the time when the weather had changed forever**.

Was Hooper right? Were the floods of 2002 just the beginning of worse and worse disasters? Or were they "normal disasters" that we should expect only once every 100 years? Right after the floods, statistical studies claimed **that floods were not getting worse, but that flood damage was increasing**. They concluded **that people ought to stop building so close to water**. Then, in 2003, thousands died in Europe in a heat wave that even statistics could not call "normal." And in 2006, while buildings damaged in the 2002 flood were still being restored, the Elbe flooded again —even higher than the 2002 "flood of the century." Just four years later, in the summer of 2010, more floods hit Central Europe. Poland suffered the most. Prime Minister Donald Tuck called it "the worst natural disaster in the nation's history."

Today more and more scientists are warning **that governments have to do something about climate change**. Recent events have already shown us how much we could lose if we don't listen.

---

[3]*slosh:* to walk noisily through water or mud
[4]*manuscript:* a document, often old and valuable, that is written by hand
[5]*masterpiece:* a work of art that is considered the best of its kind
[6]*sweep away:* to remove or destroy completely
[7]*gape:* to look at something for a long time, usually with your mouth open, because you are shocked

A | Vocabulary: *Complete the sentences with the words from the box.*

bear	collapse	damage	evacuate	optimistic	restore

1. The mayor of the city was very _____ during the storm. She believed things would turn out well.

2. Many people had to _____ the city. Some left by car and some left by public transportation.

3. I couldn't _____ to leave my grandmother's painting behind. It was too important to me.

4. Did the bridge _____ during the storm, or is it still standing?

5. A professional can _____ this old painting so that it looks almost like it did when it was first painted.

6. The _____ to the building was not too bad. They were able to fix most of it.

B | Comprehension: *Check (✓) the exact words that people from the article said.*

1. John Hooper said:
   - ☐ "It had been raining for more than 24 hours."
   - ☐ "It has been raining for more than 24 hours."

2. Dr. Irena Kopencova said:
   - ☐ "Many treasured poems in the Czech language had been lost."
   - ☐ "Many treasured poems in the Czech language have been lost."

3. Heiko Ringel said:
   - ☐ "I'm back in my hometown this summer to help."
   - ☐ "He's back in his hometown this summer to help."

4. Martin Rohl said:
   - ☐ "With another few feet of water, nothing was safe."
   - ☐ "With another few feet of water, nothing will be safe."

5. Scientists said:
   - ☐ "Governments have to do something about climate change."
   - ☐ "Governments had to do something about climate change."

INDIRECT SPEECH: TENSE CHANGES

Direct Speech			Indirect Speech				
Subject	**Reporting Verb**	**Direct Statement**	**Subject**	**Reporting Verb**	**Noun / Pronoun**	**(that)**	**Indirect Statement**
He	said,	"I **live** in Dresden." "I **moved** here in June." "I'**m looking** for an apartment." "I'**ve started** a new job." "I'**m going to stay** here." "I'**ll invite** you for the holidays." "We **can go** to the museums." "I **may look** for a roommate." "I **should get back** to work." "I **have to finish** my report." "You **must come** to visit." "We **ought to see** each other more."	He	told said	Jim me you him her us them	(that)	he **lived** in Dresden. he **had moved** there in June. he **was looking** for an apartment. he **had started** a new job. he **was going to stay** there. he **would invite** me for the holidays. we **could go** to the museums. he **might look** for a roommate. he **should get back** to work. he **had to finish** his report. I **had to come** to visit. we **ought to see** each other more.

GRAMMAR NOTES

1 As you learned in Unit 25, when the **reporting verb** is in the **simple past**, we often **change the verb tense** in the indirect speech statement.

DIRECT SPEECH		INDIRECT SPEECH
Simple present	→	Simple past
Present progressive	→	Past progressive
Simple past	→	Past perfect
Present perfect	→	Past perfect

DIRECT SPEECH	INDIRECT SPEECH
He said, "It'**s** cloudy."	He said it **was** cloudy.
She said, "A storm **is coming**."	She said that a storm **was coming**.
He said, "Klaus **called**."	He said that Klaus **had called**.
She told him, "I'**ve heard** the news."	She told him that she'**d heard** the news.

2 Modals often change in indirect speech.

Direct Speech		Indirect Speech
will	→	*would*
can	→	*could*
may	→	*might*
must	→	*had to*

Direct Speech	Indirect Speech
I said, "The winds **will be** strong."	I said the winds **would be** strong.
"You **can stay** with me," he told us.	He told us that we **could stay** with him.
He said, "The storm **may cause** severe damage."	He said that the storm **might cause** severe damage.
"You **must leave**," he told us.	He told us that we **had to leave**.

3 The following **do NOT change** in indirect speech:

a. *should*, *could*, *might*, and *ought to*

b. the **past perfect**

c. the **present** and **past unreal conditional**

d. **past modals**

Direct Speech	Indirect Speech
"You **should listen** to the news," he told us.	He told us that we **should listen** to the news.
"I **had moved** here a week before the flood," he said.	He said he **had moved** here a week before the flood.
"If I **knew**, I **would tell** you," said Jim.	Jim said if he **knew**, he **would tell** me.
"If I **had known**, I **would have told** you," said Jim.	He said that if he **had known**, he **would have told** me.
"I **should have left**."	He said that he **should have left**.
"We **couldn't have known**."	They said they **couldn't have known**.

4 **Change time words** in indirect speech to keep the speaker's <u>original meaning</u>.

Direct Speech		Indirect Speech
now	→	*then*
today	→	*that day*
tomorrow	→	*the next day*
yesterday	→	*the day before*
this week / month / year	→	*that week / month / year*
last week / month / year	→	*the week / month / year before*
next week / month / year	→	*the following week / month / year*

Uta to Klaus:
- "I just got home **yesterday**. I'll start cleaning up **tomorrow**."

Klaus to Heiko (a few days later):
- Uta told me she had just gotten home **the day before**. She said she would start cleaning up **the next day**.

Lotte to her mother (right after the storm):
- "Our electricity won't be restored until **next week**."

The family newsletter (two months later):
- Lotte reported that their electricity wouldn't be restored until **the following week**.

(continued on next page)

5 Change *here* and *this* in indirect speech to keep the speaker's <u>original meaning</u>.

DIRECT SPEECH		INDIRECT SPEECH
here	→	**there**
this	→	**that**

Jim (in Athens) to Erica (in Berlin):
• "I love it **here**. **This** climate is great."
Erica to Susan (both in Berlin):
• Jim said he loved it ***there***. He told me that ***that*** climate was great.

REFERENCE NOTES
For a list of **reporting verbs**, see Appendix 14 on page A-5.
For **punctuation rules for direct speech**, see Appendix 27 on page A-13.

STEP 3 FOCUSED PRACTICE

EXERCISE 1: Discover the Grammar

Read each numbered sentence (indirect speech). Circle the letter of each sentence (direct speech) that is similar in meaning.

1. The local weather forecaster said that it was going to be a terrible storm.
   a. "It was going to be a terrible storm."
   b. "It's going to be a terrible storm."
   c. "It was a terrible storm."

2. She said the winds might reach 60 kilometers per hour.
   a. "The winds reached 60 kilometers per hour."
   b. "The winds would reach 60 kilometers per hour."
   c. "The winds may reach 60 kilometers per hour."

3. She said there would be more rain the next day.
   a. "There will be more rain the next day."
   b. "There would be more rain tomorrow."
   c. "There will be more rain tomorrow."

4. She told people that they should try to leave the area.
   a. "You should try to leave the area."
   b. "You should have tried to leave the area."
   c. "You would leave the area."

5. She reported that people were evacuating the city.
   a. "People are evacuating the city."
   b. "People were evacuating the city."
   c. "People evacuated the city."

6. She said that they could expect a lot of damage.

    a. "We could expect a lot of damage."

    b. "We could have expected a lot of damage."

    c. "We can expect a lot of damage."

7. She said that the floods were the worst they had had there.

    a. "The floods are the worst we have here."

    b. "The floods are the worst we have had here."

    c. "The floods are the worst we have had there."

8. She told them that the emergency relief workers had arrived the day before.

    a. "Emergency relief workers arrived the day before."

    b. "Emergency relief workers arrived yesterday."

    c. "Emergency relief workers arrived today."

9. She reported that the president would be there to inspect the damage.

    a. "The president will be here to inspect the damage."

    b. "The president will be there to inspect the damage."

    c. "The president would be there to inspect the damage."

10. She said that if they hadn't had time to prepare, the danger would have been even greater.

    a. "If we hadn't had time to prepare, the danger would have been even greater."

    b. "If we don't have time to prepare, the danger will be even greater."

    c. "If we didn't have time to prepare, the danger would be even greater."

EXERCISE 2: Indirect Statements and Tense Changes   *(Grammar Notes 1–5)*

You are in Berlin. Imagine you heard these rumors yesterday about the storm in Europe. Use **They said** *to report the rumors.*

1. "The storm changed direction last night."

    They said that the storm had changed direction the night before.

2. "It's going to pass north of here."

    _____

3. "The bridge collapsed this afternoon."

    _____

4. "It's not really a hurricane, just a big storm."

    _____

(continued on next page)

5. "People in Dresden are evacuating."

_____

6. "They won't restore the electricity until tomorrow."

_____

7. "They can't reopen the schools because of the damage."

_____

8. "You ought to use bottled water for a few days."

_____

EXERCISE 3: Indirect Statements and Tense Changes (Grammar Notes 1–3)

A | _Read the interview between radio station WWEA and meteorologist Dr. Ronald Myers._

WWEA: Exactly how common are floods?

MYERS: Floods are the most common of all natural disasters except fire. They are also the most widespread. They occur everywhere.

WWEA: What causes them?

MYERS: Usually they are the result of intense, heavy rainfall. But they can also be caused by melting snow. Another cause is unusually high tides in coastal areas. Then, of course, there are tsunamis, like the one that struck Japan in 2011. These tremendous waves are often caused by earthquakes.

WWEA: And what causes these high tides?

MYERS: Severe winds over the ocean surface cause high tides. Often these winds are part of a hurricane.

WWEA: What is a _flash flood_? Is it just a very bad flood?

MYERS: No. A flash flood comes with little or no warning. Because of this, it's the most dangerous type of flood. In fact, flash floods cause almost 75 percent of all flood-related deaths.

WWEA: That's terrible. Is there anything that can be done?

MYERS: We've made progress in predicting floods. But we must get better at predicting flash floods.

WWEA: Is there anything that can be done to actually prevent floods?

MYERS: People must improve their protection of the Earth and the environment. When we replace grass and soil with roads and buildings, the ground loses its ability to absorb rainfall. This can lead to flooding. We should restore these "green" areas. In addition, many scientists believe that global warming is causing an increase in the number of floods.

WWEA: So the answer lies in better prediction and better treatment of the Earth?

MYERS: Exactly. We can't completely stop floods from happening. It's part of nature. But I'm optimistic that we _can_ predict them better and prevent flood damage from increasing.

B | *Now read the following statements. For each statement write* **That's right** *or*
That's wrong *and report what Dr. Myers said.*

1. Floods are not very common.

   That's wrong. He said floods were the most common of all natural disasters except fire.

2. They are very widespread.

   _____

3. Floods are usually caused by melting snow.

   _____

4. Tsunamis are often caused by high tides.

   _____

5. A flash flood is just a very bad flood.

   _____

6. A flash flood is the most dangerous type of flood.

   _____

7. Flash floods cause 25 percent of all flood-related deaths.

   _____

8. We have made progress in predicting floods.

   _____

9. People are doing a good job of protecting the Earth and the environment.

   _____

10. Restoring green areas can lead to flooding.

    _____

11. Many scientists believe that global warming is causing an increase in the number of floods.

    _____

12. We can completely stop floods from happening.

    _____

13. It's possible to prevent flood damage from increasing.

    _____

EXERCISE 4: Direct Speech

(Grammar Notes 1–5)

John and Eva live in Germany. Read the information that John got during the day. Then write what people said. Use direct speech.

John's mother called. She told him that she was listening to the weather report. She said that she was worried about John and Eva. She told him that if they weren't so stubborn they'd pack up and leave right then.

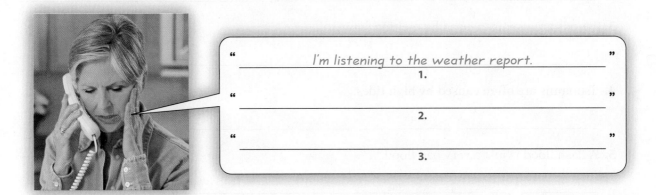

" _____ "
    I'm listening to the weather report.
    1.

" _____ "
    2.

" _____ "
    3.

John's father gave him some good advice. He said he'd had some experience with floods. He said John and Eva had to put sandbags in front of their doors. He also told John that they ought to fill the sinks and bathtubs with clean water. He said they should buy a lot of batteries.

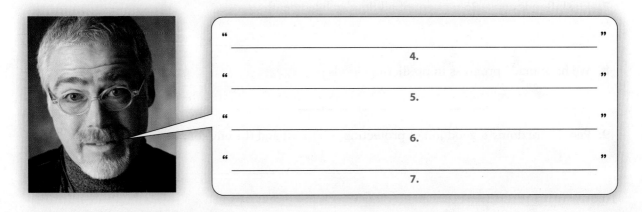

" _____ "
    4.

" _____ "
    5.

" _____ "
    6.

" _____ "
    7.

John's brother, Steve, called. He and Uta are worried. Their place is too close to the river. He said that they couldn't stay there, and he told John that they wanted to stay with him and Eva. He said they were leaving that night. Steve told John that he and Uta should have called sooner.

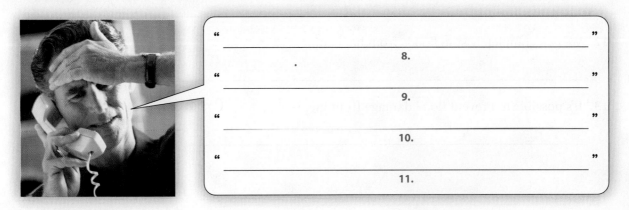

" _____ "
    8.

" _____ "
    9.

" _____ "
    10.

" _____ "
    11.

John listened to the storm warning in the afternoon. The forecaster said the storm would hit that night. She warned that the rainfall was going to be very heavy, and she said that the storm might last for several hours.

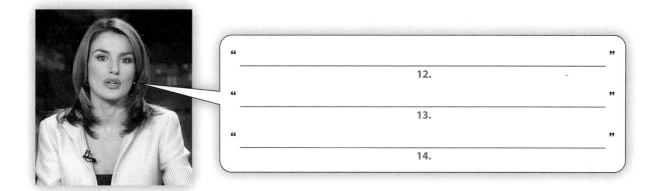

"_____"
12.

"_____"
13.

"_____"
14.

EXERCISE 5: Editing

Read this student's report. There are ten mistakes in the use of indirect speech. The first mistake is already corrected. Find and correct nine more.

What is it like to live through a flood? For my report, I interviewed the Nemec family, who

experienced last month's floods in our city. They reported that ~~we~~ *they* had experienced fear and

sadness. On September 14, the family went to a movie. Jerzy, a high school student, said

they can't drive the car home because their street was flooded. He told it had happened in

only three hours. Mrs. Nemec said that all their belongings were ruined, but that their cat

has gone to an upstairs bedroom. They were sad about losing so many valuable items, but

she said she will have been much sadder to lose the family pet. Jerzy's father also said their

home had been a complete mess and that the family had worked all this week to clean out

the house. Anna, who is in junior high school, wanted to keep her old dollhouse. It had

belonged to her mother and her mother's mother. At first, her father told her that she can't

keep it because seeing it would just make her sad. Anna replied that she saw memories in

that dollhouse—not just broken wood. She said I couldn't bear to throw it away. In the end,

they kept it. Mr. Nemec said he and Anna are able to restore the dollhouse a few weeks

later. Mrs. Nemec said that Anna had taught them something important today.

EXERCISE 6: Listening

A | *Read the sentences. Then listen to the winter storm warning. Listen again and circle the word or phrase that best completes each sentence.*

1. A foot of snow will fall / has fallen this morning.

2. Schools / Roads may remain closed tomorrow.

3. Snow and high winds are causing dangerous conditions / accidents on the roads.

4. If you must drive, you should bring extra clothes and have plenty of food / gas.

5. The post office is closed / open now.

6. You can buy food and other necessary items until this afternoon / evening.

7. Driving probably will / won't be easier tomorrow.

B | *Work in small groups. Listen again to the winter storm warning and check (✓) the correct information. It's all right to leave something blank.*

Schools

1. Today schools:	☑ closed at 10:00	☐ will close at 1:00
2. Students and teachers:	☐ should stay at school	☐ should go home immediately
3. Tomorrow schools:	☐ will open	☐ may stay closed

Roads

4. Road conditions:	☐ are safe	☐ are dangerous
5. Drivers must:	☐ drive slowly	☐ pick up passengers
6. Everyone should:	☐ avoid driving	☐ continue driving

Public Offices

7. Libraries:	☐ will stay open	☐ will close at 1:00
8. Post offices:	☐ will stay open until 5:00	☐ will close early
9. Government offices:	☐ will be closed tomorrow	☐ will remain open tomorrow

Businesses

10. Banks:	☐ will close at noon	☐ will stay open until 3:00
11. Gas stations:	☐ will close at noon	☐ will stay open until evening
12. Supermarkets:	☐ are open now	☐ are closed now

C | *Now compare your information with what other group members heard. Complete any missing information in your chart. Then listen again and check your answers.*

EXAMPLE: **A:** She said that schools would close at 1:00.
         B: That's not right. She said that schools had closed at 10:00.

EXERCISE 7: Pronunciation

A | *Read and listen to the Pronunciation Note.*

Pronunciation Note

When we speak, we usually **stress content words**.

Content words are the words in a sentence that **carry the most information**.

Some types of content words:

Nouns (*Tom, storm, gas, camera*)   **Main Verbs** (*say, tell, look, get*)

Adjectives (*big, dangerous, careful*)   **Adverbs** (*always, carefully, later, yesterday*)

***Wh*- question words** (*what, when, who*)   **Negatives** (*no, not, didn't, weren't*)

EXAMPLES: He **said** he'd **call** us **soon**.

            Jorge said we should **listen** to the **news**.

            Emma told me she **never works late**.

            They **told** us that the **storm** was **coming**.

B | *Listen to the short conversations. Listen again and put a dot (●) over the words that are stressed in the answers.*

1. **A:** Will Debra and Tom leave soon?

   B: Tom said they would leave tomorrow.

2. **A:** How are the roads?

   B: He said they weren't dangerous.

3. **A:** Has Jorge called?

   B: No. He told me he'd call us later.

4. **A:** What did they say on the weather report?

   B: They said that the storm could start soon.

5. **A:** Is there enough gas in the car?

   B: No. I told you we needed some yesterday.

6. **A:** Did you pack the camera?

   B: Definitely. You told me that I should pack it.

7. **A:** What did your father tell you?

   B: He told me to drive carefully.

C | *Listen again to the conversations and repeat the answers. Then practice the conversations with a partner.*

EXERCISE 8: Game: Telephone

Work in small groups. Student A whispers something in the ear of Student B. Student B reports (in a whisper) to Student C what he or she heard. Each student reports to the next student in a whisper and may only say the information once. The last student tells the group what he or she heard. Expect surprises.

EXAMPLE: **A:** There won't be any class tomorrow.
     B: He said that there wouldn't be any class tomorrow.
     C: She said that there wouldn't be any gas tomorrow.

EXERCISE 9: Interview

Use the questions below to interview three classmates. Report your findings to the class.

- Have you ever experienced extreme weather conditions such as the following?

a hurricane or a tornado	a flood
a heat wave	a sandstorm or a dust storm
a blizzard	wildfires
a drought	*Other*: _____

- How did you feel?
- What did you do to protect yourself?
- What advice would you give to someone in the same situation?

EXAMPLE: Arielle told me she had experienced a heat wave when temperatures reached over 40 degrees Celsius (That's 104 degrees Fahrenheit). She told me that she had felt sick a lot of the time. She said she had stayed indoors until evening every day. Arielle told me that everyone should move slowly and drink a lot of liquids in hot weather.

EXERCISE 10: Writing

A | *Write a paragraph reporting someone else's experiences with extreme weather. Use information from your interview in Exercise 9, or interview another person. Use indirect speech.*

EXAMPLE: My friend Julie told me about a dust storm in Australia. She said that one afternoon, the sky had gotten very dark, and the wind had started to blow hard. Her mother told her that they all had to go inside right away and close all the windows. Then . . .

B | *Check your work. Use the Editing Checklist.*

Editing Checklist
In indirect speech, did you make necessary changes in . . . ?   ☐ verb tenses   ☐ modals   ☐ time words (to keep the speaker's original meaning)   ☐ *here* and *this* (to keep the speaker's original meaning)

UNIT 26 **Review**

Check your answers on page UR-7.
Do you need to review anything?

A | Circle the correct words to complete the indirect speech sentences.

Direct Speech	Indirect Speech
"It's cloudy."	She said it <u>was / were</u> cloudy. **1.**
"You should take an umbrella to work."	He told me <u>she / I</u> should <u>take / have taken</u> an umbrella **2.** **3.** to work.
"The temperature may drop."	She said the temperature <u>must / might</u> drop. **4.**
"Tomorrow will be nice."	He said yesterday that <u>tomorrow / today</u> <u>will / would</u> be nice. **5.** **6.**
"We can expect a lot of damage here in Florida."	She said they <u>can / could</u> expect a lot of damage **7.** <u>here / there</u> in Florida. *(reported a week later in Texas)* **8.**

B | Rewrite each direct statement as an indirect statement. Keep the original meaning.
(The direct statement was said to you <u>two months ago</u>).

Direct Speech	Indirect Speech
1. "It's going to rain."	She said _____.
2. "It could be the worst storm this year."	He said _____.
3. "It's going to start soon."	She said _____.
4. "We should buy water."	He said _____.
5. "We must leave right now."	He told me _____.
6. "I'll call you tomorrow."	She said _____.

C | Find and correct six mistakes.

What a storm! They told it is going to be bad, but it was terrible. They said it will last two days, but it lasted four. On the first day of the storm, my mother called and told me that we should have left the house right now. (I still can hear her exact words: "You should leave the house *right now!*") We should have listened to her! We just didn't believe it was going to be so serious. I told her last night that if we had known, we would had left right away. We're lucky we survived. I just listened to the weather forecast. Good news! They said tomorrow should be sunny.

27 Indirect Instructions, Commands, Requests, and Invitations

HEALTH PROBLEMS AND REMEDIES

STEP 1 GRAMMAR IN CONTEXT

Before You Read

Look at the photo. Discuss the questions.

1. What time is it? Where is the man?
2. How does the man feel? Why does he feel that way?

Read

🎧 *Read the transcript of a radio interview with the director of a sleep clinic.*

HERE'S TO YOUR HEALTH

THE SNOOZE NEWS

CONNIE: Good morning! This is Connie Sung, bringing you "Here's to Your Health," a program about today's health issues. This morning, we've invited Dr. Thorton Ray **to talk to us about insomnia**. As you probably know, insomnia is a problem with getting to sleep or staying asleep. Dr. Ray is the director of the Sleep Disorders[1] Clinic, so he should have some good information for us. Welcome to the show!

DR. RAY: Thanks, Connie. It's great to be here.

CONNIE: Your book *Night Shift*[2] will be coming out soon. In it, you tell people **to pay more attention to sleep disorders**. But why is losing a little sleep such a big problem?

DR. RAY: I always tell people **to think of the worst industrial disaster**[3] **they've ever heard about**. Usually it was caused at least in part by sleep deprivation.[4] Then I ask them **to think about what can happen if they drive when they're tired**. Every year, more than 100,000 automobile accidents in this country are caused by sleepy drivers.

---

[1] ***disorder:*** a physical or mental problem that can affect health for a long period of time
[2] ***shift:*** a work period, especially in a factory (the night shift is often midnight to 8:00 A.M.)
[3] ***industrial disaster:*** an accident in a factory that causes a great deal of damage and loss of life
[4] ***deprivation:*** not having something that you need or want

HERE'S TO YOUR HEALTH

THE SNOOZE NEWS

CONNIE: Wow! That *is* a big problem.

DR. RAY: And a costly one. Recently, a large study of workers' fatigue reported that the problem costs U.S. employers around $136.4 billion a year in lost work time.

CONNIE: That's astonishing! But now let's talk about how individuals can deal with insomnia. For example, if I came to your clinic, what would you advise me **to do**?

DR. RAY: First, I would find out about some of your habits. If you drank coffee or cola late in the day, I would tell you **to stop**. The caffeine in these drinks interferes with sleep.

CONNIE: What about old-fashioned remedies like warm milk?

DR. RAY: Actually, a lot of home remedies do make sense. We tell patients **to have a high-carbohydrate[5] snack like a banana before they go to bed**. Warm milk helps too. But I'd advise you **not to eat a heavy meal before bed**.

CONNIE: My doctor told me **to get more exercise**, but when I run at night, I have a hard time getting to sleep.

DR. RAY: It's true that if you exercise regularly, you'll sleep better. But we always tell patients **not to exercise too close to bedtime**.

CONNIE: My mother always told me just **to get up and scrub the floor when I couldn't sleep**.

DR. RAY: That works. I advised one patient **to balance his checkbook**. He went right to sleep, just to escape from the task.

"I couldn't sleep."

CONNIE: Suppose I try these remedies and they don't help?

DR. RAY: If the problem persists, we often ask patients **to come and spend a night at our sleep clinic**. Our equipment monitors the patient through the night. In fact, if you're really interested, we can invite you **to come to the clinic for a night**.

CONNIE: Maybe I should do that.

---

[5] **high-carbohydrate:** containing a great deal of sugar or starch (for example fruit, potatoes, and rice)

A | Vocabulary: *Circle the letter of the word or phrase that best completes each sentence.*

1. An **astonishing** fact is very _____.
   a. frightening
   b. surprising
   c. uninteresting

2. **Fatigue** is a feeling of extreme _____.
   a. excitement
   b. pain
   c. tiredness

3. If someone **interferes** with your success, he or she _____ it.
   a. enjoys
   b. prevents
   c. causes

4. Hank's parents **monitored** his homework by _____ it every night.
   a. checking
   b. doing
   c. copying

5. My grandparents use traditional **remedies**. Those old _____ fascinate me.
   a. recipes
   b. stories
   c. treatments

6. After Jerry took pain medication, his headache **persisted**. It _____ for days.
   a. stopped
   b. continued
   c. improved

B | Comprehension: *Check (✓) the things Dr. Ray suggests for people with insomnia.*

☐ **1.** Stop drinking coffee and cola late in the day.

☐ **2.** Eat a heavy meal before going to bed.

☐ **3.** Get more exercise.

☐ **4.** Exercise right before bedtime.

☐ **5.** Get up from bed and balance your checkbook.

☐ **6.** Spend the night at the sleep clinic.

INDIRECT INSTRUCTIONS, COMMANDS, REQUESTS, AND INVITATIONS

Direct Speech		
Subject	**Reporting Verb**	**Direct Speech**
He	said,	"**Drink** warm milk." "**Don't drink** coffee." "Can you **turn out** the light, please?" "Why don't you **visit** the clinic?"

Indirect Speech			
Subject	**Reporting Verb**	**Noun / Pronoun**	**Indirect Speech**
He	told advised asked	Connie her	**to drink** warm milk. **not to drink** coffee. **to turn out** the light.
	said		
	invited	her	**to visit** the clinic.

GRAMMAR NOTES

1 In **indirect speech**, use an **infinitive** (*to* + **base form** of the verb) for:

- **instructions**
- **commands**
- **requests**
- **invitations**

DIRECT SPEECH	INDIRECT SPEECH
"**Come** early," said the doctor.	The doctor said *to come* early.
The doctor told her, "**Lie down**."	The doctor told her *to lie down*.
"Could you please **arrive** by 8:00?"	He asked Connie *to arrive* by 8:00.
"Could you **join** me for lunch?"	He invited us *to join* him for lunch.

2 Use a **negative infinitive** (*not* + **infinitive**) for:

- **negative instructions**
- **negative commands**
- **negative requests**

DIRECT SPEECH	INDIRECT SPEECH
"**Don't eat** after 9:00 P.M.," he said.	He told me *not to eat* after 9:00 P.M.
Mrs. Bartolotta told me, "**Don't wake** Cindy!"	Mrs. Bartolotta told me *not to wake* Cindy.
Jean said, "Please **don't set** the alarm."	Jean asked me *not to set* the alarm.

REFERENCE NOTES

For a list of **reporting verbs**, see Appendix 14 on page A-5.

For **punctuation rules for direct speech**, see Appendix 27 on page A-13.

EXERCISE 1: Discover the Grammar

Connie Sung decided to write an article about her visit to Dr. Ray's clinic. Read her notes for the article. Underline the indirect instructions, commands, requests, and invitations. Circle the reporting verbs that introduce them.

A Dream Job

2/18 11:00 A.M. The clinic called and (asked) me to arrive at 8:30 tonight. They told me to bring my nightshirt and toothbrush. They told me people also like to bring their own pillow, but I decided to travel light.

8:30 P.M. I arrived on schedule. My room was small but cozy. Only the video camera and cable told me I was in a sleep clinic. Juan Estrada, the technician for the night shift, told me to relax and watch TV for an hour.

9:30 P.M. Juan came back and got me ready for the test. He pasted 12 small metal disks to my face, legs, and stomach. I asked him to explain, and he told me that the disks, called electrodes, would be connected to a machine that records electrical activity in the brain. I felt like a character in a science fiction movie.

11:30 P.M. Juan came back and asked me to get into bed. After he hooked me up to the machine, he instructed me not to leave the bed that night. I fell asleep easily.

2/19 7:00 A.M. Juan came to awaken me and to disconnect the wires. I told him that I didn't think insomnia was my problem—those electrodes hadn't interfered with my sleep at all! He invited me to join him in the next room, where he had spent the whole night monitoring the equipment. I looked at the pages of graphs and wondered aloud whether Juan and Dr. Ray would be able to read my weird dream of the night before. Juan laughed and told me not to worry. "Those just show electrical impulses," he assured me.

8:00 A.M. Dr. Ray reviewed my data with me. He told me I had healthy sleep patterns, except for some leg movements during the night. He told me to get more exercise, and I promised I would.

EXERCISE 2: Indirect Instructions: Affirmative and Negative   (*Grammar Notes 1–2*)

Read the questions to Helen, a newspaper columnist who writes about health issues. Report her instructions using the verbs in parentheses.

Q: Do you have a remedy for insomnia? I have trouble getting to sleep.—Mike Landers, Detroit

A: Don't drink anything with caffeine after 2:00 p.m. Try exercising regularly, early in the day.

    1. (tell) *She told him not to drink anything with caffeine after 2:00 p.m.*

    2. (say) *She said to try exercising regularly, early in the day.*

Q: What can I do to soothe a sore throat? I never take medicine unless I have to.—Anne Bly, Troy

A: One remedy is hot herbal tea with honey. But don't drink black tea. It will make your throat dry.

    3. (say) _____

    4. (tell) _____

Q: I get leg cramps at night. They wake me up, and I can't get back to sleep.—Lou Rich, Dallas

A: The next time you feel a cramp, do this: Pinch the place between your upper lip and your nose. The cramp should stop right away. Sounds simple, but it's astonishing how well this works.

    5. (say) _____

Q: Do you know of an inexpensive way to remove stains on teeth?—Pete Lee, Brooklyn

A: Make a toothpaste of one tablespoon of baking soda and a little water. Brush as usual.

    6. (tell) _____

    7. (say) _____

Q: What can I do to ease an itchy poison ivy rash?—Marvin Smith, Hartford

A: Spread cool, cooked oatmeal over the rash. Also, try soaking the rash in a cool bath with a quarter cup of baking soda. Don't scratch the rash. That will make it worse.

    8. (tell) _____

    9. (say) _____

   10. (tell) _____

Q: Bugs love me. They bite me all the time.—Ed Small, Tulsa

A: There are a few things you can do to keep bugs away. Eat onions or garlic every day. Your skin will have a slight odor that bugs hate. Or ask your doctor about a vitamin B supplement.

   11. (say) _____

   12. (tell) _____

> **IMPORTANT:** A PROBLEM THAT PERSISTS MIGHT NEED MEDICAL TREATMENT. CALL YOUR DOCTOR ABOUT ANY CONDITION THAT DOESN'T IMPROVE OR GETS WORSE.

EXERCISE 3: Direct and Indirect Speech

(Grammar Notes 1–2)

A | *Connie had a dream at the sleep clinic. She wrote about it in her journal. Read her account of the dream and underline the indirect instructions, commands, requests, and invitations.*

I dreamed that an extraterrestrial came into my room. He told me <u>to get up</u>. Then he said to follow him. There was a spaceship outside the clinic. It was an astonishing sight! The creature from outer space invited me to come aboard. I asked him to lead the way! Juan, the lab technician, was on the ship. Suddenly, Juan told me to pilot the ship. He ordered me not to leave the controls. Then he went to sleep. Next, Dr. Ray was at my side giving me instructions. He told me to slow down. Then he said to point the ship toward the Earth. There was a loud knocking noise as we hit the ground, and I told everyone not to panic. Then I heard Juan tell me to wake up. I opened my eyes and saw him walking into my room at the sleep clinic.

B | *Complete the cartoon by writing what each character said.*

438 UNIT 27

EXERCISE 4: Editing

Read this entry in a student's journal. There are twelve mistakes in the use of indirect instructions, commands, requests, and invitations. The first mistake is already corrected. Find and correct eleven more. Don't forget to check punctuation. Mistakes with quotation marks count as one mistake for the sentence.

> In writing class today, the teacher asked Juan to read one of his stories. Juan, who works in a sleep clinic, read a story about someone with insomnia. It was wonderful, and everyone in class enjoyed it a lot. After class, the teacher invited me read a story in class next week. I don't feel ready to do this. I asked her no to call on me next week because I'm having trouble getting ideas. She told me that not to worry, and she said to wait for two weeks. I was still worried about coming up with an idea, so I decided to talk to Juan after class. I asked him tell me the source for his ideas. He was really helpful. He said that they came from his dreams. I was astonished — I'd never thought of using my dreams! He said me to keep a dream journal for ideas. Then he invited me "to read some of his journal." It was very interesting, so I asked him to give me some tips on remembering dreams. (Juan says that everyone dreams, but many people, like me, just don't remember their dreams in the morning.) Again, Juan was very helpful. He said getting a good night's sleep because the longer dreams came after a long period of sleep. He also tell me to keep my journal by the bed and to write as soon as I wake up. He said to no move from the sleeping position. He also told me not think about the day at first. (If you think about your day, you might forget your dreams.) Most important: Every night he tells himself that to remember his dreams. These all sound like great ideas, and I want to try them out right away. The only problem is, I'm so excited about this, I'm not sure I'll be able to fall asleep!

EXERCISE 5: Listening

A | *Read the statements. Then listen to Juan's conversation with Ann. Listen again and check (✓) True or False for each statement. Correct the false statements.*

	True	False
1. Juan just got back from a ~~sleep~~ *headache* clinic.	☐	☑
2. At the clinic, they said that too much sleep causes headaches.	☐	☐
3. Juan thinks the night shift interferes with his sleep.	☐	☐
4. Ann advised him not to use painkillers right now.	☐	☐
5. She suggested massaging around his eyes.	☐	☐
6. At the clinic, they said to eat several large meals every day.	☐	☐
7. Ann has been working at a headache clinic for a long time.	☐	☐

B | *Listen again to the conversation. Check (✓) the correct column to show what the doctors at the clinic told Juan to do, what they told him not to do, and what they didn't mention.*

	Do	Don't Do	Not Mentioned
1. Get regular exercise.	☑	☐	☐
2. Get eight hours of sleep.	☐	☐	☐
3. Take painkillers.	☐	☐	☐
4. Use an ice pack.	☐	☐	☐
5. Massage around the eyes.	☐	☐	☐
6. Eat three big meals a day.	☐	☐	☐
7. Eat chocolate.	☐	☐	☐
8. Avoid cheese.	☐	☐	☐

EXERCISE 6: Pronunciation

A | *Read and listen to the Pronunciation Note.*

Pronunciation Note

As you learned in Unit 26, **content words** are usually **stressed**.

In **affirmative** indirect instructions, commands, requests, and invitations, in addition to other content words in the sentence, we usually **stress**:

- the **reporting verb**
- the **base form** of the verb in the infinitive (**to** isn't stressed)

EXAMPLES: The doctor **invited** her to **visit** the sleep clinic.

They **asked** us to **arrive** by 8:00.

In **negative** instructions, commands, requests, and invitations, we also **stress** *not*.

EXAMPLES: They **told** him **not** to **eat** a big meal.

They **said not** to **watch** TV before bedtime.

B | *Listen to the short conversations. Circle the words you hear.*

1. **A:** What did the doctor say?

   B: She told me <u>to eat / not to eat</u> a lot of cheese.

2. **A:** What time are you going to the sleep clinic?

   B: Well, they asked me <u>to arrive / not to arrive</u> before 8:00.

3. **A:** How can I remember my dreams?

   B: I'd advise you <u>to sleep / not to sleep</u> for a long time, if possible.

4. **A:** Is Ella jogging with us today?

   B: No. Her doctor told her <u>to exercise / not to exercise</u> in the morning.

5. **A:** This article says that vinegar is good for a sunburn.

   B: Really? My mother always said <u>to use / not to use</u> that.

6. **A:** Did you tell your boss you needed a new schedule?

   B: Yes. I asked him <u>to put / not to put</u> me on the night shift.

C | *Listen again to the conversations and repeat the answers. Then practice the conversations with a partner. Use the correct stress.*

EXERCISE 7: Problem Solving

A | *What advice have you heard for the following problems? Work in pairs and talk about what to do and what not to do for them.*

- minor kitchen burns
- insomnia
- insect bites
- headaches
- snoring
- hiccups

- a cold
- blisters
- poison ivy
- a sore throat
- a tooth ache
- *Other:* _____

> EXAMPLE: **A:** My mother always told me to hold a burn under cold water.
> **B:** They say not to put butter on a burn.

B | *Choose two problems. Take turns reporting to the class.*

> EXAMPLE: **A:** My mother always told me to hold a burn under cold water.
> **B:** For insomnia, my grandparents said to . . .

EXERCISE 8: Picture Discussion

Jeff's parents went out for the evening and left a list of instructions for him. Work in pairs. Read the list and look at the picture on the next page. Talk about which instructions Jeff followed and which ones he didn't follow. Use indirect instructions.

> Dear Jeff,
>
> We'll be home late. Here are a few things to remember:
>
> Don't stay up after 10:00.
>
> Don't drink any cola —it keeps you awake. Drink some milk instead.
>
> Have some cake, but please save some for us.
>
> Please take the garbage out. Also, wash the dishes and put
> them away.
>
> And please let the cat in —then close and lock the back door.
>
> Do your homework.
>
> Don't watch any horror movies. (They give you nightmares—remember?)
>
> Don't invite your friends over tonight.
>
> Love,
> Mom and Dad

> EXAMPLE: **A:** His parents told him not to stay up after 10:00, but it's 11:30 and he's not in bed—
> he's asleep on the couch and having a nightmare.
> **B:** They also said to . . .

EXERCISE 9: Writing

A | *Write a paragraph about a dream you had or one that someone has told you about. You can even invent a dream. Use the paragraph from Connie's journal in Exercise 3 as a model. Use indirect instructions, commands, requests, and invitations.*

> **EXAMPLE:** One night I dreamed that I was in my grandmother's kitchen. In my dream, I saw a beautiful, carved wooden door. My grandmother invited me to open the door. She said that there were a lot of rooms in the house, and she invited me to explore them with her.

B | *Exchange your paragraph with a partner. Draw a sketch of your partner's dream and write the direct speech in speech bubbles. Discuss your sketch with your partner to make sure you understood the story and the indirect speech in your partner's dream. Make any changes necessary in your paragraph to make your writing clearer.*

C | *Check your work. Use the Editing Checklist.*

Editing Checklist
Did you use . . . ? ☐ affirmative infinitives to report affirmative indirect instructions, commands, requests, and invitations ☐ negative infinitives to report negative indirect instructions, commands, and requests

A | *Circle the correct words or punctuation mark to complete the sentences.*

1. I arrived at 8:00 because the doctor asked me to come early **. / ?**

2. Mr. Vance's class asked him to **give / gave** a test on Friday.

3. The teacher said, **"To sit down." / "Please sit down."**

4. Johannes advised us **don't / not to** worry.

5. Some experts **say / tell** to eat a snack before bedtime.

6. At the sleep clinic, the technician **told / said** me to relax and watch TV.

7. My neighbors **invited / advised** me to have dinner at their new home.

B | *Rewrite the direct speech as an indirect instruction, command, request, or invitation. Use an appropriate reporting verb (**advise, ask, invite,** or **tell**). Use pronouns.*

1. Officer David Zhu to Anita: "Please show me your license."

_____

2. Doctor Sue Rodriguez to Sam: "You ought to get more exercise."

_____

3. Ms. Carson to her students: "Please come to the English Department party."

_____

4. Robert to Nina: "Could you turn on the light, please?"

_____

5. Lisa to Nina and Paulo: "Why don't you hang out at my house?"

_____

C | *Find and correct eight mistakes. Remember to check punctuation.*

My teacher, Mr. Wong, told to sleep well before the test. He said to don't stay up late studying. He always invites we to ask him questions. He says, "Not to be shy." I'm glad my friend Tom advised me taking his class. He said me to register early, and he warned me "that the class filled up fast every semester." I told him don't to worry. I said I'd already registered.

UNIT 28 Indirect Questions
JOB INTERVIEWS

STEP 1 GRAMMAR IN CONTEXT

Before You Read

Look at the photo and the title of the article. Discuss the questions.

1. What are the people doing?
2. Are the man's questions typical in this situation? What is the woman's reaction?
3. What do you think a *stress interview* is?

Read

Read the excerpt from an article about job interviews.

Why can't you work under pressure?
Have you cleaned out your car recently?
Who wrote your application letter for you?

Do I really want this job?

The STRESS
Interview
By Miguel Vega

A few weeks ago, Melissa Morrow had an unusual job interview. First, the interviewer asked **why she couldn't work under pressure**. Before she could answer, he asked **if she had cleaned out her car recently**. Right after that he wanted to know **who had written her application letter for her**. Melissa was shocked, but she handled herself well. She asked the interviewer **whether he was going to ask her serious questions**. Then she politely ended the interview.

Melissa had had a *stress interview*, a type of job interview that features tough, tricky questions, long silences, and negative evaluations of the job candidate. To the unhappy candidate, this may seem unnecessarily nasty on the interviewer's part. However, some positions require an ability to handle just this kind of pressure. If there is an accident in an oil well near the coast, for example, the oil company's public relations officer[1] must remain calm when hostile[2] reporters ask **how the accident could have occurred**.

(continued on next page)

---

[1]*public relations officer:* someone hired by a company to explain to the public what the company does, so that the public will understand it and approve of it
[2]*hostile:* angry and unfriendly

The **STRESS** Interview

The uncomfortable atmosphere[3] of a stress interview gives the potential employer a chance to watch a candidate react to pressure. In one case, the interviewer ended each interview by saying, "We're really not sure that you're the right person for this job." One excellent candidate asked the interviewer angrily **if he was sure he knew how to conduct an interview**. She clearly could not handle the pressure she would encounter as a TV news reporter—the job she was interviewing for.

Stress interviews may be appropriate for some jobs, but they can also work against a company. Some excellent candidates may refuse the job after a hostile interview. Melissa Morrow handled her interview extremely well, but she later asked herself **if she really wanted to work for that company**. Her answer was *no*.

A word of warning to job candidates: Not all tough questioning is legitimate.[4] In some countries, certain questions are illegal unless the answers are directly related to the job. If an interviewer asks **how old you are, whether you are married**, or **how much money you owe**, you can refuse to answer. If you think a question isn't appropriate, then ask the interviewer **how the answer specifically relates to that job**. If you don't get a satisfactory explanation, you don't have to answer the question. And remember: Whatever happens, don't lose your cool.[5] The interview will be over before you know it!

DID YOU KNOW . . . ?

In some countries, employers must hire only on the basis of skills and experience. In Canada, most countries in Europe, and in the United States, for example, an interviewer cannot ask an applicant certain questions unless the information is related to the job. Here are some questions an interviewer may NOT ask:

X How old are you?

X What is your religion?

X Are you married?

X What does your husband (or wife) do?

X Have you ever been arrested?

X How many children do you have?

X How tall are you?

X Where were you born?

---

[3]*atmosphere:* the feeling that you get from a situation or a place
[4]*legitimate:* proper and allowable
[5]*lose your cool:* to get excited and angry

After You Read

A | Vocabulary: *Circle the letter of the word or phrase that best completes each sentence.*

1. A job **evaluation** gives a worker _____.
   a. more money
   b. more vacation time
   c. comments on his or her work

2. A bad way to **handle** an interview is to _____.
   a. say the right things
   b. get angry
   c. ask good questions

3. A **candidate** for a job promotion _____ get a better position.
   a. may
   b. will
   c. can't

4. A job with a lot of **pressure** _____.
   a. pays well
   b. is easy
   c. is difficult

5. Sara's behavior was **appropriate**. She did the _____ thing.
   a. right
   b. wrong
   c. easiest

6. A **potential** problem is one that _____.
   a. is very serious
   b. may happen
   c. has an easy solution

B | Comprehension: *Check (✓) the questions the interviewer asked Melissa Morrow.*

☐ **1.** "Does she really want to work for this company?"

☐ **2.** "Have you cleaned out your car recently?"

☐ **3.** "Is he going to ask me serious questions?"

☐ **4.** "How can the accident have occurred?"

☐ **5.** "Why can't you work under pressure?"

☐ **6.** "Are you sure you know how to conduct an interview?"

INDIRECT QUESTIONS

Direct Speech: *Yes / No* Questions

Subject	Reporting Verb	Direct Question
He	asked,	"**Do you have** any experience**?**" "**Can you create** spreadsheets**?**" "**Will you stay** for a year**?**"

Indirect Speech: *Yes / No* Questions

Subject	Reporting Verb	(Noun / Pronoun)	Indirect Question	
He	asked	(Melissa) (her)	*if* *whether (or not)*	**she had** any experience. **she could create** spreadsheets. **she would stay** for a year.

Direct Speech: *Wh-* Questions About the Subject

Subject	Reporting Verb	Direct Question
He	asked,	"*Who* **told** you about the job**?**" "*What* **happened** on your last job**?**" "*Which company* **hired** you**?**"

Indirect Speech: *Wh-* Questions About the Subject

Subject	Reporting Verb	(Noun / Pronoun)	Indirect Question	
He	asked	(Bob) (him)	*who*	**had told** him about the job.
			what	**had happened** on his last job.
			which company	**had hired** him.

Direct Speech: *Wh-* Questions About the Object

Subject	Reporting Verb	Direct Question
He	asked,	"*Who* **do you work** for**?**" "*What* **do you do** there**?**" "*Which job* **did you accept?**"

Indirect Speech: *Wh-* Questions About the Object

Subject	Reporting Verb	(Noun / Pronoun)	Indirect Question	
He	asked	(Melissa) (her)	*who*	**she worked** for.
			what	**she did** there.
			which job	**she had accepted**.

Direct Speech: *Wh-* Questions with *When, Where, Why,* and *How*		
Subject	**Reporting Verb**	**Direct Question**
He	asked,	"*When* **did you start** your new job**?**" "*Where* **do you work** now**?**" "*Why* **have you changed** jobs**?**" "*How much* **did you earn** there**?**"

Indirect Speech: *Wh-* Questions with *When, Where, Why,* and *How*				
Subject	**Reporting Verb**	**(Noun / Pronoun)**	**Indirect Question**	
He	asked	(Melissa) (her)	*when*	**she had started** her new job.
			where	**she worked** now.
			why	**she had changed** jobs.
			how much	**she had earned** there.

GRAMMAR NOTES

1

We often use **indirect speech** to report **questions**.
The most common **reporting verb** for both direct and indirect questions is *ask*.
We also use other **expressions** such as *want to know*.

REMEMBER: When the **reporting verb** is in the **simple past**, the verb tense in the **indirect question** often **changes**. For example:
The **simple present** in direct speech becomes the **simple past** in indirect speech.
The **simple past** in direct speech becomes the **past perfect** in indirect speech.

- "Did you find a new job?" she *asked*.
  She *asked* **if I had found a new job**.
- "Where do you work?" she *wanted to know*.
  She *wanted to know* **where I worked**.

- "**Do** you **like** your new job?" he asked.
  He asked me if I **liked** my new job.
- "**Did** you **find** it online?" he wanted to know.
  He wanted to know if I **had found** it online.

2

Use *if* or *whether* in **indirect *yes / no* questions**.

USAGE NOTES:

- *Whether* is more formal than *if*.

- We often use *whether or not* to report *yes / no* questions.

DIRECT QUESTION	**INDIRECT QUESTION**
"Can you type?" she asked.	She asked me *if I could type*.
"Do you know how to use a scanner?" he asked.	He wanted to know *whether I knew how to use a scanner*.

- My boss wants to know *whether the report is ready yet*.
- He wanted to know *whether or not the report was ready yet*.

3

Use **question words** in **indirect *wh-* questions**.

DIRECT QUESTION	**INDIRECT QUESTION**
"Where is your office?" I asked.	I asked *where his office was*.
I asked, "How much is the salary?"	I asked *how much the salary was*.

(continued on next page)

Indirect Questions **449**

4 Use **statement word order** (**subject** + **verb**), not question word order, for all indirect questions:

a. indirect *yes / no* questions

b. indirect *wh-* questions about the **subject**

c. indirect *wh-* questions about the **object**

d. indirect *wh-* questions with *when*, *where*, *why* and *how* or *how much / many*.

BE CAREFUL! If a direct question about the subject has the form **question word** + **be** + **noun**, then the indirect question has the form **question word** + **noun** + **be**.

SUBJECT VERB
They hired Li.

DIRECT QUESTION	INDIRECT QUESTION
"Did he hire Li?"	I asked *if* he had hired Li.
"Who hired Li?"	I asked *who* had hired Li.
"Who did he hire?"	I asked *who* he had hired.
"Why did they hire Li?"	I asked *why* they had hired Li.
"**Who** *is* the boss?"	I asked them who the boss *was*. NOT: I asked them who ~~was the boss~~.

5 In **indirect questions**:

• Do **NOT use** the auxiliary *do*, *does*, or *did*.

• Do **NOT end with a question mark** (end with a period).

DIRECT QUESTION	INDIRECT QUESTION
"Why did you leave?"	She asked me *why* I had left. NOT: She asked me why ~~did I leave~~. NOT: She asked me why I had left~~?~~

REFERENCE NOTES

The same **verb tense changes and other changes** occur in both indirect questions and indirect statements (see Units 25 and 26).

For a list of **reporting verbs** in questions, see Appendix 14 on page A-5.

For **punctuation rules for direct speech**, see Appendix 27, on page A-13.

STEP 3 FOCUSED PRACTICE

EXERCISE 1: Discover the Grammar

A | *Melissa Morrow is telling a friend about her job interview. Underline the indirect questions in the conversation.*

DON: So, how did the interview go?

MELISSA: It was very strange.

DON: What happened?

MELISSA: Well, it started off OK. He asked me <u>how much experience I'd had</u>, and I told him I'd been a public relations officer for 10 years. Let's see . . . He also asked what I would change about my current job. That was a little tricky.

Don: What did you say?

Melissa: Well, I didn't want to say anything negative, so I told him that I was ready to take on a lot more responsibility.

Don: Good. What else did he ask?

Melissa: Oh, you know, the regular things. He asked what my greatest success had been, and how much money I was making.

Don: Sounds like a normal interview to me. What was so strange about it?

Melissa: Well, at one point, he just stopped talking for a long time. Then he asked me all these questions that weren't even related to the job. I mean, *none* of them were appropriate.

Don: Like what?

Melissa: He asked me if I'd cleaned out my car recently.

Don: You're kidding.

Melissa: No, I'm not. Then he asked me why my employer didn't want me to stay.

Don: That's crazy. I hope you told him that you hadn't been fired.

Melissa: Of course. In fact, I told him I'd never even gotten a negative evaluation. Oh, and then he asked me if I was good enough to work for his company.

Don: What did you tell him?

Melissa: I told him that with my skills and experience I was one of the best in my field.

Don: That was a great answer. It sounds like you handled yourself very well.

Melissa: Thanks. But now I'm asking myself if I really want this job.

Don: Take your time. This job is a potential opportunity for you. Don't make any quick decisions.

B | Now check (✓) the direct questions that the interviewer asked Melissa.

☐ **1.** How much experience have you had?

☐ **2.** What would you change about your current job?

☐ **3.** Are you ready for more responsibility?

☐ **4.** What was your greatest success?

☐ **5.** How much are you making now?

☐ **6.** Was it a normal interview?

☐ **7.** Have you cleaned out your car recently?

☐ **8.** Have you been fired?

☐ **9.** Are you good enough to work for this company?

☐ **10.** Do you ever make quick decisions?

EXERCISE 2: Word Order

(Grammar Notes 1–4)

Jaime has an interview next week. His neighbor, Claire, wants to know all about it. Report Claire's questions using the words in parentheses in the correct order. Use **ask** *or* **want to know** *to report the questions.*

1. **CLAIRE:** I heard you're going on an interview next week. What kind of job is it?

   JAIME: It's for a job as an office assistant.

   She asked what kind of job it was.
   _____
   (kind of job / what / was / it)

2. **CLAIRE:** Oh, really? When is the interview?

   JAIME: It's on Tuesday at 9:00.

   _____
   (the interview / was / when)

3. **CLAIRE:** Where's the company?

   JAIME: It's downtown on the west side.

   _____
   (was / where / the company)

4. **CLAIRE:** Do you need directions?

   JAIME: No, I know the way.

   _____
   (needed / if / he / directions)

5. **CLAIRE:** How long does it take to get there?

   JAIME: About half an hour.

   _____
   (to get there / it / takes / how long)

6. **CLAIRE:** Are you going to drive?

   JAIME: I think so. It's probably the fastest way.

   _____
   (was going to / if / he / drive)

7. **CLAIRE:** Who's going to interview you?

   JAIME: Um. I'm not sure. Probably the manager of the department.

   _____
   (was going to / his / who / interview)

8. **CLAIRE:** Well, good luck. When will they let you know?

   JAIME: It will take a while. They have a lot of candidates.

   _____
   (his / they / would / when / let / know)

EXERCISE 3: Indirect Questions: Verb and Pronoun Changes

(Grammar Notes 1–5)

Read the questions that were asked during Jaime's interview. Jaime asked some of the questions, and the manager, Ms. Stollins, asked others. Decide who asked each question. Then rewrite each question as indirect speech.

1. "What type of training is available for the job?"

   Jaime asked (Ms. Stollins) what type of training was available for the job.

2. "What kind of experience do you have?"

   _____

3. "Is there opportunity for promotion?"

   _____

4. "Are you interviewing with other companies?"

   _____

5. "What will my responsibilities be?"

   _____

6. "How is job performance rewarded?"

   _____

7. "What was your starting salary at your last job?"

   _____

8. "Did you get along well with your last employer?"

   _____

9. "When does the job start?"

   _____

10. "Why did you apply for this position?"

    _____

EXERCISE 4: Editing

Read the memo an interviewer wrote after an interview. There are seven mistakes in the use of indirect questions. The first mistake is already corrected. Find and correct six more. Don't forget to check punctuation. Mistakes with quotation marks count as one mistake for the sentence.

May 15, 2012

TO: Francesca Giuffrida

FROM: Ken Marley

SUBJECT: Interview with Carlos Lopez

This morning I interviewed Carlos Lopez for the administrative assistant position. Since this job requires a lot of contact with the public, I did some stress questioning. I asked Mr. Lopez why

                  he couldn't
~~couldn't he~~ work under pressure. I also asked him why his supervisor disliked him. Finally, I inquired when he would quit the job with our company?

Mr. Lopez remained calm throughout the interview. He answered all my questions, and he had some excellent questions of his own. He asked "if we expected changes in the job." He also wanted to know how often do we perform employee evaluations. I was quite impressed when he asked why did I decide to join this company.

Mr. Lopez is an excellent candidate for the job, and I believe he will handle the responsibilities well. At the end of the interview, Mr. Lopez inquired when we could let him know our decision? I asked him if whether he was considering another job, and he said he was. I think we should act quickly in order not to lose this excellent potential employee.

EXERCISE 5: Listening

A | *You are going to hear a job interview that takes place in Canada. Read the checklist. Then listen to the interview. Listen again and check (✓) the topics that the interviewer asks about.*

Possible Job Interview Topics

OK to Ask

- ☐ Name
- ☐ Address
- ☐ Work experience
- ☑ Reason for leaving job
- ☐ Reason for seeking position
- ☐ Salary
- ☐ Education
- ☐ Professional affiliations
- ☐ Convictions[1] for crimes
- ☐ Skills
- ☐ Job performance
- ☐ Permission to work in Canada

Not OK to Ask[2]

- ☐ Age
- ☐ Race
- ☐ Sex
- ☐ Religion
- ☐ National origin
- ☐ Height or weight
- ☐ Marital status
- ☐ Information about spouse
- ☐ Arrest record
- ☐ Physical disabilities
- ☐ Children
- ☐ Citizenship
- ☐ English language skill
- ☐ Financial situation

[1]*conviction:* a court's decision that a person is guilty of a crime
[2]*not OK to ask:* illegal to ask if not related to the job

B | *Listen again to the interview and write the illegal questions the interviewer asks.*

1. *How old are you?*
2. _____
3. _____
4. _____
5. _____
6. _____
7. _____

C | *Now report the illegal questions to the class.*

EXAMPLE: He asked her how old she was.

EXERCISE 6: Pronunciation

A | *Read and listen to the Pronunciation Note.*

Pronunciation Note
In **direct** *yes / no* **questions**, the voice usually **rises at the end**.
EXAMPLES: Do you have a lot of experience?
Will you be able to start next week?
In **indirect** *yes / no* **questions**, the voice usually **falls at the end**.
EXAMPLES: He asked if I had a lot of experience.
She wanted to know if I'd be able to start next week.

B | *Listen to parts of a conversation. Notice how the voice rises (➚) or falls (➘) at the end of the direct and indirect questions. Draw a rising arrow or a falling arrow over the end of each direct or indirect question.*

1. A: So, **did the interview go OK**?

    B: I think so. The interviewer asked me **if she could call my old employer.**

2. A: **Did you say yes?**

    B: Of course. And she also wanted to know **whether I could start next month.**

3. A: Sounds good. **Did you ask any questions?**

    B: Yes. I asked her **if she liked working there.**

4. A: Great question. So, **does she like working there?**

    B: She said yes. But **was she telling the truth?**

5. A: Never mind. Just ask yourself **if you want the job.**

    B: I don't know. **Can we talk about something else?**

6. A: Sure. I forgot to ask you **if you wanted to eat out tonight.**

    B: Sounds good. **Do you want to try that new Japanese restaurant?**

C | *Listen again. Then practice the conversation with a partner.*

EXERCISE 7: Role Play: A Job Interview

A | *Read the résumé and the job advertisement. Work in groups to write questions for a job interview. Half of the group should write questions to ask the candidate. The other half should write questions to ask the interviewer. Write at least three questions for each.*

Pat Rogers
215 West Hill Drive
Baltimore, MD 21233
Telephone: (410) 555-7777
Fax: (410) 555-7932
progers@email.com

EDUCATION	**Taylor Community College**
	Associate's degree (Business) 2010
	Middlesex High School
	High school diploma, 2008

MEDICAL RECEPTIONIST for busy doctor's office. Mature individual needed to answer phones, greet patients, make appointments. Some filing and billing. Similar experience preferred. Computer skills necessary.

EXPERIENCE	
2010–Present **Patients Plus** Baltimore, MD	**Medical receptionist** Responsibilities: Greet patients, make appointments, answer telephones, update computer records
2008–2010 **Union Hospital** Baltimore, MD	**Admitting clerk, hospital admissions office** Responsibilities: Interviewed patients for admission, input information in computer, answered telephones

EXAMPLES: **To ask the candidate:**   Why did you leave your job at Union Hospital?
                   To ask the interviewer: How many doctors work here?

B | *Select two people to act out the interview for the class.*

C | *Discuss each group's role-play interview as a class. Use these questions to guide your discussion. Support your ideas by reporting questions that were asked in the interview.*

1. Was it a stress interview? Why or why not?

2. Did the interviewer ask any illegal questions? Which ones were illegal?

3. Which of the candidate's questions were the most useful in evaluating the job? Why do you think so?

4. Which of the interviewer's questions gave the clearest picture of the candidate? Why do you think so?

5. If you were the interviewer, would you hire this candidate? Why or why not?

6. If you were the candidate, would you want to work for this company? Why or why not?

EXAMPLE: **A:** I think it was a stress interview because the interviewer asked him why he couldn't find a new job.
           B: The interviewer asked two illegal questions. She asked when the candidate was born. She also asked . . .
           C: The candidate's most useful questions were . . .

EXERCISE 8: Questionnaire: Work Values

A | *Your values are the things that are most important to you. Take this work values quiz on your own. (If none of the answers match your values, add your own.) Then work with a partner. Ask your partner three of the questions and discuss your answers. Then answer the other three questions and discuss your answers.*

Work Values Questionnaire

1. Why do you want to work?

○ To make a lot of money. ○ To become well known.

○ To help people. ○ Other: _____

2. Where do you prefer to work?

○ I'd like to travel. ○ At home.

○ In an office. ○ Other: _____

3. When do you want to work?

○ 9–5 every day. ○ On my own schedule.

○ On a changing schedule. ○ Other: _____

4. What kind of routine do you like?

○ The same type of task all day. ○ Tasks that change often.

○ A variety of tasks every day. ○ Other: _____

5. How much job pressure can you handle?

○ I like a high-pressure job. ○ Just enough to keep me awake.

○ I can handle some, but not a lot. ○ Other: _____

6. Who would you like to work with?

○ I work best with a team. ○ I enjoy working with the public.

○ I like to work by myself. ○ Other: _____

B | *Get together with another pair and report your conversations.*

EXAMPLE: **A:** Sami asked me how much job pressure I could handle. I told him . . .
B: Ella asked why I wanted to work. I said that . . .

EXERCISE 9: What About You?

In small groups, discuss a personal experience with a school or job interview. (If you do not have a personal experience, use the experience of someone you know.) Talk about these questions:

- What did the interviewer want to find out?
- What was the most difficult question to answer? Why?
- Were there any questions that you didn't want to answer? What did you say?
- What did you ask the interviewer?

EXAMPLE: **A:** The interviewer asked me if I was married.
               B: That isn't legal, is it?
               C: What did you say?
               A: I asked him. . . .

EXERCISE 10: Writing

A | *Before you look for work, it's a good idea to talk to people who are already working in jobs that might interest you. In these kinds of "informational interviews" you can ask what the tasks in that job are, why people like or dislike the work, or how much you can expect to be paid. Write a list of questions to ask in an informational job interview.*

EXAMPLE: Do you like your job?
               How much vacation time do you get?

B | *Now interview someone and write a report about the interview. Use indirect questions.*

EXAMPLE: I interviewed Pete Ortiz, who is an assistant in the computer lab. I wanted to talk to him because I'm interested in applying for a job in the lab. I asked Pete if he liked working there, and he told me he liked it most of the time . . .

C | *Check your work. Use the Editing Checklist.*

Editing Checklist

Did you use . . . ?
- ☐ *if* or ***whether*** in indirect *yes / no* questions
- ☐ question words in indirect *wh-* questions
- ☐ statement word order for all indirect questions
- ☐ a period at the end of indirect questions

A | Circle the correct punctuation mark or words to complete the sentences.

1. She asked what my name was ./?

2. He asked me if / do I had work experience.

3. I asked them where was their office / their office was.

4. They asked where I lived / did I live.

5. They asked me why had I / I had left my last job.

B | Rewrite the direct questions in parentheses as indirect questions. (The direct questions were asked a few months ago).

1. They asked _____
   (Who did the company hire?)

2. He asked me _____
   (Did you take the job?)

3. She wanted to know _____
   (Do you like your present job?)

4. He asked me _____
   (Who is your boss?)

5. I asked _____
   (How many employees work here?)

6. They wanted to know _____
   (Why do you want to change jobs?)

7. I asked _____
   (What's the starting salary?)

8. They wanted to know _____
   (Can you start soon?)

C | Find and correct seven mistakes. Remember to check punctuation.

They asked me so many questions! They asked me where did I work. They asked who was my boss. They asked why I did want to change jobs. They asked how much money I made. They ask me who I have voted for in the last election. They even asked me what my favorite color was? Finally, I asked myself whether or no I really wanted that job!

29 Embedded Questions
TRAVEL TIPS

Before You Read

Look at the cartoon. Discuss the questions.

1. What is unusual about the vending machine?
2. What is the man worried about?

Read

Read the interview about tipping from World Travel (WT) *magazine.*

THE TIP: Who? When? and How much?

I n China it used to be illegal, in New
Zealand it's uncommon, but in
Germany it's included in the bill. In the
United States and Canada it's common,
but it isn't logical: You tip the person who
delivers flowers, but not the person who
delivers a package.

Do *you* often wonder **what to do** about
tipping? *We* do, so to help us through the
tipping maze[1] we interviewed author
Irene Frankel. Her book, *Tips on Tipping:
The Ultimate Guide to* **Who**, **When**, *and*
How Much to Tip answers all your
questions about this complicated practice.

TIPS ACCEPTED

JUICE   COLA

CANDY

"I wonder **how much we should give**."

WT: Tell me **why you decided to write a
book about tipping**.

IF: I began writing it for people from
cultures where tipping isn't a
custom. But when I started

researching, I found that Americans
were also unsure **how to tip**, so *Tips*
became a book to clarify tipping
practices for people traveling to the
U.S. *and* for people living here.

---

[1]*maze:* something that is complicated and hard to understand

(continued on next page)

THE TIP: Who? When? and How much?

WT: Does your book explain **who to tip?**

IF: Oh, absolutely. It tells you **who to tip**, **how much to tip**, and **when to tip**. And equally important, it tells you **when not to tip**.

WT: That *is* important. Suppose[2] I don't know **whether to tip someone**, and I left your book at home. Is it OK to ask?

IF: Sure. If you don't know **whether to leave a tip**, the best thing to do is ask. People usually won't tell you **what to do**, but they *will* tell you **what most customers do**.

WT: I always wonder **what to do when I get bad service**. Should I still tip?

IF: Don't tip the ordinary amount, but tip *something* so that the service person doesn't think that you just forgot to leave a tip.

WT: That makes sense. Here's another thing I've always wondered about. Is there any reason **why we tip a restaurant server but we don't a flight attendant?**

IF: Not that I know. The rules for tipping in the United States aren't very logical, and there are often contradictions in who we tip.

WT: Another thing—I've never really understood **why a restaurant tip depends on the amount of the bill rather than on the amount of work involved in serving the meal**. After all, bringing out a $20 dish of food involves the same amount of work as carrying out a $5 plate.

IF: You're right. It makes no sense. That's just the way it is.

WT: One last question. Suppose I'm planning a trip to Egypt. Tell me **how I can learn about tipping customs in that country**.

IF: There are a number of Internet sites where you can learn **what the rules are for tipping in each country**. The *World Travel* site is always reliable. You can also find that information in travel books for the country you're planning to visit.

WT: Well, thanks for all the good tips! I know our readers will find them very helpful. *I* certainly did.

IF: Thank *you*.

[2]*suppose:* to imagine that something is true and its possible results; a way to ask "What if . . . ?"

After You Read

A | **Vocabulary:** *Match the words with their definitions.*

_____ 1. clarify

_____ 2. custom

_____ 3. ultimate

_____ 4. logical

_____ 5. ordinary

_____ 6. depend on

    a. not unusual

    b. reasonable and sensible

    c. a traditional way of doing something

    d. to make clear

    e. to be affected by

    f. best

B | **Comprehension:** *Circle the word or phrase that best completes each sentence.*

1. *Tips on Tipping* is a guide to tipping customs in restaurants / Egypt / the United States.

2. A question that is NOT mentioned in the interview is: "How much / Who / Why should I tip?"

3. If you're not sure whether to tip, it's OK to ask Irene Frankel / the server / a customer.

4. When you get bad service, Frankel says to leave no / a smaller / the normal tip.

5. In the U.S., tipping customs are logical / required by law / often not logical.

6. To learn about tipping customs in Mexico, read *Tips on Tipping* / a travel website / this interview.

STEP 2 GRAMMAR PRESENTATION

EMBEDDED QUESTIONS

Direct *Yes / No* Question	Main Clause	Embedded *Yes / No* Question
Did I leave the right tip?	I don't know	*if* **I left** the right tip.
	Can you tell me	*if* **I left** the right tip?
Was five dollars enough?	I wonder	*whether* (*or not*) **five dollars was** enough.
	Do you know	*whether* (*or not*) **five dollars was** enough?
Should we leave a tip?	We're not sure	*whether* (*or not*) **to leave** a tip.

Direct *Wh-* Question	Main Clause	Embedded *Wh-* Question
Who is our server?	I don't know	*who* **our server is.**
	Can you tell me	*who* **our server is?**
Why didn't he leave a tip?	I wonder	*why* **he didn't leave** a tip.
	Do you know	*why* **he didn't leave** a tip?
How much should we give the taxi driver?	We're not sure	*how much* **to give** the taxi driver.

GRAMMAR NOTES

1 | **Embedded questions** are questions that are inside another sentence. An embedded question can be:
- inside a **statement**
- inside **another question**

BE CAREFUL! If the embedded question is inside a **statement**, use a **period** at the end of the sentence.
If the embedded question is inside a **question**, use a **question mark** at the end of the sentence.

- I don't know **who our server is**.
- Do you remember **who our server is**?

- I wonder **if that's our server**.
  Not: I wonder if that's our server?

- Do you know **if that's our server**?

---

2 | Use **embedded questions** to:

- **express** something you **do not know**

- **ask** for **information** in a **more polite** way

DIRECT QUESTION	EMBEDDED QUESTION
Why didn't he tip her?	I don't know **why he didn't tip her**.
Is the tip included?	Can you tell me **if the tip is included**?

---

3 | There are **two kinds of embedded questions**.

a. embedded *yes / no* questions
The direct questions are *yes / no* questions.

Begin **embedded *yes / no* questions** with *if*, *whether*, or *whether or not*.

USAGE NOTE: *Whether* is more **formal** than *if*.

DIRECT QUESTION	EMBEDDED QUESTION
Did they **deliver** the pizza?	I don't know **if they delivered the pizza**.

- Do you know **if they delivered the pizza**?

- Do you know **whether they delivered the pizza**? OR
- Do you know **whether or not they delivered the pizza**?

b. embedded *wh-* questions
The direct questions are *wh-* questions.

Begin **embedded *wh-* questions** with a **wh- word** (*who, what, which, whose, when, where, why, how, how many, how much*).

DIRECT QUESTION	EMBEDDED QUESTION
Who delivered the pizza?	I don't know **who delivered the pizza**.

- I wonder **who our server is**.
- Do you know **when the restaurant closes**?
- Many tourists wonder **how much they should tip their restaurant server**.

4

Use **statement word order** (**subject** + **verb**), not question word order, for all embedded questions:

a. embedded *yes / no* questions

b. embedded *wh-* questions about the **subject**

c. embedded *wh-* questions about the **object**

d. embedded *wh-* questions with *when*, *where*, *why*, *how*, *how much*, or *how many*

REMEMBER: Do NOT use question word order and auxiliary verbs *do*, *does*, or *did* in embedded questions.
Do NOT leave out *if* or *whether* in embedded *yes / no* questions.

BE CAREFUL! If a direct question about the subject has the form *be* + **noun**, then the embedded question has the form **noun** + **be**.

SUBJECT	VERB
Eva ordered	pizza.

DIRECT QUESTION	EMBEDDED QUESTION
Did Eva order pizza?	Do you know *if* **Eva ordered** pizza?
Who ordered pizza?	I can't remember *who* **ordered** pizza.
What does it cost?	Can you tell me *what* **it costs**?
When do they open?	Do you know *when* **they open**?

- I wonder *why* **they ordered** pizza.
  NOT: I wonder why ~~did they order~~ pizza.

- I don't know *if* **they ordered** pizza.
  NOT: I don't know ~~did they order~~ pizza.

DIRECT QUESTION	EMBEDDED QUESTION
Who *is* **our server**?	Do you know who **our server** *is*?
	NOT: Do you know who ~~is our server~~?
Is **our order** ready?	Do you know if **our order** *is* ready?
	NOT: Do you know ~~is our order~~ ready?

5

In embedded questions, you can also use:

- **question word** + **infinitive**

- *whether* + **infinitive**

BE CAREFUL! Do **NOT use the infinitive** after *if* or *why*.

- Let's ask where we should leave the tip. OR
- Let's ask *where* **to leave** the tip.

- I wonder whether I should leave a tip. OR
- I wonder *whether* **to leave** a tip.

- I don't understand *why* **I should tip**.
  NOT: I don't understand why ~~to tip~~.

6

Embedded questions often **follow these phrases**:

STATEMENTS:

I don't know . . .   *I'm not sure . . .*
I don't understand . . .   *I wonder . . .*
I'd like to know . . .   *Let's ask . . .*

QUESTIONS:

Do you know . . . ?   *Can you tell me . . . ?*
Can you remember . . . ?   *Could you explain . . . ?*

- *I don't know* what the name of the restaurant is.
- *I wonder* what time the restaurant closes.
- *Let's ask* what today's specials are.

- *Do you know* how much the shrimp costs?
- *Could you explain* what that sign means?

REFERENCE NOTE

For a list of **phrases introducing embedded questions**, see Appendix 16 on page A-5.

EXERCISE 1: Discover the Grammar

Read the advertisement for Tips on Tipping. *Underline the embedded questions.*

Tips on Tipping

This book is for you if . . .

- you've ever avoided a situation just because you didn't know <u>how much to tip</u>.
- you've ever realized (too late) that you were supposed to offer a tip.
- you've ever given a huge tip and then wondered if a tip was necessary at all.
- you've ever needed to know how to calculate the right tip instantly.
- you're new to the United States and you're not sure who you should tip here.
- you'd like to learn how tipping properly can get you the best service for your money.

What readers are saying . . .

"Essential, reliable information—I can't imagine how I got along without it."
—*Chris Sarton, Minneapolis, Minnesota*

"Take *Tips* along if you want a stress-free vacation."
—*Midori Otaka, Osaka, Japan*

"I took my fiancée to dinner at Deux Saisons and knew exactly how to tip everyone!"
—*S. Prasad, San Francisco, California*

"You need this book—whether you stay in hostels or five-star hotels."
—*Cuno Pumpin, Bern, Switzerland*

Send for the ultimate guide to tipping and get all the answers to your tipping questions.

- ✂ - -

Yes! I want to learn who to tip, when to tip, and how much to tip. Please send me additional information on *Tips on Tipping*. I understand that the book will be $4.95 plus $2.00 postage and handling for each copy. (New York residents: Add sales tax.) Contact Martin Unlimited, Inc. at dmifdmif@yahoo.com.

EXERCISE 2: Embedded Questions

(Grammar Notes 1–4, 6)

Complete this travel column about tipping customs around the world. Change the direct questions in parentheses to embedded questions. Use correct punctuation.

Tipping customs vary, so travelers should find out who, where, and how much to tip. Here are some frequently asked questions.

Q: Can you tell me whether *I should tip in Canada?*

1. **(Should I tip in Canada?)**

A: Yes. Tipping practices in Canada are similar to those in the United States.

Q: I know that most restaurants and cafés in France include a service charge. Could you explain

_____

2. **(How can I tell if the tip is included in the bill?)**

A: Look for the phrase *service compris* (service included) on the bill.

Q: I'm going to China next month. I understand that tipping used to be illegal there. Do you know

_____

3. **(Will restaurant servers accept tips now?)**

A: It depends on where you are. In large cities, you can leave 3 percent in a restaurant. In small cities, your tip may not be accepted.

Q: On a recent trip to Iceland, I found that most service people refused tips. Could you explain

_____

4. **(Why did this happen?)**

A: In Iceland, people often feel insulted by tips. Just say thank you—that's enough.

Q: I'm going on an eco tour[1] of Costa Rica. The guides are professional naturalists.[2] I'm not sure

_____

5. **(Should I offer them a tip or not?)**

A: Professional guides should get $10–$15 per day. Remember, your guide's knowledge will turn an ordinary experience into an extraordinary one.

Q: My husband and I are planning a trip to several cities in Australia and New Zealand. Please tell us

_____

6. **(Who expects a tip and who doesn't?)**

A: Restaurant servers expect a tip of 10 percent, but you don't need to tip taxi drivers.

Q: I'm moving to Japan, and I have a lot of luggage. I'm finding some contradictions on travel websites. One says not to tip in Japan, but another says to tip airport porters. Could you tell me

_____

7. **(Is it the custom to tip airport and train porters?)**

A: There's a fixed fee[3] per bag for airport porters, not a tip. Most train stations don't have porters. We recommend shipping your luggage from the airport. I hope that clarifies things!

---

[1] *eco tour:* a trip to see natural places such as rainforests and the animals and plants there
[2] *naturalist:* a professional who studies nature
[3] *fixed fee:* a price that does not change

EXERCISE 3: Embedded Questions

(Grammar Notes 1–4, 6)

Two foreign exchange students are visiting Rome, Italy. Complete their conversations. Choose the appropriate questions from the list and change them to embedded questions. Use correct punctuation.

- How much are we supposed to tip the taxi driver?
- Could we rent a car and drive there?
- Do they have tour buses that go there?
- How much does the subway cost?
- How far are you going?
- How are we going to choose?
- How much does a bus tour cost?
- What did they put in the sauce?
- Where is the Forum?
- ~~Where is it?~~

Rome: the Forum

DRIVER: Where do you want to go? The airport?

MARTINA: The Hotel Forte. Do you know *where it is?* _____
                                                                    1.

DRIVER: Sure. Get in and I'll take you there.

MARTINA: *(whispering)* Do you know _____
                                                              2.

MIUKI: According to the book, the custom is to leave 10 to 15 percent. I've got it.

★ ★ ★ ★ ★

MARTINA: There's so much to see in Rome. I don't know _____
                                                                       3.

MIUKI: We could take a bus tour of the city first, and then decide.

MARTINA: Does the guidebook say _____
                                                          4.

MIUKI: Yeah. About $15 per person, plus tips for the guide and the driver.

★ ★ ★ ★ ★

MARTINA: That was delicious.

MIUKI: Let's try to find out _____
                                                  5.

MARTINA: It tasted like it had a lot of garlic and basil. I'll ask the server.

★ ★ ★ ★ ★

MARTINA: Excuse me. Can you tell me _____
                                                            6.

OFFICER: Sure. Just turn right and go straight.

★ ★ ★ ★ ★

Miuki: Let's take the subway. Do you know _____
                                                                    7.

Martina: It's not expensive. I don't think it depends on _____
                                                                                      8.

★ ★ ★ ★ ★

Martina: I'd like to visit Ostia Antica. It's supposed to be like the ruins at Pompeii.

Miuki: I wonder _____
                                                    9.

Martina: I really don't want to go with a big group of people. What about you? Do you think

_____
                        10.

Miuki: Good idea! It'll be nice to drive around and see some of the countryside too.

EXERCISE 4: Question Word + Infinitive   *(Grammar Note 5)*

Complete the conversation between Martina and Miuki. Use a question word and the infinitive form of the verbs from the box.

| figure out | get | go | invite | leave | ~~wear~~ |

Martina: I can't decide ____*what to wear*____ Friday night.
                                                1.

Miuki: Your red dress. You always look great in it. By the way, where are you going?

Martina: Trattoria da Luigi. It's Janek's birthday, so I wanted to take him someplace special—not

just the ordinary places we usually go to. We're meeting there at 8:00.

Miuki: Great! You know _____ there, don't you?
                                                    2.

Martina: Yes, but I'm not sure _____.
                                                            3.

Miuki: Leave at 7:30. That'll give you enough time.

Martina: I'd like to take Janek someplace for dessert afterward, but I don't know

_____.
                        4.

Miuki: The desserts at da Luigi's are supposed to be pretty good.

Martina: Oh. By the way, since it's Janek's birthday, I'm paying. But I'm still not quite sure

_____ the tip.
                        5.

Miuki: Service is usually included in Italy. The menu should tell you. So, who else is going?

Martina: Well, I thought about asking a few people to join us, but I really didn't know

_____.
                        6.

Miuki: Don't worry. I'm sure it will be fine with just the two of you.

EXERCISE 5: Editing

Read this post to a travelers' website. There are ten mistakes in the use of embedded questions. The first mistake is already corrected. Find and correct nine more. Don't forget to check punctuation.

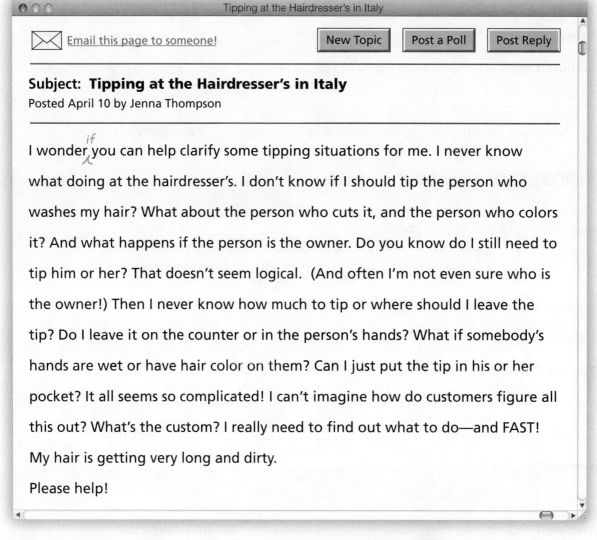

○ ○ ○   Tipping at the Hairdresser's in Italy

✉ Email this page to someone!   [New Topic] [Post a Poll] [Post Reply]

Subject: Tipping at the Hairdresser's in Italy
Posted April 10 by Jenna Thompson

I wonder ^if^ you can help clarify some tipping situations for me. I never know what doing at the hairdresser's. I don't know if I should tip the person who washes my hair? What about the person who cuts it, and the person who colors it? And what happens if the person is the owner. Do you know do I still need to tip him or her? That doesn't seem logical. (And often I'm not even sure who is the owner!) Then I never know how much to tip or where should I leave the tip? Do I leave it on the counter or in the person's hands? What if somebody's hands are wet or have hair color on them? Can I just put the tip in his or her pocket? It all seems so complicated! I can't imagine how do customers figure all this out? What's the custom? I really need to find out what to do—and FAST! My hair is getting very long and dirty.

Please help!

I wonder how much I should tip.

EXERCISE 6: Listening

A | *A travel agent is being interviewed on a call-in radio show about tipping. Read the sentences. Then listen to the callers' questions. Listen again and check (✓)* **True** *or* **False** *for each statement. Correct the false statements.*

	True	False
1. Where Caller One comes from, people usually ~~leave a 10% tip.~~ *don't leave a tip*	☐	☑
2. Caller Two thinks that she often tips taxi drivers too much.	☐	☐
3. Caller Three wants to know how much to tip the server.	☐	☐
4. Caller Four plans to go to the theater in France.	☐	☐
5. Caller Five is annoyed about the service he got in a restaurant.	☐	☐
6. Caller Six wants to know whether to tip the person who washes her hair.	☐	☐
7. Caller Seven needs cultural information for his business trip.	☐	☐
8. Caller Eight is planning to order a pizza after he hangs up.	☐	☐

B | *Listen again to the callers' questions. Then circle the letter of the correct response to each caller's question.*

1. **Caller One**
   a. between 15 and 20 percent of the bill
   b. the server

2. **Caller Two**
   a. about 15 percent of the fare
   b. only if you are happy with the ride

3. **Caller Three**
   a. before you leave
   b. on the table

4. **Caller Four**
   a. the person who takes you to your seat
   b. one euro for one person; two euros for two or more people

5. **Caller Five**
   a. the manager
   b. don't leave a tip

6. **Caller Six**
   a. one dollar
   b. at the cashier

7. **Caller Seven**
   a. Look it up on the Internet.
   b. It's included in the bill.

8. **Caller Eight**
   a. at least three dollars
   b. the person who delivers your food

EXERCISE 7: Pronunciation

A | *Read and listen to the Pronunciation Note.*

> **Pronunciation Note**
>
> In **direct *wh-* questions**, the voice usually **falls** at the end.
>
> **EXAMPLE:** How much should we tip?
>
> When a ***wh-* question** is **embedded inside a *yes / no* question**, the voice usually **rises** at the end.
>
> **EXAMPLE:** Do you know how much we should tip?

B | *Listen to the short conversations. Draw a rising arrow (↗) or a falling arrow (↘) over the end of each question.*

1. **BRAD:** Do you know when Lily's birthday is?

   EMMA: I think it's next week.

2. **BRAD:** Where should we take her?

   EMMA: Let's take her to True Blue Café.

3. **EMMA:** Can you remember where you took me last year?

   BRAD: I think it was Rustica. I bet she'd love that place.

4. **LILY:** What's the soup of the day?

   SERVER: Today it's tomato soup.

5. **LILY:** Do you know which salad you're going to order?

   BRAD: They make a great vegetable salad here.

6. **EMMA:** Could you tell me what's in the hollandaise sauce?

   SERVER: Certainly. It's made with egg yolks, butter, and lemon juice.

7. **EMMA:** Why is our server taking so long?

   BRAD: Here he comes now!

EXERCISE 8: Information Gap: Eating Out

Work in groups of three. Students A and B are customers in a restaurant. Student C is the server. **Students A and B,** *look at the menu.* **Student C,** *go to page 476 and follow the instructions there.*

Trattoria da Luigi

English version

Appetizers
Bruschetta	€1.25
Roasted vegetables	3.25

FIRST COURSE
Soup of the day (*please ask*)	€2.95
Caesar salad	3.25
Luigi's salad	2.95
Linguine with clam sauce	10.80
Spaghetti da Luigi	12.90

SECOND COURSE
Chicken
Chicken da Luigi	€7.95
Half roasted chicken	6.95

Beef
Veal parmigiano	€15.90
Steak frites	12.90

Fish
Catch of the day (*please ask*)	price varies
Shrimp marinara	€15.80
Filet of sole with sauce Dijon	13.90

Side Dishes
Vegetable of the day	€2.50
Roasted potatoes	2.50

Desserts
Fruit tart (in season)	€4.30
Ice cream	3.40
Chocolate cake	2.50
Fresh fruit	2.95
Dessert of the day (*please ask*)	price varies

Service Charge Not Included

Student A, *you are allergic to tomatoes and dairy products.* **Student B,** *you don't eat meat or chicken. Discuss the menu with your partner. Then ask your server about items on the menu and order a meal. When you get the check, figure out a 20 percent tip.*

EXAMPLE: **A:** Do you know what's in a Caesar salad?
B: Not really. We'll have to ask the server. Excuse me. Can you tell us what's in the Caesar salad?
C: Sure. It has lettuce, parmesan cheese, and croutons.

EXERCISE 9: Discussion

Work in small groups. Discuss these questions.

1. Do you think tipping is a good system? Why or why not?
2. Were you ever in a situation where you didn't know what to do about a tip? What did you do?
3. How do people tip in your country and in other countries you know?

EXAMPLE: **A:** I'm not sure whether tipping is good or not. I think people should get paid enough so that they don't have to count on tips to live.
           B: I wonder if you would still get good service if the tip were included.
           C: Sure you would. A service charge is included in a lot of countries, and the service is still good.

EXERCISE 10: What About You?

A | *Think about the first time you did something—such as the following:*

- traveled to a foreign country
- went on a job interview
- drove a car
- became a parent

B | *Work in pairs. Discuss what problems you had.*

EXAMPLE: **A:** I remember the first time I went to a restaurant in Italy. I didn't know how to get the server's attention.
           B: I didn't know whether to tip or not.

EXERCISE 11: Role Play: Information Please!

*Work in pairs (A and B). **Student A**, you are a desk clerk at a hotel. **Student B**, you are a guest at the hotel. Use embedded questions to find out information about the following:*

- restaurants
- interesting sights
- transportation
- entertainment
- banks
- shopping
- tipping
- laundry

EXAMPLE: **A:** Can I help you?
           B: Yes. Could you tell me where to find a good, inexpensive restaurant around here?
           A: There are some nice restaurants around the university.

EXERCISE 12: Writing

A | *Write a paragraph about a situation that confused or surprised you. It could be a time when you were traveling or another unfamiliar situation. Use embedded questions.*

EXAMPLE: When I was an exchange student in China, my Chinese friends always wanted to know how old I was. I couldn't understand why my new friends needed to know my age. I wasn't sure whether to tell the truth, because I was younger than them . . .

B | *Check your work. Use the Editing Checklist.*

Editing Checklist

Did you use . . . ?
- ☐ *if*, *whether (or not)*, or a **wh-** word to begin an embedded question
- ☐ statement word order (**subject** + **verb**) for embedded questions
- ☐ correct punctuation at the end of sentences with embedded questions

---

Student C, read the notes about today's menu.

Trattoria da Luigi

Appetizers
Bruschetta (toasted bread with chopped tomatoes, garlic, olive oil)
Roasted vegetables (onions, red pepper, zucchini, eggplant)

FIRST COURSE
Soup of the day
Monday: vegetable soup (carrots, peas, string beans in a tomato broth)
Tuesday: tomato soup
Wednesday: pea soup
Thursday: onion soup
Friday: fish soup
Saturday: potato soup (includes cream)

Caesar salad (lettuce, parmesan cheese,
croutons—cubes of bread toasted in olive oil and garlic)
Luigi's salad (spinach, mushrooms, tomatoes, onions)
Spaghetti da Luigi (spaghetti with spinach, fresh
tomatoes, and mushrooms in a light cream sauce)

SECOND COURSE
Chicken da Luigi (chicken baked in a tomato sauce
with olives and basil)
Steak frites (steak cooked in pan with butter,
served with french fried potatoes)
Catch of the day: grilled flounder—€6.95
Shrimp marinara (shrimp in tomato sauce)
Filet of sole with sauce Dijon (mustard sauce)

Side Dishes
Vegetable of the day: broccoli

Desserts
Fruit tart (cherry, apple, blueberry)
Ice cream (chocolate, strawberry, vanilla)
Fresh fruit (apples, bananas, strawberries)
Dessert of the day: strawberry shortcake (yellow cake
with fresh strawberries and whipped cream—€3.25)

Answer your customers' questions. When they are done ordering, look at the menu on
page 473. *Write up a check. Include the items ordered and the prices. Use your own paper.*

EXAMPLE: **A:** Do you know what's in a Caesar salad?
B: Not really. We'll have to ask the server. Excuse me. Can you tell us what's in the Caesar salad?
C: Sure. It has lettuce, parmesan cheese, and croutons.

Check your answers on page UR-8.

Do you need to review anything?

A | Circle the correct words and punctuation marks to complete the sentences.

1. I wonder whether <u>should we / we should</u> tip the driver.

2. Do you remember who <u>is our server / our server is</u>?

3. I don't know why she ordered pizza <u>? / .</u>

4. Let's ask how <u>can we / to</u> get to the museum.

5. I wonder if <u>to / I should</u> take a taxi.

6. Can you tell me whether I need to tip the owner of a hair salon <u>? / .</u>

7. I'm not sure <u>whether / did</u> they read the tipping book.

B | Rewrite the questions in parentheses to complete the embedded questions. Use correct punctuation.

1. Can you remember _____
   (Where is the restaurant?)

2. I don't know _____
   (Does the subway go to the museum?)

3. We're not sure _____
   (Should we tip the porter?)

4. I can't imagine _____
   (Why didn't we buy the book on tipping?)

5. Let's ask _____
   (How much should we tip the tour guide?)

6. I'd like to know _____
   (Do you have any travel books?)

7. Could you explain _____
   (What does this sign say?)

C | Find and correct six mistakes. Remember to check punctuation.

A: Hi. Is this a good time to call? I wasn't sure what time you have dinner?

B: This is fine. I didn't know were you back from your trip.

A: We got back two days ago. I can't remember did I email you some photographs.

B: Yes. They were great. Can you tell me where took you that picture of the lake? I want to go!

A: Hmm. I'm not sure which one was that. We saw a lot of lakes in Switzerland.

B: I'll show it to you. I'd really like to find out where is it.

From Grammar to Writing

USING DIRECT AND INDIRECT SPEECH

A letter of complaint often includes both direct and indirect speech to describe a problem. We use **direct speech** only when it is important (**for 100 percent accuracy**) to report someone's exact words or to communicate a speaker's attitude. Otherwise, we use indirect speech.

1 | *Read this letter of complaint. Underline once examples of indirect speech. Underline twice examples of direct speech.*

Computer Town, Inc.
Customer Service Department
One Swell Way
Dallas, TX 75201

Dear Customer Service Manager:

In September 2012, I purchased a computer from your company. After the one-year warranty expired, I bought an extended service contract every year. I always received a renewal notice in the mail that told me that my policy was going to expire in a few weeks. This year, however, I did not receive the notice, and, as a result, I missed the deadline.

Upon realizing this mistake, I immediately called your company and asked if I could renew the service contract. The representative said, "It's too late, Miss." He said that if I wanted to extend my contract, the company would have to send someone to my home to inspect my computer. He also told me I would have to pay $160 for this visit. He said that my only other option was to ship my computer back to the company for inspection. I told him that neither of these options was acceptable.

When I asked him why I hadn't been notified that my contract was going to expire, he said, "We don't send notices out anymore." I said that I wanted to make a complaint. He said, "Don't complain to me. I don't even park the cars of the people who make these decisions." I think that your representatives should be more polite when speaking

---

to customers. I also think that your customers should have been told that they would no longer receive renewal notices in the mail. That way, I would not have missed the deadline. I would, therefore, greatly appreciate it if I could have my service contract renewed without having to go through the inconvenience and expense of having my computer inspected.

Thank you for your attention.

Sincerely yours,

Anne Marie Clarke

Anne Marie Clarke
Customer No. 5378593

2 | *Look at the letter in Exercise 1. Circle the correct words to complete these sentences. Give an example of each item.*

1. The word *that* often introduces direct / (indirect) speech.

He told me that my policy was going to expire in a few weeks.

2. Use quotation marks for direct / indirect speech.

_____

3. Put final punctuation inside / outside the quotation marks.

_____

4. Don't use a comma before direct / indirect speech.

_____

5. Capitalize the first word of direct / indirect speech.

_____

6. You can leave out the word *that* / question word when it introduces an indirect statement.

_____

7. The writer used direct / indirect speech to show that the representative was rude.

_____

3 | *Before you write . . .*

    1. Think of an incident you would like to complain about, or make one up.

    2. Work with a partner. Discuss each other's incidents and ask questions. Talk about where to use direct speech most effectively.

4 | *Write your letter of complaint. Remember to use indirect speech, and, if appropriate, direct speech. Be sure to capitalize and punctuate correctly.*

5 | *Exchange letters with a different partner. Then answer the following questions.*

	Yes	No
1. Do you understand the writer's complaint?	☐	☐
2. Did the writer choose direct speech to show the other person's attitude?	☐	☐
3. Did the writer choose direct speech for 100 percent accuracy?	☐	☐
4. Did the writer use quotation marks for direct speech only?	☐	☐
5. Is the direct speech punctuated correctly?	☐	☐

6 | *Work with your partner. Discuss each other's editing questions from Exercise 5. Then rewrite your own letter and make any necessary corrections.*

APPENDICES

1 Irregular Verbs

Base Form	Simple Past	Past Participle
arise	arose	arisen
awake	awoke	awoken
be	was/were	been
beat	beat	beaten/beat
become	became	become
begin	began	begun
bend	bent	bent
bet	bet	bet
bite	bit	bitten
bleed	bled	bled
blow	blew	blown
break	broke	broken
bring	brought	brought
build	built	built
burn	burned/burnt	burned/burnt
burst	burst	burst
buy	bought	bought
catch	caught	caught
choose	chose	chosen
cling	clung	clung
come	came	come
cost	cost	cost
creep	crept	crept
cut	cut	cut
deal	dealt	dealt
dig	dug	dug
dive	dived/dove	dived
do	did	done
draw	drew	drawn
dream	dreamed/dreamt	dreamed/dreamt
drink	drank	drunk
drive	drove	driven
eat	ate	eaten
fall	fell	fallen
feed	fed	fed
feel	felt	felt
fight	fought	fought
find	found	found
fit	fit/fitted	fit
flee	fled	fled
fling	flung	flung
fly	flew	flown
forbid	forbade/forbid	forbidden
forget	forgot	forgotten
forgive	forgave	forgiven
freeze	froze	frozen
get	got	gotten/got
give	gave	given
go	went	gone
grind	ground	ground
grow	grew	grown

Base Form	Simple Past	Past Participle
hang	hung*/hanged**	hung*/hanged**
have	had	had
hear	heard	heard
hide	hid	hidden
hit	hit	hit
hold	held	held
hurt	hurt	hurt
keep	kept	kept
kneel	knelt/kneeled	knelt/kneeled
knit	knit/knitted	knit/knitted
know	knew	known
lay	laid	laid
lead	led	led
leap	leaped/leapt	leaped/leapt
leave	left	left
lend	lent	lent
let	let	let
lie (*lie down*)	lay	lain
light	lit/lighted	lit/lighted
lose	lost	lost
make	made	made
mean	meant	meant
meet	met	met
pay	paid	paid
prove	proved	proved/proven
put	put	put
quit	quit	quit
read /rid/	read /rɛd/	read /rɛd/
ride	rode	ridden
ring	rang	rung
rise	rose	risen
run	ran	run
say	said	said
see	saw	seen
seek	sought	sought
sell	sold	sold
send	sent	sent
set	set	set
sew	sewed	sewn/sewed
shake	shook	shaken
shave	shaved	shaved/shaven
shine (*intransitive*)	shone/shined	shone/shined
shoot	shot	shot
show	showed	shown
shrink	shrank/shrunk	shrunk/shrunken
shut	shut	shut
sing	sang	sung
sink	sank/sunk	sunk

* hung = *hung an object*
** hanged = *executed by hanging*

(continued on next page)

Base Form	Simple Past	Past Participle
sit	sat	sat
sleep	slept	slept
slide	slid	slid
speak	spoke	spoken
speed	sped/speeded	sped/speeded
spend	spent	spent
spill	spilled/spilt	spilled/spilt
spin	spun	spun
spit	spit/spat	spat
split	split	split
spread	spread	spread
spring	sprang	sprung
stand	stood	stood
steal	stole	stolen
stick	stuck	stuck
sting	stung	stung
stink	stank/stunk	stunk
strike	struck	struck/stricken
swear	swore	sworn
sweep	swept	swept
swim	swam	swum
swing	swung	swung
take	took	taken
teach	taught	taught
tear	tore	torn
tell	told	told
think	thought	thought
throw	threw	thrown
understand	understood	understood
upset	upset	upset
wake	woke	woken
wear	wore	worn
weave	wove/weaved	woven/weaved
weep	wept	wept
win	won	won
wind	wound	wound
withdraw	withdrew	withdrawn
wring	wrung	wrung
write	wrote	written

2 Non-Action Verbs

EMOTIONS	MENTAL STATES		WANTS AND PREFERENCES	SENSES AND PERCEPTION	APPEARANCE AND VALUE	POSSESSION AND RELATIONSHIP
admire	agree	imagine	desire	feel	appear	belong
adore	assume	know	hope	hear	be	come from (origin)
appreciate	believe	mean	need	notice	cost	contain
care	consider	mind	prefer	observe	equal	have
detest	disagree	presume	want	perceive	look (seem)	own
dislike	disbelieve	realize	wish	see	matter	possess
doubt	estimate	recognize		smell	represent	
envy	expect	remember		sound	resemble	
fear	feel (believe)	see (understand)		taste	seem	
hate	find (believe)	suppose			signify	
like	forget	suspect			weigh	
love	guess	think (believe)				
miss	hesitate	understand				
regret	hope	wonder				
respect						
trust						

3 Verbs Followed by Gerunds (Base Form of Verb + -ing)

acknowledge	celebrate	endure	give up (stop)	permit	quit	resist
admit	consider	enjoy	go	postpone	recall	risk
advise	delay	escape	imagine	practice	recommend	suggest
allow	deny	excuse	justify	prevent	regret	support
appreciate	detest	explain	keep (continue)	prohibit	report	tolerate
avoid	discontinue	feel like	mention	propose	resent	understand
ban	discuss	finish	mind (object to)			
can't help	dislike	forgive	miss			

4 Verbs Followed by Infinitives (*To* + Base Form of Verb)

afford	can('t) afford	expect	hurry	neglect	promise	volunteer
agree	can't wait	fail	intend	offer	refuse	wait
appear	choose	grow	learn	pay	request	want
arrange	consent	help	manage	plan	seem	wish
ask	decide	hesitate	mean (*intend*)	prepare	struggle	would like
attempt	deserve	hope	need	pretend	swear	yearn

5 Verbs Followed by Object + Infinitive

advise	challenge	encourage	help*	order	remind	urge
allow	choose*	expect*	hire	pay*	request	want*
ask*	convince	forbid	instruct	permit	require	warn
beg*	dare*	force	invite	persuade	teach	wish*
cause	enable	get*	need*	promise*	tell	would like*

*These verbs can also be followed by an infinitive without an object (EXAMPLE: *ask to leave* or *ask someone to leave*).

6 Verbs Followed by Gerunds or Infinitives

begin	forget*	love	start
can't stand	hate	prefer	stop*
continue	like	remember*	try

*These verbs can also be followed by either a gerund or an infinitive, but there is a big difference in meaning.

7 Verb + Preposition Combinations

admit to	choose between	feel like/about	pay for	talk about
advise against	complain about	go along with	plan on	thank s.o. for
apologize for	deal with	insist on	rely on	think about
approve of	decide on	look forward to	resort to	wonder about
believe in	dream about/of	object to	succeed in	worry about

8 Adjective + Preposition Combinations

accustomed to	awful at	concerned about	fed up with	known for	sad about	sorry for/about
afraid of	bad at	content with	fond of	nervous about	safe from	surprised at/about/by
amazed at/by	bored with/by	curious about	glad about	opposed to	satisfied with	terrible at
angry at	capable of	different from	good at	pleased about	shocked at/by	tired of
ashamed of	careful of	excited about	happy about	ready for	sick of	used to
aware of	certain about	famous for	interested in	responsible for	slow at/in	worried about

9 Adjectives Followed by Infinitives

afraid	ashamed	difficult	easy	glad	pleased	reluctant	surprised
alarmed	curious	disappointed	embarrassed	happy	prepared	right	touched
amazed	delighted	distressed	encouraged	hesitant	proud	sad	upset
angry	depressed	disturbed	excited	likely	ready	shocked	willing
anxious	determined	eager	fortunate	lucky	relieved	sorry	wrong

10 Nouns Followed by Infinitives

attempt	desire	offer	price	right
chance	dream	opportunity	promise	time
choice	failure	permission	reason	trouble
decision	need	plan	request	way

11 Irregular Comparisons of Adjectives, Adverbs, and Quantifiers

ADJECTIVE	ADVERB	COMPARATIVE	SUPERLATIVE
bad	badly	worse	the worst
far	far	farther/further	the farthest/furthest
good	well	better	the best
little	little	less	the least
many/a lot of	—	more	the most
much*/a lot of	much*/a lot	more	the most

*Much is usually only used in questions and negative statements.

12 Adjectives that Form the Comparative and Superlative in Two Ways

ADJECTIVE	COMPARATIVE	SUPERLATIVE
common	commoner/more common	commonest/most common
cruel	crueler/more cruel	cruelest/most cruel
deadly	deadlier/more deadly	deadliest/most deadly
friendly	friendlier/more friendly	friendliest/most friendly
handsome	handsomer/more handsome	handsomest/most handsome
happy	happier/more happy	happiest/most happy
likely	likelier/more likely	likeliest/most likely
lively	livelier/more lively	liveliest/most lively
lonely	lonelier/more lonely	loneliest/most lonely
lovely	lovelier/more lovely	loveliest/most lovely
narrow	narrower/more narrow	narrowest/most narrow
pleasant	pleasanter/more pleasant	pleasantest/most pleasant
polite	politer/more polite	politest/most polite
quiet	quieter/more quiet	quietest/most quiet
shallow	shallower/more shallow	shallowest/most shallow
sincere	sincerer/more sincere	sincerest/most sincere
stupid	stupider/more stupid	stupidest/most stupid
true	truer/more true	truest/most true

13 Participial Adjectives

-ed	-ing	-ed	-ing	-ed	-ing
alarmed	alarming	disturbed	disturbing	moved	moving
amazed	amazing	embarrassed	embarrassing	paralyzed	paralyzing
amused	amusing	entertained	entertaining	pleased	pleasing
annoyed	annoying	excited	exciting	relaxed	relaxing
astonished	astonishing	exhausted	exhausting	satisfied	satisfying
bored	boring	fascinated	fascinating	shocked	shocking
confused	confusing	frightened	frightening	surprised	surprising
depressed	depressing	horrified	horrifying	terrified	terrifying
disappointed	disappointing	inspired	inspiring	tired	tiring
disgusted	disgusting	interested	interesting	touched	touching
distressed	distressing	irritated	irritating	troubled	troubling

14 Reporting Verbs

STATEMENTS				INSTRUCTIONS, COMMANDS, REQUESTS, AND INVITATIONS		QUESTIONS
acknowledge	complain	note	state	advise	invite	ask
add	conclude	observe	suggest	ask	order	inquire
admit	confess	promise	tell	caution	say	question
announce	declare	remark	warn	command	tell	want to know
answer	deny	repeat	whisper	demand	urge	wonder
argue	exclaim	reply	write	instruct	warn	
assert	explain	report	yell			
believe	indicate	respond				
claim	maintain	say				
comment	mean	shout				

15 Time Word Changes in Indirect Speech

DIRECT SPEECH		INDIRECT SPEECH
now	→	then
today	→	that day
tomorrow	→	the next day OR the following day OR the day after
yesterday	→	the day before OR the previous day
this week/month/year	→	that week/month/year
last week/month/year	→	the week/month/year before
next week/month/year	→	the following week/month/year

16 Phrases Introducing Embedded Questions

I don't know . . .	I'd like to know . . .	Do you know . . . ?
I don't understand . . .	I want to understand . . .	Do you understand . . . ?
I wonder . . .	I'd like to find out . . .	Can you tell me . . . ?
I'm not sure . . .	We need to find out . . .	Could you explain . . . ?
I can't remember . . .	Let's ask . . .	Can you remember . . . ?
I can't imagine . . .		Would you show me . . . ?
It doesn't say . . .		Who knows . . . ?

17 Verbs and Expressions Used Reflexively

allow yourself	be proud of yourself	enjoy yourself	keep yourself (busy)	remind yourself
amuse yourself	behave yourself	feel sorry for yourself	kill yourself	see yourself
ask yourself	believe in yourself	forgive yourself	look after yourself	take care of yourself
avail yourself of	blame yourself	help yourself	look at yourself	talk to yourself
be hard on yourself	cut yourself	hurt yourself	prepare yourself	teach yourself
be yourself	deprive yourself of	imagine yourself	pride yourself on	tell yourself
be pleased with yourself	dry yourself	introduce yourself	push yourself	treat yourself

18 Transitive Phrasal Verbs

(s.o. = someone   s.t. = something)
- **Separable phrasal verbs** show the object between the verb and the particle: **call** s.o. **up**.
- **Verbs that must be separated** have an asterisk (*): **do** s.t. **over***
- **Inseparable phrasal verbs** show the object after the particle: **carry on** s.t.

REMEMBER: You can put a **noun object** between the verb and the particle of **separable** two-word verbs (*call Jan up* OR *call up Jan*). You <u>must</u> put a **pronoun object** between the verb and the particle of separable verbs (*call her up* NOT ~~call up her~~).

PHRASAL VERB	MEANING	PHRASAL VERB	MEANING
ask s.o. **over***	invite to one's home	**draw** s.t. **together**	unite
block s.t. **out**	stop from passing through (light/ noise)	**dream** s.t. **up**	invent
		drink s.t. **up**	drink completely
blow s.t. **out**	stop burning by blowing air on it	**drop** s.o. or s.t. **off**	take someplace
blow s.t. **up**	1. make explode	**drop out of** s.t.	quit
	2. fill with air (a balloon)	**empty** s.t. **out**	empty completely
	3. make something larger (a photo)	**end up with** s.t.	have an unexpected result
bring s.t. **about**	make happen	**fall for** s.o.	feel romantic love for
bring s.o. or s.t. **back**	return	**fall for** s.t.	be tricked by, believe
bring s.o. **down***	depress	**figure** s.o. or s.t. **out**	understand (after thinking about)
bring s.t. **out**	introduce (a new product/book)	**fill** s.t. **in**	complete with information
bring s.o. **up**	raise (children)	**fill** s.t. **out**	complete (a form)
bring s.t. **up**	bring attention to	**fill** s.t. **up**	fill completely
build s.t. **up**	increase	**find** s.t. **out**	learn information
burn s.t. **down**	burn completely	**fix** s.t. **up**	redecorate (a home)
call s.o. **back***	return a phone call	**follow through with** s.t.	complete
call s.o. **in**	ask for help with a problem	**get** s.t. **across**	get people to understand an idea
call s.t. **off**	cancel	**get off** s.t.	leave (a bus/a train)
call s.o. **up**	contact by phone	**get on** s.t.	board (a bus/a train)
carry on s.t.	continue	**get out of** s.t.	leave (a car/taxi)
carry s.t. **out**	conduct (an experiment/a plan)	**get** s.t. **out of** s.t.*	benefit from
cash in on s.t.	profit from	**get through with** s.t.	finish
charge s.t. **up**	charge with electricity	**get to** s.o. or s.t.	1. reach s.o. or s.t.
check s.t. **out**	examine		2. upset s.o.
cheer s.o. **up**	cause to feel happier	**get together with** s.o.	meet
clean s.o. or s.t. **up**	clean completely	**give** s.t. **away**	give without charging money
clear s.t. **up**	explain	**give** s.t. **back**	return
close s.t. **down**	close by force	**give** s.t. **out**	distribute
come off s.t.	become unattached	**give** s.t. **up**	quit, abandon
come up with s.t.	invent	**go after** s.o. or s.t.	try to get or win, pursue
count on s.o. or s.t.	depend on	**go along with** s.t.	support
cover s.o. or s.t. **up**	cover completely	**go over** s.t.	review
cross s.t. **out**	draw a line through	**hand** s.t. **in**	submit, give work (to a boss/teacher)
cut s.t. **down**	1. bring down by cutting (a tree)		
	2. reduce	**hand** s.t. **out**	distribute
cut s.t. **off**	1. stop the supply of	**hang** s.t. **up**	put on a hook or hanger
	2. remove by cutting	**help** s.o. **out**	assist
cut s.t. **out**	remove by cutting	**hold** s.t. **on**	keep attached
cut s.t. **up**	cut into small pieces	**keep** s.o. or s.t. **away**	cause to stay at a distance
do s.t. **over***	do again	**keep** s.t. **on***	not remove (a piece of clothing/jewelry)
do s.o. or s.t. **up**	make more beautiful		

PHRASAL VERB	MEANING	PHRASAL VERB	MEANING
keep s.o. or s.t. **out**	*prevent from entering*	**show up on** s.t.	*appear*
keep up with s.o. or s.t.	*go as fast as*	**shut** s.t. **off**	*stop (a machine/light)*
lay s.o. **off**	*end employment*	**sign** s.o. **up** (for s.t.)	*register*
lay s.t. **out**	1. *arrange according to a plan*	**start** s.t. **over***	*start again*
	2. *spend money*	**stick with/to** s.o. or s.t.	*not quit, not leave, persevere*
leave s.t. **on**	1. *not turn off (a light/radio)*	**straighten** s.t. **up**	*make neat*
	2. *not remove (a piece of clothing/jewelry)*	**switch** s.t. **on**	*start (a machine/light)*
		take s.t. **away**	*remove*
leave s.t. **out**	*omit, not include*	**take** s.o. or s.t. **back**	*return*
let s.o. **down**	*disappoint*	**take** s.t. **down**	*remove*
let s.o. or s.t. **in**	*allow to enter*	**take** s.t. **in**	1. *notice, understand, and remember*
let s.o. **off**	1. *allow to leave (a bus/car)*		
	2. *not punish*		2. *earn (money)*
let s.o. or s.t. **out**	*allow to leave*	**take** s.t. **off**	*remove*
light s.t. **up**	*illuminate*	**take** s.o. **on**	*hire*
look after s.o. or s.t.	*take care of*	**take** s.t. **on**	*agree to do*
look into s.t.	*research*	**take** s.t. **out**	*borrow from a library*
look s.o. or s.t. **over**	*examine*	**take** s.t. **up**	*begin a job or activity*
look s.t. **up**	*try to find (in a book/on the Internet)*	**talk** s.o. **into***	*persuade*
		talk s.t. **over**	*discuss*
make s.t. **up**	*create*	**team up with** s.o.	*start to work with*
miss out on s.t.	*lose the chance for something good*	**tear** s.t. **down**	*destroy*
		tear s.t. **up**	*tear into small pieces*
move s.t. **around***	*change the location*	**think back on** s.o. or s.t.	*remember*
pass s.t. **out**	*distribute*	**think** s.t. **over**	*consider*
pass s.o. or s.t. **up**	*decide not to use*	**think** s.t. **up**	*invent*
pay s.o. or s.t. **back**	*repay*	**throw** s.t. **away/out**	*discard, put in the trash*
pick s.o. or s.t. **out**	1. *choose*	**touch** s.t. **up**	*improve by making small changes*
	2. *identify*		
pick s.o. or s.t. **up**	*lift*	**try** s.t. **on**	*put clothing on to see if it fits*
pick s.t. **up**	1. *buy, purchase*	**try** s.t. **out**	*use to see if it works*
	2. *get (an idea/an interest)*	**turn** s.t. **around***	*change the direction so the front is at the back*
	3. *answer the phone*		
point s.o. or s.t. **out**	*indicate*	**turn** s.o. **down**	*reject*
put s.t. **away**	*put in an appropriate place*	**turn** s.t. **down**	1. *lower the volume (a TV/radio)*
put s.t. **back**	*return to its original place*		2. *reject (a job/an idea)*
put s.o. or s.t. **down**	*stop holding*	**turn** s.t. **in**	*submit, give work (to a boss/teacher)*
put s.o. **off**	*discourage*		
put s.t. **off**	*delay*	**turn** s.o. or s.t. **into***	*change from one form to another*
put s.t. **on**	*cover the body (with clothes or jewelry)*	**turn** s.o. **off***	*[slang] destroy interest*
		turn s.t. **off**	*stop (a machine), extinguish (a light)*
put s.t. **together**	*assemble*		
put s.t. **up**	*erect*	**turn** s.t. **on**	*start (a machine/light)*
run into s.o.	*meet accidentally*	**turn** s.t. **over**	*turn something so the top side is at the bottom*
see s.t. **through***	*complete*		
send s.t. **back**	*return*	**turn** s.t. **up**	*make louder (a TV/radio)*
send s.t. **out**	*mail*	**use** s.t. **up**	*use completely, consume*
set s.t. **off**	*cause to explode*	**wake** s.o. **up**	*awaken*
set s.t. **up**	1. *prepare for use*	**watch out for** s.o. or s.t.	*be careful about*
	2. *establish (a business/an organization)*	**work** s.t. **off**	*remove by work or activity*
		work s.t. **out**	*solve, understand*
settle on s.t.	*choose s.t. after thinking about many possibilities*	**write** s.t. **down**	*write on a piece of paper*
		write s.t. **up**	*write in a finished form*
show s.o. or s.t. **off**	*display the best qualities*		

Phrasal Verb	Meaning
act up	cause problems
blow up	explode
break down	stop working (a machine)
break out	happen suddenly
burn down	burn completely
call back	return a phone call
catch on	1. become popular
	2. understand
cheer up	make happier
clean up	clean completely
clear up	become clear
close down	stop operating
come about	happen
come along	come with, accompany
come around	happen
come back	return
come down	become less (price)
come in	enter
come off	become unattached
come out	appear
come up	arise
dress up	wear special clothes
drop in	visit by surprise
drop out	quit
eat out	eat in a restaurant
empty out	empty completely
end up	1. do something unexpected or unintended
	2. reach a final place or condition
fall off	become detached
find out	learn information
follow through	complete
fool around	act playful
get ahead	make progress, succeed
get along	have a good relationship
get back	return
get by	survive
get off	1. leave (a bus, the Internet)
	2. end a phone conversation
get on	enter, board (a bus, a train)
get through	finish
get together	meet
get up	rise from bed, arise
give up	quit

Phrasal Verb	Meaning
go away	leave a place or person
go back	return
go down	become less (price, number), decrease
go off	explode (a gun/fireworks)
go on	continue
go out	leave
go over	succeed with an audience
go up	1. be built
	2. become more (price, number), increase
grow up	become an adult
hang up	end a phone call
hold on	1. wait
	2. not hang up the phone
keep away	stay at a distance
keep on	continue
keep out	not enter
keep up	go as fast as
lie down	recline
light up	illuminate
look out	be careful
make up	end a disagreement, reconcile
miss out	lose the chance for something good
pay off	be worthwhile
pick up	improve
play around	have fun
run out	not have enough of
show up	appear
sign up	register
sit down	take a seat
slip up	make a mistake
stand up	rise
start over	start again
stay up	remain awake
straighten up	make neat
take off	depart (a plane)
turn out	have a particular result
turn up	appear
wake up	stop sleeping
watch out	be careful
work out	1. be resolved
	2. exercise

A. Social Modals and Expressions

Function	Modal or Expression	Time	Examples
Ability	can can't	Present	• Sam **can swim**. • He **can't skate**.
	could couldn't	Past	• We **could swim** last year. • We **couldn't skate**.
	be able to* not be able to*	All Verb Forms	• Lea **is able to run** fast. • She **wasn't able to run** fast last year.
Advice	should shouldn't ought to had better** had better not**	Present or Future	• You **should study** more. • You **shouldn't miss** class. • We **ought to leave**. • We**'d better go**. • We**'d better not stay**.
Advisability in the Past and Regret or Blame	should have shouldn't have ought to have could have might have	Past	• I **should have become** a doctor. • I **shouldn't have wasted** time. • He **ought to have told** me. • She **could have gone** to college. • You **might have called**. I waited for hours.
Necessity	have to* not have to*	All Verb Forms	• He **has to go** now. • He **doesn't have to go** yet. • I **had to go** yesterday. • I **will have to go** soon.
	have got to* must	Present or Future	• He**'s got** to leave! • You **must use** a pen for the test.
Permission	can can't could may may not	Present or Future	• **Can** I **sit** here? • **Can** I **call** tomorrow? • Yes, you **can**. • No, you **can't**. Sorry. • **Could** he **leave** now? • **May** I **borrow** your pen? • Yes, you **may**. • No, you **may not**. Sorry.
Prohibition	must not can't	Present or Future	• You **must not drive** without a license. • You **can't drive** without a license.
Requests	can can't could will would	Present or Future	• **Can** you **close** the door, please? • Sure, I **can**. • Sorry, I **can't**. • **Could** you please **answer** the phone? • **Will** you **wash** the dishes, please? • **Would** you please **mail** this letter?

*The meaning of this expression is similar to the meaning of a modal. Unlike a modal, it has -s for third-person singular.

**The meaning of this expression is similar to the meaning of a modal. Like a modal, it has no -s for third-person singular.

FUNCTION	MODAL OR EXPRESSION	TIME	EXAMPLES
Conclusions and Possibility	must must not have to* have got to*	Present	• This **must be** her house. Her name is on the door. • She **must not be** home. I don't see her car. • She **has to know** him. They went to school together. • He's **got to be** guilty. We saw him do it.
	may may not might might not could	Present or Future	• She **may be** home now. • It **may not rain** tomorrow. • Lee **might be sick** today. • He **might not come** to class. • They **could be** at the library. • It **could rain** tomorrow.
	may have may not have might have might not have could have	Past	• They **may have left** already. I don't see them. • They **may not have arrived** yet. • He **might have called.** I'll check my phone messages. • He **might not have left** a message. • She **could have forgotten** to mail the letter.
Impossibility	can't	Present or Future	• That **can't be** Ana. She left for France yesterday. • It **can't snow** tomorrow. It's going to be too warm.
	couldn't	Present	• He **couldn't be** guilty. He wasn't in town when the crime occurred. • The teacher **couldn't give** the test tomorrow. Tomorrow's Saturday.
	couldn't have	Past	• You **couldn't have failed.** You studied so hard.

*The meaning of this expression is similar to the meaning of a modal. Unlike a modal, it has -s for third-person singular.

21 Irregular Plural Nouns

SINGULAR	PLURAL	SINGULAR	PLURAL	SINGULAR	PLURAL	SINGULAR	PLURAL
analysis	analyses	half	halves	person	people	deer	deer
basis	bases	knife	knives	man	men	fish	fish
crisis	crises	leaf	leaves	woman	women	sheep	sheep
hypothesis	hypotheses	life	lives	child	children		
		loaf	loaves	foot	feet		
		shelf	shelves	tooth	teeth		
		wife	wives	goose	geese		
				mouse	mice		

22 Spelling Rules for the Simple Present: Third-Person Singular (*He, She, It*)

1. Add *-s* for most verbs.

work	work**s**
buy	buy**s**
ride	ride**s**
return	return**s**

2. Add *-es* for verbs that end in *-ch*, *-s*, *-sh*, *-x*, or *-z*.

watch	watch**es**
pass	pass**es**
rush	rush**es**
relax	relax**es**
buzz	buzz**es**

3. Change the *y* to *i* and add *-es* when the base form ends in a **consonant** + *y*.

study	stud**ies**
hurry	hurr**ies**
dry	dr**ies**

Do not change the *y* when the base form ends in a vowel + *y*. Add *-s*.

play	play**s**
enjoy	enjoy**s**

4. A few verbs are irregular.

be	**is**
do	**does**
go	**goes**
have	**has**

23 Spelling Rules for Base Form of Verb + *-ing* (Progressive and Gerund)

1. Add *-ing* to the base form of the verb.

read	read**ing**
stand	stand**ing**

2. If the verb ends in a silent *-e*, drop the final *-e* and add *-ing*.

leave	leav**ing**
take	tak**ing**

3. In **one-syllable verbs**, if the last three letters are a consonant-vowel-consonant combination (CVC), double the last consonant and add *-ing*.

```
C V C
↓ ↓ ↓
s i t     sit**ting**

C V C
↓ ↓ ↓
p l a n   plan**ning**
```

4. In verbs of **two or more syllables** that end in a consonant-vowel-consonant combination, double the last consonant only if the last syllable is stressed.*

ad'mit	admit**ting**	*(The last syllable is stressed.)*
'whisper	whisper**ing**	*(The last syllable is not stressed, so don't double the -r.)*

5. If the verb ends in *-ie*, change the *ie* to *y* before adding *-ing*.

die	d**ying**
lie	l**ying**

---

*The symbol ' shows main stress.

Do not double the last consonant in verbs that end in *-w*, *-x*, or *-y*.

sew	sew**ing**
fix	fix**ing**
play	play**ing**

---

24 Spelling Rules for Base Form of Verb + -ed (Simple Past and Past Participle of Regular Verbs)

1. If the verb ends in a consonant, add -ed.

   return   returned
   help   helped

2. If the verb ends in -e, add -d.

   live   lived
   create   created
   die   died

3. In **one-syllable verbs**, if the last three letters are a consonant-vowel-consonant combination (CVC), double the last consonant before adding -ed.

   C V C
   ↓ ↓ ↓
   h o p   hopped

   C V C
   ↓ ↓ ↓
   p l a n   planned

   Do not double the last consonant of one-syllable words ending in -w, -x, or -y.

   bow   bowed
   mix   mixed
   play   played

4. In verbs of **two or more syllables** that end in a consonant-vowel-consonant combination, double the last consonant only if the last syllable is stressed.*

   prefér   preferred   *(The last syllable is stressed, so double the r.)*

   vísit   visited   *(The last syllable is not stressed, don't double the -t.)*

5. If the verb ends in **consonant + y**, change the y to i and add -ed.

   worry   worried
   carry   carried

6. If the verb ends in **vowel + y**, add -ed. (Do not change the y to i.)

   play   played
   annoy   annoyed
   EXCEPTIONS: pay—paid
                   lay—laid
                   say—said

   *The symbol ' shows main stress.

25 Spelling Rules for the Comparative (-er) and Superlative (-est) of Adjectives

1. With **one-syllable** adjectives add -er to form the comparative. Add -est to form the superlative.

   cheap   cheaper   cheapest
   bright   brighter   brightest

2. If the adjective ends in -e, add -r or -st.

   nice   nicer   nicest

3. If the adjective ends in a **consonant + y**, change y to i before you add -er or -est.

   pretty   prettier   prettiest

   EXCEPTION:
   shy   shyer   shyest

4. In one-syllable adjectives, if the last three letters are a consonant-vowel-consonant combination (CVC), double the last consonant before adding -er or -est.

   C V C
   ↓ ↓ ↓
   b i g   bigger   biggest

   Do not double the consonant in words ending in -w or -y.

   slow   slower   slowest
   gray   grayer   grayest

26   Spelling Rules for Adverbs Ending in *-ly*

1. Add *-ly* to the corresponding adjective.

nice	nice**ly**
quiet	quiet**ly**
beautiful	beautifu**lly**

2. If the adjective ends in **consonant** + *y*, change the *y* to *i* before adding *-ly*.

easy	eas**ily**

3. If the adjective ends in *-le*, drop the *e* and add *-y*.

possible	possib**ly**

Do not drop the *e* for other adjectives ending in *-e*.

extreme	extreme**ly**

EXCEPTION:

true	tru**ly**

4. If the adjective ends in *-ic*, add *-ally*.

basic	basic**ally**
fantastic	fantastic**ally**

27   Direct Speech: Punctuation Rules

Direct speech may either follow or come before the reporting verb.

When direct speech follows the reporting verb:
a. Put a comma after the reporting verb.
b. Use opening quotation marks (") before the first word of the direct speech.
c. Begin the quotation with a capital letter.
d. Use the appropriate end punctuation for the direct speech. It may be a period (.), a question mark (?), or an exclamation point (!).
e. Put closing quotation marks (") after the end punctuation of the quotation.

> **EXAMPLES:**   He said, "I had a good time."
>   She asked, "Where's the party?"
>   They shouted, "Be careful!"

When direct speech comes before the reporting verb:
a. Begin the sentence with opening quotation marks (").
b. Use the appropriate end punctuation for the direct speech. If the direct speech is a statement, use a comma (,). If the direct speech is a question, use a question mark (?). If the direct speech is an exclamation, use an exclamation point (!).
c. Use closing quotation marks after the end punctuation for the direct speech (").
d. Begin the reporting clause with a lowercase letter.
e. Use a period at the end of the main sentence (.).

> **EXAMPLES:**   "I had a good time," he said.
>   "Where's the party?" she asked.
>   "Be careful!" they shouted.

28 Pronunciation Table

These are the pronunciation symbols used in this text. Listen to the pronunciation of the key words.

VOWELS

Symbol	Key Word	Symbol	Key Word
i	beat, feed	ə	banana, among
ɪ	bit, did	ɚ	shirt, murder
eɪ	date, paid	aɪ	bite, cry, buy, eye
ɛ	bet, bed	aʊ	about, how
æ	bat, bad	ɔɪ	voice, boy
ɑ	box, odd, father	ɪr	beer
ɔ	bought, dog	ɛr	bare
oʊ	boat, road	ɑr	bar
ʊ	book, good	ɔr	door
u	boot, food, student	ʊr	tour
ʌ	but, mud, mother		

CONSONANTS

Symbol	Key Word	Symbol	Key Word
p	pack, happy	ʃ	ship, machine, station, special, discussion
b	back, rubber		
t	tie	ʒ	measure, vision
d	die	h	hot, who
k	came, key, quick	m	men, some
g	game, guest	n	sun, know, pneumonia
tʃ	church, nature, watch	ŋ	sung, ringing
dʒ	judge, general, major	w	wet, white
f	fan, photograph	l	light, long
v	van	r	right, wrong
θ	thing, breath	y	yes, use, music
ð	then, breathe	t̬	butter, bottle
s	sip, city, psychology		
z	zip, please, goes		

29 Pronunciation Rules for the Simple Present: Third-Person Singular (He, She, It)

1. The third-person singular in the simple present always ends in the letter -s. There are three different pronunciations for the final sound of the third-person singular.

/s/	/z/	/ɪz/
talks	loves	dances

2. The final sound is pronounced /s/ after the voiceless sounds /p/, /t/, /k/, and /f/.

top	tops
get	gets
take	takes
laugh	laughs

3. The final sound is pronounced /z/ after the voiced sounds /b/, /d/, /g/, /v/, /m/, /n/, /ŋ/, /l/, /r/, and /ð/.

describe	describes
spend	spends
hug	hugs
live	lives
bathe	bathes
seem	seems
remain	remains
sing	sings
tell	tells
lower	lowers

4. The final sound is pronounced /z/ after all **vowel sounds**.

agree	agrees
try	tries
stay	stays
know	knows

5. The final sound is pronounced /ɪz/ after the sounds /s/, /z/, /ʃ/, /ʒ/, and /tʃ/. /dʒ/ adds a syllable to the verb.

relax	relaxes
freeze	freezes
rush	rushes
massage	massages
watch	watches
judge	judges

6. Do and say have a change in vowel sound.

do	/du/	does	/dʌz/
say	/seɪ/	says	/sɛz/

30 Pronunciation Rules for the Simple Past and Past Participle of Regular Verbs

1. The regular simple past and past participle always ends in the letter *-d*. There are three different pronunciations for the final sound of the regular simple past and past participle.

/t/	/d/	/ɪd/
ra**ced**	li**ved**	atten**ded**

2. The final sound is pronounced /t/ after the voiceless sounds /**p**/, /**k**/, /**f**/, /**s**/, /**ʃ**/, and /**tʃ**/.

hop	ho**pped**
work	wor**ked**
laugh	lau**ghed**
address	addre**ssed**
publish	publi**shed**
watch	wa**tched**

3. The final sound is pronounced /d/ after the voiced sounds /**b**/, /**g**/, /**v**/, /**z**/, /**ʒ**/, /**dʒ**/, /**m**/, /**n**/, /**ŋ**/, /**l**/, /**r**/, and /**ð**/.

rub	ru**bbed**
hug	hu**gged**
live	li**ved**
surprise	surpri**sed**
massage	massa**ged**
change	chan**ged**
rhyme	rhy**med**
return	retur**ned**
bang	ba**nged**
enroll	enro**lled**
appear	appea**red**
bathe	ba**thed**

4. The final sound is pronounced /**d**/ after all **vowel sounds**.

agree	agr**eed**
play	pl**ayed**
die	d**ied**
enjoy	enj**oyed**
row	r**owed**

5. The final sound is pronounced /**ɪd**/ after /**t**/ and /**d**/. /**ɪd**/ adds a syllable to the verb.

start	star**ted**
decide	deci**ded**

31 Capitalization and Punctuation Rules

	USE FOR . . .	EXAMPLES
capital letter	• the pronoun *I* • proper nouns • the first word of a sentence	Tomorrow **I** will be here at 2:00. His name is **Karl**. He lives in **Germany**. **When** does the train leave? **At** 2:00.
apostrophe (')	• possessive nouns • contractions	Is that **Marta's** coat? **That's** not hers. **It's** mine.
comma (,)	• after items in a list • before sentence connectors *and*, *but*, *or*, and *so* • after the first part of a sentence that begins with *because* • after the first part of a sentence that begins with a preposition • after the first part of a sentence that begins with a time clause or an *if* clause • before and after a non-identifying adjective clause in the middle of a sentence. • before a non-identifying adjective clause at the end of a sentence	He bought **apples, pears, oranges**, and **bananas**. They watched TV, **and** she played video games. **Because it's raining**, we're not walking to work. **Across from the post office**, there's a good restaurant. **After he arrived**, we ate dinner. *If* **it rains**, we won't go. Tony, **who lives in Paris**, emails me every day. I get emails every day from Tony, **who lives in Paris**.
exclamation mark (!)	• at the end of a sentence to show surprise or a strong feeling	You're here! That's great! Stop! A car is coming!
period (.)	• at the end of a statement	Today is Wednesday.
question mark (?)	• at the end of a question	What day is today**?**

GLOSSARY OF GRAMMAR TERMS

action verb   A verb that describes an action.
- *Alicia **ran** home.*

active sentence   A sentence that focuses on the agent (the person or thing doing the action).
- ***Ari kicked** the ball.*

addition   A clause or a short sentence that follows a statement and expresses similarity or contrast with the information in the statement.
- *Pedro is tall, **and so is Alex**.*
- *Trish doesn't like sports. **Neither does her sister**.*

adjective   A word that describes a noun or pronoun.
- *It's a **good** plan, and it's not **difficult**.*

adjective clause   A clause that identifies or gives additional information about a noun.
- *The woman **who called you** didn't leave her name.*
- *Samir, **who you met yesterday**, works in the lab.*

adverb   A word that describes a verb, an adjective, or another adverb.
- *She drives **carefully**.*
- *She's a **very** good driver.*
- *She drives **really** well.*

affirmative   A statement or answer meaning *Yes*.
- *He **works**. (affirmative statement)*
- ***Yes**, he **does**. (affirmative short answer)*

agent   The person or thing doing the action in a sentence. In passive sentences, the word *by* is used before the agent.
- *This magazine is published **by National Geographic**.*

article   A word that goes before a noun. The **indefinite** articles are *a* and ***an***.
- *I ate **a** sandwich and **an** apple.*

The **definite** article is ***the***.
- *I didn't like **the** sandwich. **The** apple was good.*

auxiliary verb   (also called **helping verb**) A verb used with a main verb. *Be*, *do*, and *have* are often auxiliary verbs. Modals (*can*, *should*, *may*, *must* . . .) are also auxiliary verbs.
- *I **am** exercising right now.*
- *I **should** exercise every day.*
- ***Do** you like to exercise?*

base form   The simple form of a verb without any endings (*-s, -ed, -ing*) or other changes.
- ***be**, **have**, **go**, **drive***

clause   A group of words that has a subject and a verb. A sentence can have one or more clauses.
- ***We are leaving now.** (one clause)*
- ***If it rains, we won't go.** (two clauses)*

common noun   A word for a person, place, or thing (but not the name of the person, place, or thing).
- *Teresa lives in a **house** near the **beach**.*

comparative   The form of an adjective or adverb that shows the difference between two people, places, or things.
- *Alain is **shorter** than Brendan. (adjective)*
- *Brendan runs **faster** than Alain. (adverb)*

conditional sentence   A sentence that describes a condition and its result. The sentence can be about the past, the present, or the future. The condition and result can be real or unreal.
- *If it **rains**, I **won't go**. (future, real)*
- *If it **had rained**, I **wouldn't have gone**. (past, unreal)*

continuous   See **progressive**.

contraction   A short form of a word or words. An apostrophe (') replaces the missing letter or letters.
- ***she's** = she is*
- ***can't** = cannot*

count noun   A noun that you can count. It has a singular and a plural form.
- *one **book**, two **books***

definite article *the* This article goes before a noun that refers to a specific person, place, or thing.

- *Please bring me **the book** on **the table**. I'm almost finished reading it.*

dependent clause (also called **subordinate clause**) A clause that needs a main clause for its meaning.

- ***If I get home early**, I'll call you.*

direct object A noun or pronoun that receives the action of a verb.

- *Marta kicked **the ball**. I saw **her**.*

direct speech Language that gives the exact words a speaker used. In writing, quotation marks come before and after the speaker's words.

- *"**I saw Bob yesterday**," she said.*
- *"**Is he in school?**"*

embedded question A question that is inside another sentence.

- *I don't know **where the restaurant is**.*
- *Do you know **if it's on Tenth Street**?*

formal Language used in business situations or with adults you do not know.

- *Good afternoon, Mr. Rivera. Please have a seat.*

gerund A noun formed with verb + *-ing* that can be used as a subject or an object.

- ***Swimming** is great exercise.*
- *I enjoy **swimming**.*

helping verb See **auxiliary verb**.

identifying adjective clause A clause that identifies which member of a group the sentence is about.

- *There are 10 students in the class. The student **who sits in front of me** is from Russia.*

if clause The clause that states the condition in a conditional sentence.

- ***If I had known you were here**, I would have called you.*

imperative A sentence that gives a command or instructions.

- ***Hurry!***
- ***Turn left on Main Street.***

indefinite article *a or an* These articles go before a noun that does not refer to a specific person, place, or thing.

- *Can you bring me **a book**? I'm looking for something to read.*

indefinite pronoun A pronoun such as *someone, something, anyone, anything, anywhere, no one, nothing, nowhere, everyone,* and *everything*. An indefinite pronoun does not refer to a specific person, place, or thing.

- ***Someone** called you last night.*
- *Did **anything** happen?*

indirect object A noun or pronoun (often a person) that receives something as the result of the action of the verb.

- *I told **John** the story.*
- *He gave **me** some good advice.*

indirect speech Language that reports what a speaker said without using the exact words.

- *Ann said **she had seen Bob the day before**.*
- *She asked **if he was in school**.*

infinitive *to* + base form of the verb.

- *I want **to leave** now.*

infinitive of purpose *(in order) to* + base form. This form gives the reason for an action.

- *I go to school **(in order) to learn** English.*

informal Language used with family, friends, and children.

- *Hi, Pete. Sit down.*

information question See **wh- question**.

inseparable phrasal verb A phrasal verb whose parts must stay together.

- *We **ran into** Tomás at the supermarket. (Not: We ran Tomás into . . .)*

intransitive verb A verb that does not have an object.

- *She **paints**.*
- *We **fell**.*

irregular A word that does not change its form in the usual way.

- ***good → well***
- ***bad → worse***
- ***go → went***

main clause   A clause that can stand alone as a sentence.
- *I called my friend Tom*, who lives in Chicago.

main verb   A verb that describes an action or state. It is often used with an auxiliary verb.
- *Jared is **calling**.*
- *Does he **call** every day?*

modal   A type of auxiliary verb. It goes before a main verb or stands alone as a short answer. It expresses ideas such as ability, advice, permission, and possibility. *Can, could, will, would, may, might, should,* and *must* are modals.
- ***Can** you swim?*
- *Yes, I **can**.*
- *You really **should** learn to swim.*

negative   A statement or answer meaning *No*.
- *He **doesn't** work.* (negative statement)
- ***No**, he **doesn't**.* (negative short answer)

non-action verb   (also called **stative verb**). A verb that does not describe an action. It describes such things as thoughts, feelings, and senses.
- *I **remember** that word.*
- *Chris **loves** ice cream.*
- *It **tastes** great.*

non-count noun   A noun you usually do not count (*air, water, rice, love . . .*). It has only a singular form.
- *The **rice** is delicious.*

nonidentifying adjective clause   (also called **nonrestrictive adjective clause**) A clause that gives additional information about the noun it refers to. The information is not necessary to identify the noun.
- *My sister Diana, **who usually hates sports**, recently started tennis lessons.*

nonrestrictive adjective clause   See **nonidentifying adjective clause**.

noun   A word for a person, place, or thing.
- *My **sister**, **Anne**, works in an **office**.*
- *She uses a **computer**.*

object   A noun or a pronoun that receives the action of a verb. Sometimes a verb has two objects.
- *Layla threw **the ball**.*
- *She threw **it** to Tom.*
- *She threw **him the ball**.*

object pronoun   A pronoun (*me, you, him, her, it, us, them*) that receives the action of the verb.
- *I gave **her** a book.*
- *I gave **it** to **her**.*

object relative pronoun   A relative pronoun that is an object in an adjective clause.
- *I'm reading a book **that** I really like.*

paragraph   A group of sentences, usually about one topic.

particle   A word that looks like a preposition and combines with a main verb to form a phrasal verb. It often changes the meaning of the main verb.
- *He looked the word **up**.* (He looked for the meaning of the word in the dictionary.)

passive causative   A sentence formed with *have* or *get* + object + past participle. It is used to talk about services that you arrange for someone to do for you.
- *She **had the car checked** at the service station.*
- *He's going to **get his hair cut** by André.*

passive sentence   A sentence that focuses on the object (the person or thing receiving the action). The passive is formed with *be* + past participle.
- ***The ball was kicked** by Ari.*

past participle   A verb form (verb + *-ed*). It can also be irregular. It is used to form the present perfect, past perfect, and future perfect. It can also be an adjective.
- *We've **lived** here since April.*
- *They had **spoken** before.*
- *She's **interested** in math.*

phrasal verb   (also called **two-word verb**) A verb that has two parts (verb + particle). The meaning is often different from the meaning of its separate parts.
- *He **grew up** in Texas.* (became an adult)
- *His parents **brought** him **up** to be honest.* (raised)

phrase   A group of words that forms a unit but does not have a main verb. Many phrases give information about time or place.
- ***Last year**, we were living **in Canada**.*

plural   A form that means *two or more*.
- *There **are** three **people** in the restaurant.*
- ***They are** eating dinner.*
- ***We** saw **them**.*

possessive   Nouns, pronouns, or adjectives that show a relationship or show that someone owns something.

- *Zach is **Megan's** brother.* (possessive noun)
- *Is that car **his**?* (possessive pronoun)
- *That's **his** car.* (possessive adjective)

predicate   The part of a sentence that has the main verb. It tells what the subject is doing or describes the subject.

- *My sister **works for a travel agency**.*

preposition   A word that goes before a noun or a pronoun to show time, place, or direction.

- *I went **to** the bank **on** Monday. It's **next to** my office.*

progressive   (also called **continuous**) The verb form *be* + verb + *-ing*. It focuses on the continuation (not the completion) of an action.

- *She**'s reading** the paper.*
- *We **were watching** TV when you called.*

pronoun   A word used in place of a noun.

- *That's my brother. You met **him** at my party.*

proper noun   A noun that is the name of a person, place, or thing. It begins with a capital letter.

- ***Maria** goes to **Central High School**.*
- *It's on **High Street**.*

punctuation   Marks used in writing (period, comma, . . .) that make the meaning clear. For example, a period **(.)** shows the end of a sentence. It also shows that the sentence is a statement, not a question.

quantifier   A word or phrase that shows an amount (but not an exact amount). It often comes before a noun.

- *Josh bought **a lot of** books last year.*
- *He doesn't have **much** money.*

question   See *yes / no* **question** and *wh-* **question**.

question word   See *wh-* **word**.

quoted speech   See **direct speech**.

real conditional sentence   A sentence that talks about general truths, habits, or things that happen again and again. It can also talk about things that will happen in the future under certain circumstances.

- *If it rains, he takes the bus.*
- *If it rains tomorrow, we'll take the bus with him.*

regular   A word that changes its form in the usual way.

- *play → played*
- *fast → faster*
- *quick → quickly*

relative pronoun   A word that connects an adjective clause to a noun in the main clause.

- *He's the man **who** lives next door.*
- *I'm reading a book **that** I really like.*

reported speech   See **indirect speech**.

reporting verb   A verb such as *said, told,* or *asked*. It introduces direct and indirect speech. It can also come after the quotation in direct speech.

- *She **said**, "I'm going to be late." OR "I'm going to be late," she **said**.*
- *She **told** me that she was going to be late.*

restrictive adjective clause   See **identifying adjective clause**.

result clause   The clause in a conditional sentence that talks about what happens if the condition occurs.

- *If it rains, **I'll stay home**.*
- *If I had a million dollars, **I would travel**.*
- *If I had had your phone number, **I would have called you**.*

sentence   A group of words that has a subject and a main verb.

- ***Computers are** very useful.*

separable phrasal verb   A phrasal verb whose parts can separate.

- *Tom **looked** the word **up** in a dictionary.*
- *He **looked** it **up**.*

short answer   An answer to a *yes / no* question.

   A: *Did you call me last night?*
   B: ***No, I didn't.*** OR ***No.***

singular   A form that means *one*.

- *They have **a sister**.*
- ***She works** in **a hospital**.*

statement   A sentence that gives information. In writing, it ends in a period.

- *Today is Monday.*

stative verb   See **non-action verb**.

subject The person, place, or thing that the sentence is about.
- *Ms. Chen teaches English.*
- *Her class is interesting.*

subject pronoun A pronoun that shows the person (*I, you, he, she, it, we, they*) that the sentence is about.
- *I read a lot.*
- *She reads a lot too.*

subject relative pronoun A relative pronoun that is the subject of an adjective clause.
- *He's the man who lives next door.*

subordinate clause See **dependent clause**.

superlative The form of an adjective or adverb that is used to compare a person, place, or thing to a group of people, places, or things.
- *Cindi is the shortest player on the team.* (adjective)
- *She dances the most gracefully.* (adverb)

tag question A statement + tag. The **tag** is a short question at the end of the statement. Tag questions check information or comment on a situation.
- *You're Jack Thompson, aren't you?*
- *It's a nice day, isn't it?*

tense The form of a verb that shows the time of the action.
- **simple present**: *Fabio talks to his friend every day.*
- **simple past**: *Fabio talked to his teacher yesterday.*

third-person singular The pronouns *he, she,* and *it* or a singular noun. In the simple present, the third-person-singular verb ends in *-s*.
- *Tomás works in an office.* (Tomás = he)

three-word verb A phrasal verb + preposition.
- *Slow down! I can't keep up with you.*

time clause A clause that begins with a time word such as *when, before, after, while,* or *as soon as.*
- *I'll call you when I get home.*

transitive verb A verb that has an object.
- *She likes apples.*

two-word verb See **phrasal verb**.

unreal conditional sentence A sentence that talks about unreal conditions and their unreal results. The condition and its result can be untrue, imagined, or impossible.
- *If I were a bird, I would fly around the world.*
- *If you had called, I would have invited you to the party.*

verb A word that describes what the subject of the sentence does, thinks, feels, senses, or owns.
- *They run two miles every day.*
- *She loved that movie.*
- *He has a new camera.*

wh- question (also called **information question**) A question that begins with a *wh-* word. You answer a *wh-* question with information.
- **A:** *Where are you going?*
- **B:** *To the store.*

wh- word A question word such as *who, what, when, where, which, why, how,* and *how much.* It can begin a *wh-* question or an embedded question.
- *Who is that?*
- *What did you see?*
- *When does the movie usually start?*
- *I don't know how much it costs.*

yes/no question A question that begins with a form of *be* or an auxiliary verb. You can answer a *yes/no* question with *yes* or *no.*
- **A:** *Are you a student?*
- **B:** *Yes, I am.* OR *No, I'm not.*

UNIT REVIEW ANSWER KEY

Note: In this answer key, where a short or contracted form is given, the full or long form is also correct (unless the purpose of the exercise is to practice the short or contracted forms).

UNIT 1

A
1. helps
2. is working
3. Do
4. understand
5. usually go

B
1. 'm looking for
2. think
3. isn't carrying
4. need
5. see
6. 's standing
7. 's waiting
8. sounds
9. don't believe
10. wants

C Hi Leda,

How ~~do you do~~ *are you doing* these days? We're all fine. I'm writing to tell you that we ~~not~~ *aren't* living in California anymore. We just moved to Oregon. Also, we ~~expect~~ *'re expecting* a baby! We're looking for an interesting name for our new daughter. Do you have any ideas? Right now, we're thinking about *Gabriella* because it~~'s having~~ *has* good nicknames. For example, *Gabby*, *Bree*, and *Ella* all seem good to us. How ~~are~~ *do* those nicknames sound to you? We hope you'll write soon and tell us your news.
Love,
Samantha

UNIT 2

A
1. met
2. was working
3. saw
4. had
5. When
6. was thinking
7. gave

B
1. were . . . doing
2. met
3. were waiting
4. met
5. were studying
6. noticed
7. entered

C It was 2005. I ~~studied~~ *was studying* French in Paris ~~while~~ *when* I met Paul. Like me, Paul was from California. We were both taking the same 9:00 A.M. conversation class.

After class we always ~~were going~~ *went* to a café with some of our classmates. One day, while we ~~was~~ *were* drinking café au lait, Paul ~~was asking~~ *asked* me to go to a movie with him. After that, we started to spend most of our free time together. We really got to know each other well, and we discovered that we had a lot of similar interests. When the course was over, we left Paris and ~~were going~~ *went* back to California together. The next year we got married!

UNIT 3

A
1. got
2. has been living
3. since
4. read
5. been playing
6. has
7. 've been studying

B
1. has been working OR has worked
2. discovered
3. didn't know
4. found out
5. did OR 'd done
6. 's gone OR 's been going
7. hasn't found
8. 's had OR 's been having

C **A:** How long ~~did~~ *have* you been doing adventure sports?

B: I've ~~gotten~~ *got* interested five years ago, and I haven't stopped since then.

A: You're lucky to live here in Colorado. It's a great place for adventure sports. ~~Did you live~~ *Have you lived* OR *Have you been living* here long?

B: No, not long. I moved here last year. Before that, I~~'ve been living~~ *lived* in Alaska.

A: I haven't ~~go~~ *been* there yet, but I've heard it's great.

B: It *is* great. When you go, be sure to visit Denali National Park.

UNIT 4

A
1. had gotten
2. had been studying
3. had graduated
4. moved
5. hadn't given

B
1. had . . . been playing
2. joined
3. 'd decided
4. 'd been practicing
5. 'd taught
6. Had . . . come
7. 'd . . . moved
8. 'd been living
9. hadn't expected

C When five-year-old Sarah Chang enrolled in the Juilliard School of Music, she ~~has~~ *had* already been playing the violin for more than a year. Her parents, both musicians, had ~~been moving~~ *moved* from Korea to further their careers. They had ~~gave~~ *given* their daughter a violin as a fourth birthday present, and Sarah had been ~~practiced~~ *practicing* hard since then. By seven, she already performed with several local orchestras. A child prodigy, Sarah became the youngest person to receive the Hollywood Bowl's Hall of Fame Award.

She had already ~~been receiving~~ *received* several awards including the Nan Pa Award—South Korea's highest prize for musical talent.

UNIT 5

A
1. turn
2. Are
3. doing
4. is
5. is going to
6. 're
7. finishes

B
1. will . . . be doing OR are . . . going to be doing
2. is going to be leaving OR will be leaving
3. 'll be sitting OR 'm going to be sitting
4. won't be coming OR 're not going to be coming
5. Is . . . going to cause OR Will . . . cause
6. No . . . isn't. OR No . . . won't.
7. 's going to be OR 'll be
8. 'll see

C **A:** How long are you going to ⌃*be* staying in Beijing?

B: I'm not sure. I'll let you know just as soon as I⌃ find out, OK?

A: OK. It's going to be a long flight. What will you ~~did~~ *do* OR *be doing* to pass the time?

B: I'll be ~~work~~ *working* a lot of the time. And I'm going to try to sleep.

A: Good idea. Have fun, and I'm ~~emailing~~ *'ll email* you all the office news. I promise.

UNIT 6

A
1. have saved
2. get
3. have been exercising
4. 'll have read
5. By

B
1. 'll have been living
2. 'll have been studying
3. 'll have graduated
4. graduate
5. 'll have found
6. 'll have made
7. 'll have saved

C I'm so excited about your news! By the time you read this, you'll have already ~~moving~~ *moved* into your new house! And I have some good news too. By the end of this month, I will ~~have been saving~~ *have saved* $3,000. That's enough for me to buy a used car! And that means that by this time next year, I ~~drive~~ *'ll have driven* to California to visit you! I have more news too. By the time I ~~will~~ graduate, I will have ~~been~~ started my new part-time job. I hope that by this time next year, I'll also ~~had~~ *have* paid off some of my loans.

It's hard to believe that in June, we will have been ~~being~~ friends for 10 years. Time sure flies! And we'll have ~~been~~ stayed friends even though we live 3,000 miles apart. Isn't the Internet a great thing?

UNIT 7

A
1. isn't
2. Didn't
3. 've
4. it
5. Hasn't
6. she
7. Shouldn't

B
1. haven't
2. No, I haven't
3. Can't
4. are
5. Yes, I am
6. won't
7. Yes, you will

C **A:** Ken hasn't come back from Korea yet, has ~~Ken~~ *he*?

B: ~~No~~ *Yes*, he has. He got back last week. Didn't he call you when he got back?

A: No, he didn't. He's probably busy. There are a lot of things to do when you move, ~~isn't it~~ *aren't there*?

B: Definitely. And I guess his family ~~wanted~~ *will want* to spend a lot of time with him, won't they?

A: I'm sure they will. You know, I think I'll just call him. You have his phone number, ~~have~~ *don't* you?

B: Yes, I do. Could you wait while I get it off my computer? You're not in a hurry, ~~aren't~~ *are* you?

UNIT 8

A
1. does
2. So
3. isn't either
4. but
5. doesn't
6. too

B
1. I speak Spanish, and so does my brother. OR . . . and my brother does too.
2. Jaime lives in Chicago, but his brother doesn't.
3. Chicago is an exciting city, and so is New York. OR . . . and New York is too.
4. Chen doesn't play tennis, but his sister does.
5. Diego doesn't eat meat, and neither does Lila. OR . . . and Lila doesn't either.

C My friend Alicia and I have a lot in common. She comes from Los Angeles, and so ~~I do~~ *do I*. She speaks Spanish. I ~~speak~~ *do* OR *I speak Spanish* too. Her parents are both teachers, ~~but~~ *and* mine are too. (My mother teaches math, and her father ~~do~~ *does* too.) I don't have any brothers or sisters. ~~Either~~ *Neither* does she. There are some differences too. Alicia is very outgoing, ~~and~~ *but* I'm not. I like to spend more time alone. I don't enjoy sports, but she ~~doesn't~~ *does*. She's on several school teams, but ~~not I'm~~ *I'm not*.

I just think our differences make things more

interesting, and so ~~my friend does~~! *does my friend*

UNIT 9

A 1. to use
2. (in order) to save
3. ordering
4. to relax
5. to study OR study
6. preparing
7. Stopping
8. to eat
9. having
10. Cooking

B 1. doesn't OR didn't remember eating

2. wants OR wanted him to take

3. wonders OR wondered about Chu's OR Chu eating

4. didn't stop to have OR is going to stop to have

5. forgot to mail

C **A:** I was happy to hear that the cafeteria is serving

salads now. I'm eager ~~trying~~ them. *to try*

B: Me too. Someone recommended eating more

salads in order ~~for losing~~ weight. *to lose*

A: It was that TV doctor, right? He's always urging

~~we~~ to exercise more too. *us*

B: That's the one. He's actually convinced me to

stop ~~to eat~~ meat. *eating*

A: Interesting! It would be a hard decision for us

~~making~~, though. We love to barbecue. *to make*

UNIT 10

A 1. helped
2. had
3. made
4. let
5. got

B 1. didn't OR wouldn't let me have

2. got them to give

3. made me walk

4. had me feed

5. didn't OR wouldn't help me take / to take

6. got him to give

7. let them have

C Lately I've been thinking a lot about all the people

who helped me ~~adjusting~~ to moving here when I was *adjust OR to adjust*

a kid. My parents got me ⁀ join some school clubs so *to*

that I met other kids. Then my dad helped me

~~improves~~ my soccer game so I could join the team. *improve OR to improve*

And my mom never let me ✗ stay home. She made

me ✗ get out and do things. My parents also spoke

to my new teacher, and they had her ~~called~~ on me a *call*

lot so the other kids got to know me quickly. The

neighbors helped too. They got ~~I~~ to walk their dog *me*

Red, and Red introduced me to all her human

friends! The fact that so many people wanted to

help me made me ✗ realize that I was not alone.

Before long I felt part of my new school, my new

neighborhood, and my new life.

UNIT 11

A 1. off
2. it down
3. ahead
4. up
5. away
6. back
7. it up

B 1. take down
2. touch up
3. settle on
4. figure . . . out
5. show up
6. find out
7. left . . . on
8. turn . . . off

C **A:** This apartment is bringing me down. Let's do

~~over it.~~ *it over*

B: It *is* depressing. Let's put ~~around~~ a list and *together*

figure out what to do first.

A: OK. Write this down: Pick ~~on~~ new paint colors. *out*

We can look at some online.

B: The new streetlight shines into the bedroom.

We need to block ~~up~~ the light somehow. *out*

A: We could put ~~on~~ some dark curtains in that *up*

room. That should take care of the problem.

UNIT 12

A 1. f   3. a   5. b   7. g
2. e   4. c   6. d

B 1. woke Jason up
2. pick it up
3. count on her
4. call me back
5. got off the phone
6. put my nightshirt on
7. turned the lights off

C I'm so tired of telemarketers calling me up as

soon as I get ~~from work back~~ or just when I sit ~~up~~ for *back from work* *down*

a relaxing dinner! It's gotten to the point that I've

stopped picking ⁀ the phone when it rings between *up*

6:00 to 8:00 P.M. ~~up~~. I know I can count on it being a ⁀

telemarketer who will try to talk me into spending

money on something I don't want. But it's still

annoying to hear the phone ring, so sometimes I

turn ~~off it~~. Then, of course, I worry that it may be *it off*

someone important. So I end up checking caller ID

to find out. I think the Do Not Call list is a great idea.

Who thought ~~up it~~? I'm going to sign ~~for it up~~ *it up* *up for it*

tomorrow!

A 1. are   3. thinks   5. which
   2. whose   4. which   6. who

B 1. who OR that behave   5. that OR which hurt
   2. who makes   6. which . . . upset
   3. which . . . convince   7. whose . . . is
   4. who OR that . . . speaks

C It's true that we are often attracted to people
who OR *that*
~~whose~~ are very different from ourselves. An

whose
extrovert, ~~which~~ personality is very outgoing, will

is
often connect with a romantic partner who ~~are~~ an
introvert. They are both attracted to someone that
has
~~have~~ different strengths. My cousin Valerie, who is an
extreme extrovert, recently married Bill, whose idea
of a party is a Scrabble game on the Internet. Can
this marriage succeed? Will Bill learn the salsa,
which
~~that~~ is Valerie's favorite dance? Will Valerie start
who
collecting unusual words? Their friends, ~~what~~ care
about both of them, are hoping for the best.

A 1. whose   3. where   5. when
   2. that   4. who   6. who

B 1. where   5. whose
   2. that OR which   6. who(m)
   3. that OR which   7. that OR which
   4. who(m) OR that

C I grew up in an apartment building *that* OR *which* ~~who~~ my
grandparents owned. There was a small dining room
where OR *in which*   *in which* OR *where*
~~when~~ we had family meals and a kitchen ~~in that~~ I ate
whose
my breakfast. My aunt, uncle, and cousin, in ~~who~~

home I spent a lot of my time, lived in an identical
apartment on the fourth floor. I remember the time
my parents gave me a toy phone set that we set up
so I could talk to my cousin. There weren't many
children in the building, but I often visited the
whose
building manager, ~~who's~~ son I liked. I enjoyed living
in the apartment, but for me it was a happy day
when OR *that*
~~where~~ we moved into our own house.

A 1. get   4. can't   7. post
   2. may   5. help   8. must not
   3. 've got   6. might   9. be able to

B 1. 'd better not OR shouldn't OR ought not to give
   2. 'd better OR 've got to OR must register
   3. must not be

4. has got to OR must get
5. can't OR must not eat
6. may OR might OR could come

be
C 1. Could that ~~being~~ Amelie in this photograph?
   2. No, that's impossible. It doesn't look anything
can't OR *couldn't*
like Amelie. It ~~doesn't have to~~ be her.
better not
   3. I don't know this person. I guess I'd ~~not better~~
accept him as a friend on my Facebook page.
don't have to
   4. With MySpace, I ~~must not~~ call to keep in touch
with friends. It's just not necessary.
Will
   5. ~~May~~ hi5 be as popular as Facebook someday?

A 1. have   3. could   5. shouldn't
   2. ought   4. given   6. should I

B 1. I should've studied for the math test.
   2. You could've shown me your class notes.
   3. I shouldn't have stayed up so late the night
before the test.
   4. John ought to have called you.
   5. You might've invited me to join the study
group.

stayed
C I shouldn't have ~~stay~~ up so late. I overslept and
to
missed my bus. I ought have asked Erik for a ride. I
got to the office late, and my boss said, "You might
have   *should*
~~had~~ called." She was right. I ~~shouldn't~~ have called. At
lunch my co-workers went out together. They really
have   *I have*
could ~~of~~ invited me to join them. Should ~~have I~~ said
something to them? Then, after lunch, my mother
called. She said, "Yesterday was Aunt Em's birthday.
sent
You could've ~~sending~~ her a card!" I really think my
have
mother might ~~has~~ reminded me. Not a good day! I
should've
~~shouldn't have~~ just stayed in bed.

A 1. must   5. may
   2. might not have   6. have
   3. have   7. couldn't
   4. taken

B 1. might OR may not have gotten my message
   2. must not have studied
   3. couldn't OR can't have forgotten our date
   4. may OR might OR could have been at the movies
   5. must have forgotten
   6. must not have seen me

C Why did the Aztecs build their capital city in the middle of a lake? Could they ~~had~~ *have* wanted the protection of the water? They might have ~~been~~. Or the location may ~~has~~ *have* helped them to control nearby societies. At first it must have ~~being~~ *been* an awful place, full of mosquitoes and fog. But it must ~~no~~ *not* have been a bad idea—the island city became the center of a very powerful empire. To succeed, the Aztecs had to have ~~became~~ *become* fantastic engineers quite quickly. When the Spanish arrived, they couldn't have ~~expect~~ *expected* the amazing palaces, floating gardens, and well-built canals. Unfortunately, they destroyed the city anyway.

UNIT 18

A 1. Spanish is spoken in Bolivia.
2. They play soccer in Bolivia.
3. Reza Deghati took the photo.
4. The articles were translated into Spanish.
5. Quinoa is grown in the mountains.
6. They named the main street El Prado.

B 1. was discovered
2. is spoken
3. is grown
4. is exported
5. are OR have been employed
6. was made
7. has been performed
8. is attended

C Photojournalist Alexandra Avakian was born and ~~raise~~ *raised* in New York. Since she began her career, she has covered many of the world's most important stories. Her work ~~have~~ *has* been published in many newspapers and magazines including *National Geographic*, and her photographs have ~~being~~ *been* exhibited around the world. Avakian has also written a book, *Window of the Soul: My Journey in the Muslim World*, which was ~~been~~ published in 2008. It has not yet been translated ~~by translators~~ into other languages, but the chapter titles appear in both English and Arabic. Avakian's book ~~have be~~ *has been* discussed on international TV, radio, and numerous websites.

UNIT 19

A 1. done 3. could 5. be 7. has
2. be replaced 4. had 6. won't 8. are

B 1. should be trained
2. have to be given
3. must . . . be tested
4. can be experienced
5. will be provided
6. may be sent
7. could . . . be developed

C The new spacesuits are going to be ~~testing~~ *tested* underwater today. They've got to ~~been~~ *be* improved before they can be used on the Moon or Mars. Two astronauts are going to be wearing them while they're working, and they'll *be* watched by the engineers. This morning communication was lost with the Earth's surface, and all decisions had to be ~~make~~ *made* by the astronauts themselves. It was a very realistic situation. This crew ~~will got~~ *will have* OR *has got* to be very well prepared for space travel. They're going to the Moon in a few years.

UNIT 20

A 1. have it cut 4. your house painted
2. done 5. by
3. get

B 1. have OR get it repaired
2. have OR get them cleaned
3. have OR get them shortened
4. have OR get it colored
5. have OR get it fixed
6. had OR got it removed
7. have OR get it renewed
8. 'll have OR get OR 'm going to have OR 'm having OR getting it checked

C I'm going on vacation next week. I'd like to have ~~done some work~~ *some work done* in my office, and this seems like a good time for it. Please have my carpet ~~clean~~ *cleaned* while I'm gone. And could you have my computer and printer looked at? It's been quite a while since they've been serviced. Ted wants to have my office painted ~~by a painter~~ while I'm gone. Please tell him any color is fine except pink! Last week, I ~~had designed some new brochures~~ *had some new brochures designed* by Perfect Print. Please call the printer and have them delivered directly to the sales reps. And could you ~~get made up more business cards~~ *get more business cards made up* too? When I get back, it'll be time to plan the holiday party. I think we should have it catered this year ~~from~~ *by* a professional. While I'm gone, why don't you call around and get some estimates from caterers? ~~Has~~ *Have* the estimates sent to Ted. Thanks.

UNIT 21

A
1. do . . . do
2. are
3. is
4. shop
5. happens
6. doesn't stay
7. closes
8. go
9. feel
10. think

B
1. When OR If it's 7:00 A.M. in Honolulu, what time is it in Mumbai?
2. If you love jewelry, you should visit an international jewelry show.
3. A tourist might have more fun if she tries bargaining.
4. If OR When you're shopping at an outdoor market, you can always bargain for a good price.
5. But don't try to bargain if OR when you're shopping in a big department store.

C
1. If I don't like something I bought online, then I ~~returned~~ *return* it.
2. Don't buy from an online site if you don't know anything about the company.
3. When he shops online, Frank always saves a lot of time.
4. I always ~~fell~~ *fall* asleep if I fly at night. It happens every time.
5. Isabel always has a wonderful time when she visits Istanbul.

UNIT 22

A
1. d
2. f
3. a
4. c
5. b
6. e

B
1. take
2. 'll be OR 'm going to be
3. will . . . do OR are . . . going to do
4. don't get
5. 'll stay OR 'm going to stay
6. get
7. pass
8. 'll celebrate OR 'm going to celebrate

C It's been a hard week, and I'm looking forward to the weekend. If the weather ~~will be~~ *is* nice tomorrow, Marco and I are going to go to the beach. The ocean is usually too cold for swimming at this time of year, so I probably ~~don't~~ *won't* go in the water unless it's really hot outside. But I love walking along the beach and breathing in the fresh sea air.

If Marco has time, he might ~~makes~~ *make* some sandwiches to bring along. Otherwise, we'll just get some pizza. I hope it'll be a nice day. I just listened to the weather report, and there may be some rain in the afternoon. ~~Unless~~ *If* it rains, we'll probably go to the movies instead. That's our Plan B. But I really want to go to the beach, so I'm keeping my fingers crossed!

UNIT 23

A
1. 'd feel
2. were
3. could
4. found
5. could
6. weren't
7. 'd

B
1. would . . . do
2. found
3. Would . . . take
4. knew
5. would become
6. put
7. made
8. would learn

C
1. Pablo wishes he ~~can~~ *could* speak German.
2. If he had the time, he'~~ll~~*d* study in Germany. But he doesn't have the time right now.
3. He could get a promotion ~~when~~ *if* he spoke another language.
4. His company ~~may~~ *might* pay the tuition if he took a course.
5. What would you do if you ~~are~~ *were* in Pablo's situation?

UNIT 24

A
1. hadn't told
2. had
3. would have been
4. If
5. gone

B
1. would've been
2. hadn't missed
3. had been
4. wouldn't have discovered
5. hadn't accepted
6. had taken
7. wouldn't have met
8. hadn't seen
9. wouldn't have believed

C Tonight we watched the movie *Back to the Future* starring Michael J. Fox. I might never ~~had~~ *have* seen it if I hadn't read his autobiography, *Lucky Man*. His book was so good that I wanted to see his most famous movie. Now I wish I ~~saw~~ *had seen* it in the theater when it first came out, but I hadn't even been born yet! It would have been better if we ~~would have~~ *had* watched it on a big screen. Fox was great. He looked really young—

just like a teenager. But I would have recognized him even ~~when~~ *if* I hadn't known he was in the film. In real life, when Fox was a teenager, he was too small to become a professional hockey player. But if he hadn't looked so young, he ~~can't~~ *couldn't* OR *wouldn't* have gotten his role in the TV hit series *Family Ties*. In Hollywood, he had to sell his furniture to pay his bills, but he kept trying to find an acting job. If he ~~wouldn't have~~ *hadn't*, he might never have become a star.

UNIT 25

A
1. says
2. "I'd love to."
3. planned
4. he
5. 'd
6. told
7. had been
8. his

B
1. (that) she always gets OR got up early.
2. (that) water boils OR boiled at 100 degrees Celsius.
3. (that) he liked OR likes my haircut.
4. (that) she loved OR 'd loved the pasta.
5. (that) it was OR is his own recipe.
6. (that) she mailed OR 'd mailed him the check.
7. (that) his boss had liked OR liked his work.

C
1. A psychologist I know often tells me ✗ that people today tell hundreds of lies every day. ✗
2. Yesterday Marcia's boyfriend ~~said her~~ *said* OR *told her* that he liked her new dress.
3. When she heard that, Marcia said she didn't really believe ~~you~~ *him*.
4. I didn't think that was so bad. I said that her boyfriend ~~tells~~ *had told* OR *told* her a white lie.
5. But Marcia hates lying. She said that to ~~me~~ *her*, all lies are wrong.

UNIT 26

A
1. was
2. I
3. take
4. might
5. today
6. would
7. could
8. there

B
1. (that) it was going to rain
2. (that) it could be the worst storm this year
3. (that) it was going to start soon
4. (that) they should buy water
5. (that) they had to leave right then
6. (that) she would call me the next day

C What a storm! They ~~told~~ *said* it ~~is~~ *was* going to be bad, but it was terrible. They said it ~~will~~ *would* last two days, but it lasted four. On the first day of the storm, my mother called and told me that we should ~~have left~~ *leave* the house right ~~now~~ *then*. (I still can hear her exact words: "You should leave the house *right now*!") We should have listened to her! We just didn't believe it was going to be so serious. I told her last night that if we had known, we would ~~had~~ *have* left right away. We're lucky we survived. I just listened to the weather forecast. Good news! They said tomorrow should be sunny.

UNIT 27

A
1. . [*period*]
2. give
3. "Please sit down."
4. not to
5. say
6. told
7. invited

B
1. He told OR asked her to show him her license.
2. She advised OR told him to get more exercise.
3. She invited OR asked them to come to the English Department party.
4. He asked her to turn on the light.
5. She invited OR asked them to hang out at her house.

C My teacher, Mr. Wong, ~~told~~ *said* OR *told us* to sleep well before the test. He said ~~to don't~~ *not to* stay up late studying. He always invites ~~we~~ *us* to ask him questions. He says, "~~Not to~~ *Don't* be shy." I'm glad my friend Tom advised me ~~taking~~ *to take* his class. He ~~said me~~ *said* OR *told me* to register early, and he warned me ✗ that the class filled up fast every semester. ✗ I told him ~~don't~~ *not* to worry. I said I'd already registered.

UNIT 28

A
1. . [*period*]
2. if
3. their office was
4. I lived
5. I had

B
1. who the company had hired.
2. if OR whether I had taken the job.
3. if OR whether I liked my present job.
4. who my boss was.
5. how many employees worked there.
6. why I wanted to change jobs.
7. what the starting salary was.
8. if OR whether I could start soon.

C They asked me so many questions! They asked me
where ~~did I work~~ *I worked*. They asked who ~~was my boss~~ *my boss was*.
They asked why I ~~did want~~ *wanted* to change jobs. They
asked how much money I made. They ~~ask~~ *asked* me who I
~~have~~ *had* voted for in the last election. They even asked
me what my favorite color was. Finally, I asked
myself whether or ~~no~~ *not* I really wanted that job!

UNIT 29

A 1. we should   5. I should
    2. our server is   6. ? [*question mark*]
    3. . [*period*]   7. whether
    4. to

B 1. where the restaurant is?

    2. if OR whether the subway goes to the museum.

    3. if OR whether we should tip the porter.

    4. why we didn't buy the book on tipping.

    5. how much we should tip the tour guide.

    6. if OR whether you have any travel books.

    7. what this sign says?

C **A:** Hi. Is this a good time to call? I wasn't sure

what time you have dinner.

B: This is fine. I didn't know ~~were you~~ *if* OR *whether you were* back from
your trip.

A: We got back two days ago. I can't remember
if OR *whether I emailed* ~~did I email~~ you some photographs.

B: Yes. They were great. Can you tell me where
~~took you~~ *you took* that picture of the lake? I want to go!

A: Hmm. I'm not sure which one ~~was that~~ *that was*. We
saw a lot of lakes in Switzerland.

B: I'll show it to you. I'd really like to find out
where ~~is it~~ *it is*.

INDEX

This index is for the full and split editions. All entries are in the full book. Entries for Volume A of the split edition are in black. Entries for Volume B are in red.

CREDITS